The Cross-Platform Mac Handbook

D1770510

ISBN 0-13-085088-8

9 780130 850881

The Cross-Platform Mac Handbook

Keeping Your Mac in a Digital World

David L. Hart

Prentice Hall PTR
Upper Saddle River, New Jersey 07458
www.phptr.com

Library of Congress Cataloging-in-Publication Data

Hart, David L.
　The cross-platform Mac handbook: keeping your Mac in a digital world / David L. Hart.
　　p. cm.
　ISBN 0-13-085088-8 (alk. paper)
　 1. Macintosh (Computer) 2. Cross-platform software development. I. Title.

QA76.8.M3 H365 1999
004.165--dc21　　　　　　　　　　　　　　　　　　　　　　　　　99-051984

Editorial/production supervision: *Jane Bonnell*
Cover design director: *Jayne Conte*
Cover design: *Bruce Kenselaar*
Manufacturing manager: *Maura Goldstaub*
Acquisitions editor: *Michael Meehan*
Editorial assistant: *Diane Spina*
Marketing manager: *Bryan Gambrel*

© 2000 by Prentice Hall PTR
Prentice-Hall, Inc.
Upper Saddle River, New Jersey 07458

Prentice Hall books are widely used by corporations and government agencies for training, marketing, and resale.
The publisher offers discounts on this book when ordered in bulk quantities. For more information, contact Corporate Sales Department, Phone: 800-382-3419; FAX: 201-236-7141;
E-mail: corpsales@prenhall.com
Or write: Prentice Hall PTR, Corporate Sales Dept., One Lake Street, Upper Saddle River, NJ 07458.

Apple, AppleWorks, FireWire, iBook, iMac, Mac, Macintosh, Mac OS, PowerBook, Power Mac, and QuickTime are trademarks of Apple Computer, Inc., registered in the U.S.A. and other countries. Other company and product names mentioned herein are the trademarks or registered trademarks of their respective owners.

All rights reserved. No part of this book may be
reproduced, in any form or by any means,
without permission in writing from the publisher.

Printed in the United States of America
10　9　8　7　6　5　4　3　2

ISBN 0-13-085088-8

Prentice-Hall International (UK) Limited, *London*
Prentice-Hall of Australia Pty. Limited, *Sydney*
Prentice-Hall Canada Inc., *Toronto*
Prentice-Hall Hispanoamericana, S.A., *Mexico*
Prentice-Hall of India Private Limited, *New Delhi*
Prentice-Hall of Japan, Inc., *Tokyo*
Pearson Education Asia Pte. Ltd., *Singapore*
Editora Prentice-Hall do Brasil, Ltda., *Rio de Janeiro*

For Casey

Contents

Preface	*xiii*
Acknowledgments	*xix*

Chapter 1. A Digital World   1

Keep Your Mac—It's a Digital World	2
Looking Ahead	2
Does It Really Work?	4
A Moving Target	5
A Well-Connected Mac	5

Chapter 2. Sneaker Net   7

Removable Media	8
File Exchange	8
PC Disks on a Mac	8
Mac Disks on a PC	11
UNIX Disks on a Mac	12
Virus Software	13
File Conversion	14
File Names and Types	14
General Files	16

Graphics	17
Sound	18
Movies	19
Compression	19
In Short, You Need...	**22**

Chapter 3. Basic Mac Networking — 23

Mac Networking Pros and Cons	**24**
Mac OS and AppleTalk Advantages	24
Mac OS and AppleTalk Disadvantages	25
Configuring Mac Networking	**26**
AppleTalk	26
Configuration Manager	28
DialAssist	29
Infrared	29
Internet	29
Internet Config	29
Location Manager	30
MacTCP	31
Modem	31
Network	32
PPP	32
Remote Access	33
Remote Access Setup	33
TCP/IP	34
High-Performance Mac Networking	**35**
Networking Summary	**37**

Chapter 4. Local-Area Networks — 39

Mac Servers	**40**
Sharing over TCP/IP Networks	42
Sharing with Windows and UNIX	44
Printing	47
Mac OS X Server	**48**

Windows NT Servers	**48**
NetWare Servers	**51**
UNIX Servers	**53**
Network Administration	**55**
Simple Network Management Protocol	56
Tools for Network Administration	56
SDSC's Cross-Platform Installation	**59**
AppleTalk	59
File Sharing	59
Printing	60
LAN Summary	**61**

Chapter 5. The Internet   63

Internet Basics	**64**
Clients and Servers	65
Internet Services	66
Using Internet Config	67
The World Wide Web	**68**
Web Browsers	69
Netscape Communicator	70
Microsoft Internet Explorer	72
Web Servers	73
Personal Web Sharing	74
File Transfer Protocol	**76**
FTP Clients	77
FTP Servers	79
E-mail	**81**
The Most Common E-mail Problem	82
E-mail Clients	83
E-mail Servers	86
Mailing List Servers	86
An Internet Recap	**89**

Chapter 6. Applications, File Formats, and Web Standards — 91

It Should Work Just Fine… — 92
Applications — 93
- E-mail File Exchange — 93
- Windows (and Web) File Names — 93
- The Font Problem — 95
  - *A Font Solution?* — *96*
- Specific Applications — 97
  - *Adobe Photoshop* — *98*
  - *AppleWorks* — *99*
  - *FileMaker Pro* — *99*
  - *Microsoft Office* — *101*
  - *QuarkXPress* — *105*
  - *Quicken* — *106*

File Formats — 107
- "Plain" Text — 108
- Rich Text Format — 111
- Portable Document Format — 112
- PostScript — 114
- Spreadsheets and Databases — 116
- Graphics — 117

Web Standards — 120
- HTML — 121
- Beyond HTML — 122
  - *CSS* — *123*
  - *DHTML* — *123*
  - *XML and XSL* — *124*
  - *VRML and X3D* — *125*
  - *JavaScript* — *125*
  - *Java* — *126*
  - *Perl* — *127*

In Short, You Should… — 127

Chapter 7. Camouflaging Your Mac — 131

- **Simple Windows Tricks** — 132
  - GUI Orientation — 132
  - GUI Adjustments — 134
- **Terminal Emulators** — 138
- **Application Servers and Clients** — 140
  - X Window System — 141
  - Windows Terminal Server — 141
  - Remote Control — 143
- **Non-Mac Operating Systems** — 145
  - Windows Emulators — 145
  - UNIX and Linux for Mac — 146
  - Other Emulators — 148
- **PC Cards and Cheap PCs** — 149
- **Camouflage Recap** — 150

Chapter 8. The Expanding Digital World — 151

- **Peripheral Matters** — 152
  - ADB — 152
  - USB — 153
  - SCSI — 153
  - FireWire — 153
- **Accessibility and Assistive Technology** — 155
- **Computing Devices** — 156
  - Palm Computing Organizers — 156
  - Windows CE Devices — 158
  - Newton — 160
  - Desktops and Laptops — 161
- **Telephonic Mac** — 162
- **Audio-Visual Mac** — 166
  - MP3 Players — 166
  - TV Tuners and Video Capture Cards — 167
  - Digital Cameras — 168

Macs at Work	**169**
Bar Code Readers and Point-of-Sale Software	170
Data Acquisition Interfaces	171
Global Positioning System	172
Macs at Home	**174**
Home Automation	174
Home Security	176
Amateur Radio	177
For More Information	**178**

Appendix. Mac OS Networking Primer   179

General Network Terms	**180**
Mac Networking and Internet Terms	**180**
The Networking Layer Cake	**181**
A Note on "Classic" Macintosh Networking	**184**

Index   187

Preface

*I*f you use a Macintosh either at home or at the office, you almost certainly have had to work with a person who, poor soul, doesn't use a Mac. You may need to exchange files, revise documents, or share the same network printer. This book is written for those of you who have ever faced situations in which you've wanted to interact with users on other platforms and have been told, "You can't do that with a Mac." *The Cross-Platform Mac Handbook* shows you that you can.

As one of the Macintosh "power users" at the San Diego Supercomputer Center, I find myself interacting with my colleagues on Windows NT and UNIX systems daily. Whether the file is going between a UNIX, Windows NT, or Mac system, however, I have found that I rarely have to leave my desk to work with, or even on, the other systems. This capability is due not just to my efforts, though. The networking and facilities staffs provide the Ethernet that allows Mac users to exchange files and print over an AppleTalk network. The Desktop Systems group has installed and configured the tools that let Mac users move files between the Windows NT and UNIX servers in the building. As a user I take advantage of these, but I need to know how best to convert and work with files that arrive in a UNIX or Windows format.

In a large organization, the networking, system administration, and user applications that comprise a well-connected, cross-platform Mac are not maintained by a single person, but it helps to know a little about how all the parts work. The goal of *The Cross-Platform Mac Handbook* is to pull together enough information in these three areas to help you get your work done on your Mac.

This book does not cover all of these areas in great depth, but rather focuses on those areas that are particular to Macs. For example, it doesn't discuss how to configure Windows NT Server from start to finish, but it does cover how to find the settings that allow Windows NT Server to support Macintosh services. Again, let me emphasize: This book is a starting point for the wide variety of subjects described here, not a definitive reference on any of them.

PREREQUISITES

First of all, you should have a Mac. This Mac can be yours or can simply be on your network.

Second, this book will focus on Mac OS 8 and above. This is mainly a practical matter. I use Mac OS 8.5 at work and Mac OS 8.1 at home. If you use a version of System 7, I can't guarantee that everything in this book will work, but most tips will work. On the other hand, Mac OS 8 has a number of cross-platform features built in. If you need to work cross-platform today, an upgrade of your operating system or perhaps even your hardware is probably in order.

Third, you'll need an Internet account that gives you Web access. If you're still feeling your way around the Mac, you may need to follow the Web pointers in this book to more information. But even if you're an experienced Mac user and can follow the limited instructions in this book, you'll still need to get to the Web to find much of the software you're going to need.

Finally, you don't need to be an expert to make the most of this book, but you should be comfortable using a Mac. You might learn a few tips or tricks here, but for the most part the book assumes you can navigate your way through the Finder, select an option from a menu, choose a printer, and configure a control panel. Nothing terribly complex, but a skill level beyond Square 1 is required. If you are an expert in a particular area—say, a UNIX networking expert who has to support Macs on your network—you should also find this book helpful. If you are looking for an introduction to the Mac OS, you have a number of excellent books to choose from.

WHY THIS BOOK?

The main reason I'm writing this book is because there is really no other book out there quite like it. Most computer books cover one operating system or one application (or a single application that has versions on more than one operating system). But in today's Internet world, just about every computer and user comes in contact with many operating systems, at least through files, disks, or communications that began on another platform.

In my reading of Mac mailing lists and electronic and print magazines, I occasionally see a really useful cross-platform tip that resolves an annoyance for which, up to that point, I had found only a clumsy work-around. (I sure wish I had saved all those little snippets of information.) And in answering questions from my co-workers, I have come to realize that a lot of Mac users run into the same problems but may not have the answers.

There ought to be a book, I thought to myself. So I searched through the virtual shelves at *Amazon.com* and *BarnesandNoble.com,* and—lo and behold—there was none. So here you go.

Now, let it not be said that this idea is totally unique. When I began writing this book there were some related titles scheduled to be released. But none planned to cover the breadth of material in this book, such as UNIX-related integration, for example, or sneaker-net file exchange and conversion topics. Or cross-platform standards and applications. Or Internet and Web serving. If you have a cross-platform problem, chances are this book can tell you how to solve it, or at least point you to the resources that can.

Conventions

Before we get to the book proper, I need to explain a few words about notation. This book would have been a monumental undertaking without the Web and the many resources out there. Therefore, you will find a lot of URLs and references to Web sites in this book.

URLs will be printed in *italics*. And to save a lot of repetitive typing, a lot of ink, and maybe a few trees, I've omitted the leading "http://" and trailing "/" from URLs. This is becoming more common these days because many URLs already begin with "www." So if the book refers you to something that looks like *blithering.com*, you'll have the best luck by entering that notation into the Location area of your Web browser. Finally, I tried to avoid breaking a URL across lines, but if it could not be avoided, long URLs are hyphenated following a slash (/); hyphens located elsewhere in a URL are part of the URL.

Also, from my previous book, the *Mac OS 8 Web Server Cookbook*, I learned an important fact about the life span of URLs. They are always decaying and turning into file-not-found messages, so I've tried to limit my use of long, very specific URLs. This may require you to click on a link or two when you arrive at a site, but it will save you the frustration of chasing down broken links. However, despite my precautions, some of these URLs will break. If you find a broken link, visit the book's Web site and send me an e-mail message.

One final note. Although 95 percent of the Internet references in the book point to Web pages, there are a few that don't. To distinguish non-Web references, I have written out the full URL. For reference, the following table shows how the various Internet references appear in the book.

Description	Internet Reference
Basic Web site references.	*www.stalker.com* *emulation.net* *whatis.com/www.htm*
Long URL that spans two lines. The hyphen is not part of the URL.	*www.filemaker.com/support/techinfo/-articles/102453.html*
E-mail addresses contain the "@" sign.	*bourne@sdsc.edu*
ftp references begin with "ftp://".	*ftp://ftp.sdsc.edu/pub/*
News group references begin with "news:".	*news:comp.databases.filemaker*

SO, FINALLY...

In a nutshell, I like my Mac. I like the fact that, from my Mac, I can work with colleagues who use Windows 95/98/NT or UNIX systems, and I don't have to use them. Networking and applications software developers have provided tools to let all these systems work together. If there's one message I hope to send with this book, it's this: Keep your Mac. It's a digital world.

Acknowledgments

This book started when I thought to myself, "Somebody ought to write a book." So I searched *Amazon.com* and *BarnesandNoble.com*, and it turned out that no one had written a book on cross-platform solutions for the Mac. A few months of caffeine, research, late nights, and writing resulted in the book you're holding.

No project of this scale is a totally individual effort, and I would like to take this opportunity to thank a few people who contributed to the existence of this book. Even though they may not have written a word, their support and contributions helped me get it done. Thanks first to my editor Mike Meehan for taking the chance on another Mac book and seeing the process through from contract to publication. Phil Bourne at the San Diego Supercomputer Center probably isn't aware of his contribution, but by letting me co-author the *Mac OS 8 Web Server Cookbook* with him, he set the stage for this opportunity. Nick Pearce in the Desktop Systems group at SDSC helped me out specifically by describing how

Macs were supported on the local-area networks and by providing some Windows NT expertise where it was needed. The entire Desktop Systems group gets my thanks for putting up with my adventuresome Mac antics and requests. Greg Johnson provided a NeXTSTEP-formatted floppy disk in response to an off-the-wall request. I'd like to thank SDSC in general for providing an environment that supports my efforts on projects like this book, for still treating Macs as equal network citizens, for letting me host the book's Web site, and for the Desktop Systems group that keeps it all running.

A special thanks goes out to the software developers who produce the software that keeps the Mac OS connected to the digital world, particularly those who answered my questions during the book's creation and allowed their screen shots to appear in the book.

Finally, I'd like to send out a big thank you to Deborah Casey—now Deborah Casey Hart—who stuck it out as my fiancée while I wrote the book and we simultaneously planned a wedding, remodeled a house, lived without a kitchen, and worked our day jobs for several months. The book wouldn't have happened on schedule, or possibly at all, without her.

CHAPTER 1

A Digital World

The computer you're using at work or at home was chosen, more often than not, for political or compatibility reasons. If you have a Mac at the office, for example, you probably wanted a Mac at home. The same goes for Windows. Or, it may have been mandated that you give up your office Mac in the name of corporate-wide consistency. Even more common is the dilemma that I faced: If I buy a Mac, will I be cut off from the Windows world?

Even though I used a Mac at work, I worried that I would be giving up some intangible warm-and-fuzzy safety by giving away my old Windows 3.1-based PC at home and buying a Mac. Could I survive with a Mac in a Microsoft world?

Keep Your Mac—It's a Digital World

In the end, I bought a Mac—actually a now-discontinued Mac clone—with this question still hanging over my head. I soon realized that I felt much better having bought the computer I wanted rather than the computer "they" said I ought to have. Only slowly did it dawn on me that I had been worried about the wrong question. It's not a Microsoft world—it's a *digital* world. There are Web TVs, Palm OS organizers, old Commodore Amigas, Newtons, fax machines, UNIX workstations, pagers, cell phones, and even watches out there flourishing and exchanging information—digital information.

The beauty of digital information is that it all looks the same at the most basic level—a long series of zeroes and ones. A computer or any digital device works by translating those zeroes and ones into understandable instructions. Understanding information from a similar device—a Mac talking with a Mac, for example—is straightforward because both devices speak the same digital language. Exchanging messages between devices that speak different digital languages—a Mac and a Palm OS organizer, for example—requires two things: a way to move the zeroes and ones from point A to point B, such as a cable, a disk drive, or network, and software to translate between digital languages.

In some sense, all software performs this digital translation. A word processing program, for example, is the translator that turns keystrokes and mouse clicks into digital information that is both displayed on screen and saved to disk. Software and the proper connections let your Mac send a fax and upload information from your personal digital assistant.

So the right question to ask is really, "Can I survive with a Mac in a digital world?" This book is actually an extended *yes* answer to that question.

Looking Ahead

This book tackles the digital world, starting with your Mac itself and expanding outward to networks and other devices. We'll start with a short discussion of networking to lay the groundwork for later chapters. Next, we'll cover the software that a cross-platform Mac needs, then broaden our discussion to local-area networks, the Internet, and external devices. The book also has an associated

Looking Ahead

Web site with all of the book's URLs and links, as well as late-breaking updates to the information in the book. See

www.sdsc.edu/Books/Mac

Chapter 2: Sneaker Net. If your only means of moving files between computers is to manually carry floppy disks, Zip disks, CD-ROMs, or other removable media from one computer to another, you're connected to what's known as a sneaker net. The sneaker net is a very old (but very reliable) transport technology. On a sneaker net and networks in general, a cross-platform Mac needs to open and work with files of just about any format. So we look at tools you need to read disks, open files, or convert between formats that you're likely to encounter when working in a cross-platform environment.

Chapter 3: Basic Mac Networking. Now that you've mastered bipedal data transport, we can describe the digital networking technologies that allow Macs and other computers to communicate. This chapter will run through a quick primer on how Macs network. We introduce some network terms that you probably have heard or even toss around yourself on a regular basis, but may have only vague notions of what they mean—AppleTalk, TCP/IP, Ethernet, PPP, and Open Transport, to name a few.

Chapter 4: Local-Area Networks. Properly configured, your Mac can be a good neighbor on a local network in your office or school. Maybe you're in a Mac-based office and it becomes necessary to run a Windows machine on the network. Or, more commonly, you're fighting to hold on to your Mac in a workplace where the information systems department is clamoring for Windows conformity. We talk about how Mac, Windows, and UNIX servers can support file sharing, backups, printing, and other features among multiple platforms.

Chapter 5: The Internet. The Internet is the ultimate cross-platform environment. With a Mac, a network connection, and a few pieces of free or inexpensive software, you can set up your own Internet service, including Web, FTP, and e-mail. At the very least, you can communicate with systems that are running Internet services.

Chapter 6: Applications, File Formats, and Web Standards. Here we discuss some common applications that have versions for Mac and Windows, and let you know which work well as cross-platform tools. We also discuss standard file formats for exchanging information between platforms with a minimum of fuss.

Chapter 7: Camouflaging Your Mac. If all else fails, we discuss some of the emulation software that can turn your Mac, at least temporarily, into another type of computer. We also talk a little about tricks for making your Mac appear to be more like a Windows machine.

Chapter 8: The Expanding Digital World. While the bulk of the book discusses more traditional computer networks, more and more devices are cropping up that make it easier to carry your connection to the digital world. In this chapter, we discuss personal digital assistants and devices ranging from pagers to lamps that you might want to integrate with your Mac.

DOES IT REALLY WORK?

Yes, it works. If you want to get to the good parts and create your cross-platform Mac environment, you can skip ahead to Chapter 2. This section is here to help address any lingering questions about how the tools and techniques in this book were tested. You may have read some of this in the Preface.

The San Diego Supercomputer Center (SDSC) probably has one of the most diverse computing environments around. The staff has UNIX workstations (from IBM, Sun, SGI, Hewlett-Packard, and Compaq/Digital), Windows NT workstations, and Macintosh systems on their desks, and many staffers have two or more systems. The center also operates, as its name implies, high-end computer systems from IBM, Sun Microsystems, Cray, Compaq/Digital, and Tera. All these computers are connected to the center's networks, and the center is linked to the Internet and to several high-speed research networks, such as the National Science Foundation's vBNS and the California Research and Education Network (CalREN). In other words, you won't easily find a more cross-platform, better-connected place, and that's where I work.

I use a Mac as a writer, editor, and Web content provider at SDSC. I interact with co-workers using Macintosh, Windows NT, and UNIX workstations. The Networking group at SDSC has connected all these systems to the building's Ethernet. The Desktop Systems group has the Macs communicating via Apple-Talk with one another and with Apple LaserWriters, and via Windows NT Servers with Windows workstations and other printers. All the Windows NT and

Macintosh systems are automatically backed up several times a week. The center's e-mail, Web, and ftp services are provided by UNIX servers, while I run a Web server from my own Mac for sharing files and for this book's Web site.

What I'm saying is this: I know that it's not only possible but also straightforward to use a Mac in a cross-platform environment, because I work every day in just such a workplace. And not just a handful of computers, but hundreds of Mac, Windows NT, and UNIX workstations work in concert along with a lot of esoteric, high-end, and one-of-a-kind computer, storage, and network hardware. All the credit for the robust environment's existence and the Mac's acceptance goes to the excellent staff at SDSC.

A Moving Target

Although I did my best to make the information in this book as current as possible, Apple and the many software developers always seemed to be one step ahead of me. To name a few examples in the hardware arena, the iBook portable and the G4 desktop "supercomputers" were announced as the book was going to press. As for software, QuickTime 4 and Mac OS 8.6 arrived, with Mac OS 9 just over the horizon and Mac OS X due next year.

Third-party developers weren't standing still either. A flurry of MP3 players—both hardware devices and software applications—made their debuts, and the software houses that released new versions of their applications are too numerous to count.

So keep in mind that the one constant in the digital world is that things change, and this book is just a snapshot of a moving target. Visit the Web site for this book and the Web sites listed throughout the book for updates.

A Well-Connected Mac

By the end of the book, you should have a very well-connected Mac. I have to admit that my quixotic goal in writing this book was that the information in it would help some fellow Mac lovers keep their Macs in the face of pressure to conform. At the very least, I hope the information here pays off for you by making your work a little easier. Enjoy your Mac. It's a digital world!

CHAPTER 2

Sneaker Net

The "sneaker net" has been connecting computers for as long as there have been computers. In the early days, the sneaker net transported stacks of punched cards down to the mainframe operators. Later, magnetic tape reels were shuttled from racks to tape drives. As removable media evolved, the sneaker net transported floppy disks—back when floppies were still floppy and up to eight inches across—from computer to computer.

Today the sneaker net is liable to bring you a Zip disk from the cubicle next door or a CD-ROM through the mail, and a cross-platform Mac needs to be able to deal with these and other sneaker net packages. And, if you're exchanging data across one of those newfangled "networks," you need much of the same software to convert files back and forth between formats.

This chapter first shows some of the removable media options you might want to connect to your Mac, in case you need to work with disks that your Mac does not have the hardware to handle. Then, we cover the software that lets you exchange files that you might encounter on PC-formatted disks (or even a rare UNIX disk). Last, but certainly not least, we talk about the key software you should consider for creating, converting, or compressing file formats.

REMOVABLE MEDIA

Today, the options in removable media have gone way beyond the now-quaint choice between disks that are $3^1/_2$ or $5^1/_4$ inches across. Virtually all of today's options are available for Macintosh computers. Table 2-1 provides a reference for media type and corresponding vendors. (My apologies if a company has been omitted.) While this book was being written, many of these companies released new products, so the table is almost certainly incomplete. Check each company's Web site for their current product offerings. These products can be purchased from on-line mail-order companies.

FILE EXCHANGE

Once you have the disk drive you need to read a particular disk, the next step is to brace yourself and place the disk in the drive. If it's a Mac disk, it will hum and whir and an icon will appear on your Mac desktop. That's the easy way.

And it turns out that, with a Mac, the hard way isn't that difficult either. This section describes software to help you if you find yourself with a PC-formatted disk on your Mac, if you have a Mac disk that you must open on a PC, and what the heck to do in the unlikely event that someone hands you a UNIX floppy or CD-ROM.

PC Disks on a Mac

For most cases, reading PC-formatted disks on your Mac is not a problem for Mac OS versions newer than 7.5. PC Exchange (in Mac OS 7.5–8.1) and File

File Exchange

Table 2-1. Macintosh Removable Media

Medium	Vendor	Web	Connector(s)
Floppy Disk	Apple Computer	*www.apple.com*	Internal
	VST Technologies	*www.vsttech.com*	USB
CD-ROM	Apple Computer	*www.apple.com*	Internal
	(many others)		SCSI
CD-R/CD-RW	APS Technologies	*www.apstech.com*	SCSI
	Fantom Drives	*www.fantomdrives.com*	SCSI
	LaCie	*www.lacie.com*	SCSI, USB
	Microboards	*www.microboards.com*	SCSI
	Nomai	*www.nomai.com*	SCSI
	Que!	*www.qps-inc.com*	USB
DVD-ROM	Apple Computer	*www.apple.com*	Internal
	EZQuest	*www.ezq.com*	Internal (PCI)
DVD-RAM	Apple	*www.apple.com*	Internal
	LaCie	*www.lacie.com*	SCSI, fast SCSI
	Panasonic	*www.panasonic.com/-oemdvd-ram*	SCSI
Jaz, Zip	Iomega	*www.iomega.com*	SCSI, USB
	VST Technologies	*www.vsttech.com*	PowerBook bay
SparQ, SyJet	SyQuest	*www.syquest.com*	SCSI, USB
SuperDisk	Imation	*www.superdisk.com*	USB, SCSI
	VST Technologies	*www.vsttech.com*	PowerBook bay
Digital Tape	APS Technologies	*www.apstech.com*	SCSI
	Tecmar Technologies	*www.tecmar.com*	SCSI
Optical and magneto-optical disk	Fantom Drives	*www.fantomdrives.com*	SCSI
	Formac	*www.formac.com*	SCSI
	LaCie	*www.lacie.com*	SCSI
	VST Technologies	*www.vsttech.com*	Firewire

Exchange (renamed for Mac OS 8.5) allow your Mac to see and read most PC-formatted removable media, and even PC-formatted internal hard drives.

PC Exchange 2.2, shown in Figure 2-1, is one reason to upgrade to Mac OS 8.1. Older versions of PC Exchange do not support PC disks with FAT32 formatting, handle Windows long file names, or support PC-formatted Iomega Zip and Jaz disks.

File Exchange 3.0, shown in Figure 2-2, is one reason to upgrade to Mac OS 8.5. Apple merged PC Exchange and the Mac OS Easy Open control panel into File Exchange, which adds support for PC SCSI disks and adds a database of file extension mappings. Mac OS Easy Open helps identify applications that might open a file for which you don't have the application that created it. (See the section on file names and types.)

Software Architects also produces utilities that let Macs read and format PC removable media. DOS Mounter 98 reads PC-formatted disks, while Formatter-Five provides DOS Mounter functions plus enhanced formatting options. According to *MacWorld*, DOS Mounter has better cross-platform file mapping than PC Exchange, although File Exchange in Mac OS 8.5 makes significant improvements in this area. DOS Mounter will also let you create Mac and PC partitions on the same disk. Note that both the Apple and Software Architects products display only the Mac-allowed 31 characters of Windows long file names, but do not change them, so the full 253 character names are retained. Table 2-2 lists utilities for reading PC disks on a Mac.

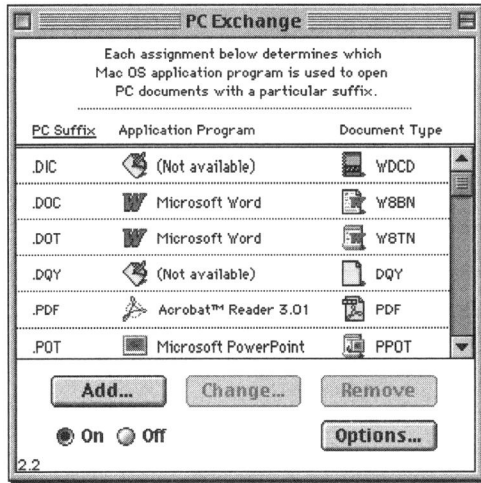

Figure 2-1. PC Exchange 2.2

File Exchange

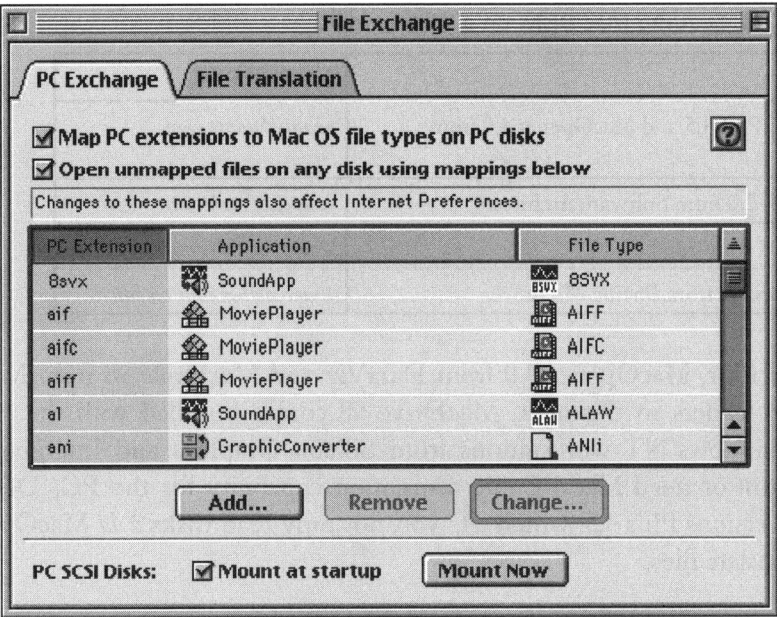

Figure 2-2. File Exchange 3.0

Table 2-2. Reading PC Disks on a Mac

Description	Location
File Exchange 3.0	Included with Mac OS 8.5
PC Exchange. Version 2.2 included with OS 8.1.	Included with Mac OS 7.5-8.1
DOS Mounter 98 and FormatterFive from Software Architects	*www.softarch.com*

Mac Disks on a PC

Although Windows does not have the native ability to read and write Mac OS disks, there are utilities that get Windows over that hurdle. The April 1998 *MacWorld* gave a brief run-down of the options, which are listed in Table 2-3. Since the *MacWorld* review, three of the four have been upgraded to support Windows 98 (the exception being Here & Now), and the upgrades handle most forms of removable media on Windows 3.1, 95, 98, and NT.

Table 2-3. Reading Mac Disks on a Windows PC

Description	Location
Conversions Plus 4.5 and MacOpener 4.0 from DataViz	*www.dataviz.com*
Here & Now 2.0 from Software Architects	*www.softarch.com*
MacDrive 98 from Media4	*www.media4.com*
Mac-in-DOS 3.0 from Pacific Micro	*www.netusa.com/pacmicro*

Of the four, MacOpener 4.0 from DataViz and MacDrive 98 from Media4 are the two leaders in this area. MacDrive 98 comes bundled with the "Mac-friendly" Windows NT workstations from Silicon Graphics and Intergraph. If you also want or need Mac-PC file translation capability for the PC, DataViz offers Conversions Plus 4.5, which lets you not only read disks *à la* MacOpener, but also translate files.

UNIX Disks on a Mac

Theoretically, you could possibly at some point have to read files off of a UNIX disk, either a 3.5-inch disk or a CD-ROM. It's not likely, since the easiest way to exchange files with a UNIX machine is via FTP (see Chapter 5). But if either your Mac or the UNIX machine is, for some reason, not on a network, you might choose to exchange files via disk.

If you have a UNIX CD-ROM, get ready for a challenge: UNIX CD-ROMs are (or at least should be) in ISO 9660 format, and you can read them simply by inserting them in your Mac's CD-ROM drive. The icon will appear, and you can access the files. (If you can't open such a CD-ROM, the ISO 9660 File Access extension, installed with the Mac OS, needs to be in your Extensions folder.)

As for regular 3.5-inch floppy disks, that's a different story. First of all, they're not easy to find. I was unable to locate a UNIX machine at SDSC with a floppy drive, and I got some funny looks when I asked.

Second, the UNIX machine may be using DOS-formatted disks. In that case, the tools and tricks for PC disks should serve you well on your Mac. There are also UNIX utilities, free and commercial, for reading and writing Mac disks.

Third, the UNIX machine may treat the floppy drive as if it were a tape drive. In this case, the best solution is the freeware utility called Suntar. Suntar will read from and write to UNIX disks that hold .tar or .bar archives. In fact, Suntar will let you mount and read tapes connected to a UNIX workstation. The main goal of this software is to extract files and folders from UNIX .tar (tape archive) files.

Fourth, I'll call this option "other." Although there were no UNIX disks at SDSC, a co-worker, Greg Johnson, was able to create a disk on his NeXT system at home. NeXTStep, unlike older variants of UNIX, actually understood the concept of floppy disk and has its own format. The Mac OS thought the disk was unformatted, and Suntar saw it was initialized but that it wasn't in .tar or .bar format. So I end this section with a request: If you know how to open disks that are formatted for platforms other than Macs or PCs, I encourage you to visit the book's Web site and add your tip. You can also send me e-mail.

VIRUS SOFTWARE

If you are going to be exchanging files with other computers via networks or disks, it behooves you to have anti-virus software for your Mac. There are not nearly as many Mac viruses as there are for Windows platforms, but there are some.

Worse than system viruses are the macro viruses, which spread through infected data files. Macros are custom functions that programmers and experienced users can create in applications such as those in Microsoft Office. Macro *viruses* are macros gone bad, and macro viruses that originate on Windows machines can infect your Mac. By default, Microsoft Office 98 for the Mac has the "Macro virus protection" option turned on—under the Tools menu, choose Preferences... and then the General tab. This protection will display an alert if you try to open a file that has a macro attached. To be safe, don't open any file with an unexpected macro. Either throw it away or run one of the anti-virus packages available for the Mac.

Table 2-4 lists some Macintosh anti-virus resources and software. The Mac Virus Web site offers the latest scoop on Mac viruses and software. Some freeware options target specific viruses or the AutoStart Worm, and Dr. Solo-

Table 2-4. Macintosh Anti-Virus Software

Description	Location
Disinfectant 3.7.1—retired and no longer being updated	*ftp.nwu.edu/ftp-archive/pub/disinfectant/-README-IMPORTANT*
Mac Virus Web site, with software, news, and reference resources	*www.macvirus.com*
Norton Anti-Virus 5.0 from Symantec	*www.symantec.com/nav/fs_navmac5.html*
Rival 3.0 from Rival	*www.intego.com*
Virex from Dr. Solomon	*www.drsolomon.com/products/virex/index.cfm*
VirusScan from McAfee is no longer being updated. Owners offered upgrade to Virex.	*www.nai.com/products/antivirus/virex_mac.asp*

mon's Virex, Norton Anti-Virus, and Intego Rival are the three main commercial packages. McAfee VirusScan for Macintosh is no longer being updated, and the freeware Disinfectant, while still available for download, has also been retired.

Since the virus situation will undoubtedly change between the time I write this and the time you read it, I will end the discussion here and point you to the Mac Virus Web site, created and maintained by Susan Lesch.

FILE CONVERSION

Once you move those files from a PC disk to your Mac, then what? If the file happens to be from an application that has Mac and PC versions, such as Microsoft Word or Adobe PhotoShop, you're probably in good shape. The Mac application should be smart enough to open a file from the Windows version. See Chapter 6 for a more detailed discussion of this situation.

Even if you don't have the Mac version of an application, there are tools for converting the common types of files you will most likely need to exchange.

File Names and Types

Microsoft Windows, as you may know, requires a user to name a file a certain way so that the operating system knows what to do with it. I'm talking about the "file extension," usually three (or four) letters tacked on to the rest of the name that clues Windows in on the file type. For example, *horse.gif* is a GIF graphics file, *resume.txt* is a text file, *memo.doc* is a Microsoft Word file, and so on. You may recognize some of these extensions from the Web, which uses a similar naming convention.

The Mac, on the other hand, doesn't care about file extensions. In the Mac OS, each file has an internal area (called a resource fork) that stores labels (called resources) for all sorts of information about a file. Two important labels are the Creator and Type, four-letter codes that identify which application created the file and what type of file it is. For example, the TEXT file type, not surprisingly, identifies a text file, and the "ttxt" code refers to SimpleText.

Plus, you should be sure to avoid special characters—\/ : * ? " < > |—in your Mac file names that will throw Windows into a snit. NameCleaner from Sig Software will help you identify and fix potential file name problems before exchanging files.

Up through Mac OS 8.1, PC Exchange did not include much information about mapping Windows file extensions to Mac file types; you have to add that information yourself. (Microsoft Office 98 does, however, install the mappings for Word, PowerPoint, and Excel file types.) If you don't know too many Windows file extensions, you can still avoid trial-and-error guessing with a few handy upgrades or utilities. Table 2-5 points you to their Web sites.

- File Exchange in Mac OS 8.5 provides an extensive database of mappings that PC Exchange lacks and includes the Mac OS Easy Open features to open a file in the application best suited to handle it.

- DOS Mounter 98 also includes an extensive database of file mappings. However, if you have to update the mappings on more than one Mac, you have to do it manually on each computer.

- The shareware Mac Type/Creator Database from Ilan Szekely includes a database that PC Exchange can use.

- The FileTyper, A Better Finder Creators and Types, and TypeRighter shareware can assign Type and Creator codes on a file-by-file basis. **A word of caution:** Take care when changing Type and Creator codes with such tools. Changing the contents of a file's resource fork can have unintended consequences if you aren't sure what you're doing.

- On the PC side, MacOpener from DataViz can perform the mapping when a PC saves a file to a Mac disk. And if your PC is connected to a

Table 2-5. Mac-PC File Name and Type Mapping

Description	Location
A Better Finder Creators and Types shareware lets you change the Creator and Type of multiple files all at once.	*www.publicspace.net/ABetterFinderCreatorsAndTypes*
FileTyper, shareware by Daniel Azuma that lets you assign Creator and Type codes (and other resource information)	*www.ugcs.caltech.edu/~dazuma/filetyper*
Mac Type/Creator Database, shareware databases including PC extension mappings from Ilan Szekely	*www.geocities.com/SiliconValley/Bay/5677*
MacOpener, Windows file extension mapping software from DataViz	*www.dataviz.com/products/MOW/MOHome.html*
NameCleaner from Sig Software analyzes file names for cross-platform suitability.	*www.sigsoftware.com*
PC Migrator, a file extension mapping plug-in for the Windows PC MAC-LAN software from Miramar Systems	*www.miramarsys.com/products/ov-migrator.htm*
TypeRighter Suite, shareware from the Lightning Foundry, for changing Creator and Type codes	*www.pict.demon.co.uk/products/typerighter*

Mac network with PC MACLAN (see Chapter 4), PC Migrator for PC MACLAN will automatically look at Mac file type and creator information and add the appropriate PC file extension when transferring Mac files to a Windows machine.

General Files

The Cross Platform utility from Sig Software (see Table 2-6) helps you analyze the files that you're exchanging between a PC and a Mac to determine which application on the PC can open it. But what if you find yourself with a file created in Lotus WordPro (formerly AmiPro)—a Windows-only word processor—or some ancient version of MacWrite? That's when you turn to MacLinkPlus from

File Conversion

DataViz. Up through Mac OS 8.1, MacLinkPlus was bundled with the system; the latest bundled version was MacLinkPlus 9.0. With Mac OS 8.5, Apple unbundled the DataViz tool, so you must purchase it separately.

The latest version, MacLinkPlus 10.0, can translate nearly 100 different word processing, spreadsheet, database, and graphics file formats, has an updated user interface, and includes the ability to open common compressed file types (see the Compression section later in this chapter).

However, converting files from one application's format to another's should not be viewed as a cure-all. Because some formatting features depend on the capabilities of the application used to create a file, don't expect that converting a heavily formatted Corel WordPerfect document to a ClarisWorks 3.0 document will preserve the exact look and feel of the original. In general, you should expect conversion to retain the readable text and basic formatting; anything more than that, you should feel very satisfied. Chapter 6 discusses some of the other issues in moving files between platforms.

Table 2-6. Mac File Conversion Software

Description	Location
Cross Platform file compatibility tool from Sig Software	*www.sigsoftware.com*
MacLinkPlus, the *de facto* standard for Mac file conversion from DataViz	*www.dataviz.com*

Graphics

This section will be shorter than you expected because there is *no way* I can hope to cover the oodles of graphics tools for the Mac. Forget about it. On fourth and long, you punt.

Most image creation and editing software can open a variety of common graphics formats. If you find yourself with an uncommon file format, try your favorite graphics program; it may just be able to open it.

If that fails, for converting graphics files, it's hard to go wrong with the shareware GraphicConverter from Lemke Software. It can open about 100 graphics file types, from Atari PIC to VOXEL, and can export about 40 graphics types. DeBabelizer from Equilibrium is a comparable commercial package that, in addition to converting between graphics formats, also has scripting and automation features.

About the only file types that give GraphicConverter pause are PostScript, Encapsulated PostScript (EPS), and Adobe's Portable Document Format (PDF). In fairness, PostScript and PDF are designed for printing pages, not graphics. Table 2-7 lists some additional software utilities.

Table 2-7. Mac Graphic Conversion Tools

Description	Location
DeBabelizer, commercial software from Equilibrium, converts graphics files and has scripting and automation features.	*www.equilibrium.com*
EPStoPICT for converting PostScript and Encapsulated PostScript files to PICT images	*www.artage.com*
GhostScript freeware allows you to view and save PostScript files as PICT files.	*www.cs.wisc.edu/~ghost/mac*
GraphicConverter shareware from Lemke Software	*www.lemkesoft.de*
Transverter Pro from TechPool Software for viewing and editing PostScript and PDF files	*www.techpool.com*

Sound

If you desperately need to convert that Microsoft .WAV file of Homer Simpson's "D'oh!" into an alert sound for your Mac, there is hope. My favorite is the freeware SoundApp by Norman Franke. This utility will read more than 20 sound types and save sounds in a half dozen formats.

QuickTime software also provides some sound conversion capability, and you should have it for viewing a variety of movie formats anyway (see the next section). If these sound tools don't suffice, there are many Mac sound utilities, not to mention sound editing tools, and Table 2-8 provides a starting point.

Table 2-8. Mac Sound Conversion Tools

Description	Location
SoundApp, freeware by Norman Franke	*www-cs-students.stanford.edu/~franke/SoundApp*
QuickTime from Apple	*www.apple.com/quicktime*
More sound utilities in the Info-Mac archive	*www.macinsearch.com/infomac2/sound/snd/-menu.shtml*

Movies

We're just flying through these sections now. Movie formats are also easy to deal with: Get QuickTime 4 from Apple Computer. The most recent releases of the Mac OS include QuickTime 4, and if you have older versions of the Mac OS, you should consider upgrading to the latest version of QuickTime. The latest version lets you view many movie types, including MPEG (common on UNIX machines) and AVI (Microsoft's own movie format).

A tip: The basic QuickTime 4 includes the QuickTime Player, which can play many movie formats but cannot convert them to other formats. To get conversion capability, you need QuickTime 4 Pro, which is about $30. However, there is a partial fix. If you have QuickTime 2.5, before installing QuickTime 4, move and rename the MoviePlayer 2.5 folder. MoviePlayer 2.5 lets you view and save movies in several common formats.

Table 2-9 points you to the QuickTime Web site, and to a few utilities that are useful for converting MPEG and AVI movies to QuickTime format.

Table 2-9. Mac Movie Conversion Tools

Description	Location
QuickTime from Apple	*www.apple.com/quicktime*
MacZilla, shareware for viewing AVI and MPEG movies	*maczilla.com*
AVI->QT for AVI files and Sparkle for MPEG are just two utilities in the Info-Mac archive.	*www.macinsearch.com/infomac2/-graphics/mov/menu.shtml*

Compression

File compression is a big deal. Compression techniques crunch a file so that it can be stored in fewer, sometimes many fewer, bits. The better the compression, the more information that can be stored on a disk, or the shorter the time to download a file across the Internet. And believe it or not, there are dozens of file compression methods. In a cross-platform environment, you need to be able to decompress most of them.

Some compressed file types are so common that decompression techniques are built right into the software that reads the files. GIF and JPEG image formats and MPEG video and audio formats, for example, are actually named for the compression method used. QuickTime software is actually a set of tools for reading audio and video stored with a variety of CODECs (COmpression-DECompression techniques).

But in general, when we talk about compressed files we mean images, text and data files, applications, or folders of such files that have been further crunched and bundled together to make them easier to distribute. Table 2-10 lists some common compression formats for Macs, PCs, and UNIX machines, and the file name extensions that (usually) identify them.

Technically, I'm treading in a gray area here among compression, archiving, and encoding. Compression means storing a file's data in fewer bits or bytes. Archiving means bundling a folder and all the files and subfolders it contains into one file, which makes distribution and installation easier. Encoding lets you transmit files across the Internet. In practice, however, you are more likely to encounter files that have been compressed, archived, and encoded, and you want to get them back to their original, usable formats.

When you have a file in one of these formats, you want to decode, decompress, and unarchive it. There are plenty of options. To help you sort them out, I'll give a few recommendations.

Table 2-10. Common Compression and Archive Formats

Platform	File Type	File Extension
Mac OS	StuffIt archive	.sit
	MacBinary	.bin
	BinHex archive	.hqx
	Self-extracting archive	.sea
	Compact Pro	.cpt
Windows 98/NT	Zip	.zip
	Archive	.arc
	LHA archive	.lzh, .lha, .lzs
	Self-extracting archive	.exe, .com, .x
UNIX	UNIX compress	.Z
	Gzip	.gz
	Tape archive	.tar

File Conversion

The long-time standard file compression tool for the Mac OS is the free StuffIt Expander from Aladdin Systems. You probably have it on your Mac now. By itself, StuffIt Expander opens .sit, .bin, and .hqx files. For smoother cross-platform operation, you'll want to purchase the shareware DropStuff with Expander Enhancer, which can open common Windows and UNIX file formats as well as create .sit archives. To cover all the bases for decompressing most cross-platform formats, try the full version of StuffIt Deluxe. StuffIt Deluxe has additional Mac features and also includes a copy of Aladdin Expander and DropStuff for Windows.

A new entry into the fray is the MindExpander utility from MindVision Software, which is better known for its Installer VISE software. MindExpander opens standard Mac formats and will use other utilities on your disk to open cross-platform formats.

The Pure Mac page of compression and encoding utilities lists more tools, some of which can create archives in Windows or UNIX formats. Table 2-11 lists a few key utilities and sources for others.

Table 2-11. Mac File Compression Software Tools

Description	Location
General compression pointers to people, techniques, mailing lists, and FAQs	*www.internz.com/compression-pointers.html*
Mac compression and encoding utilities, compiled by Pure Mac	*www.mactimes.com/puremac/compen.shtml*
MacTar, freeware from Jim Strout for reading UNIX .tar archives	*strout.net/macsoft*
MindExpander freeware from MindVision Software	*www.mindvision.com*
StuffIt Expander, StuffIt Deluxe, and other tools from Aladdin Systems	*www.aladdinsys.com*
Suntar, freeware by Sauro and Gabriele Speranza for reading UNIX .tar and .bar archives. It will also read from .tar disks and tapes.	*ftp://uiarchive.uiuc.edu/pub/systems/mac/-info-maccmp/suntar-214.hqx*

In Short, You Need...

"Blah, blah, blah," you're saying to yourself. "Cut to the chase." I hear you. For your cross-platform, sneaker net–ready Mac, get yourself these tools:

- **Reading disks.** Get Mac OS 8.5.1 to get the upgrade to File Exchange 3.0.
- **File conversion.** For word processing, spreadsheet, and database files, you need DataViz MacLinkPlus. For graphics, Lemke Software's GraphicConverter. For sounds, Norman Franke's SoundApp. For movies, the latest version of QuickTime.
- **File compression.** Get StuffIt Expander and DropStuff with Expander Enhancer.

For download information, or if these don't cut it for some reason, check out the relevant preceding sections. Table 2-12 also points you to some additional resources that discuss some of the material described in this chapter.

Table 2-12. Additional Web Resources

Description	Location
The Business Mac	*www.applelinks.com/business_mac*
MacWorld, April 1998	*macworld.zdnet.com/pages/april.98*
Pure Mac, "All the software you really need"	*www.pure-mac.com*

CHAPTER 3

Basic Mac Networking

This chapter is designed to give you a basic understanding of computer networking from a Mac perspective, explain how to configure your Mac for a network, and give you some ammunition to counter some general criticisms of Macs as networked computers.

If you are new to the whole area of computer networking, you may want to have a look at the Appendix—Mac OS Networking Primer—before you charge ahead. The Appendix defines a lot of common networking terms that appear throughout the book and gives you some idea of how they fit together. On the other hand, if you believe networking ignorance is bliss, you can probably survive without the Appendix if you use the following oversimplified definitions:

Network: a bunch of connected computers

Protocol: a networking language

AppleTalk: the native protocol of Macintosh computers

TCP/IP: the native protocol of the Internet

If you run into other terms you don't recognize, you can either fake it or refer to the Appendix. That's what it's there for.

MAC NETWORKING PROS AND CONS

Macintosh computers and the Mac OS have a reputation, with both users and administrators, for being a poor system for network use. Like most reputations, there is a mixture of myth and truth to it. As with most things in life, there are advantages and disadvantages to the Mac OS networking technologies.

Mac OS and AppleTalk Advantages

Ease of Use. AppleTalk protocols were designed with the end user in mind; TCP/IP was designed for computers. AppleTalk is easy to set up and makes it easy for users to share files, use networked printers, and access other services. Every Macintosh ever built has been able to communicate with other Macs over AppleTalk-based LocalTalk networks, and with the iPort network adapter from Griffin Technology (*www.griffintechnology.com*), the iMac can be connected to LocalTalk networks. In fact, the Internet Engineering Task Force (IETF) is developing a Service Location Protocol (SLP), similar to the AppleTalk naming system, which should bring some of AppleTalk's ease-of-use to IP-based networks.

Security. The high-level AppleTalk Filing Protocol (AFP) does not send passwords as clear text as do a number of high-level protocols, such as FTP, on the TCP/IP side.

Compatibility. Because AppleTalk and TCP/IP are built in independent layers, the high-level AppleTalk protocols can be implemented using the low-level IP protocol. For example, recent upgrades to software such as AppleShare IP allow AppleTalk file sharing over IP. (See Chapter 4.)

Mac OS and AppleTalk Disadvantages

"Chattiness." The original version of AppleTalk talked too much, according to some, and gained a reputation as a "chatty" set of protocols. Some network administrators may be under the impression that this is still true. However, years ago AppleTalk Phase 2 addressed this drawback. AppleTalk's chattiness is no longer a bottleneck. A more relevant complaint would be that managing both AppleTalk traffic and TCP/IP traffic potentially incurs a greater administrative effort.

Performance. The early releases of Open Transport had many bugs and quickly earned the Mac a reputation for being a slower Internet device than Windows and UNIX systems. With Mac OS 8.5 and Open Transport 2.0, however, Macintoshes can exchange files at rates comparable to and often faster than Windows NT machines. Other perceived sluggishness—in Web browsing, for example—is being addressed by Mac OS improvements and Apple's work with developers to improve application performance.

Management. For some time, the Mac OS has lacked support for the Simple Network Management Protocol (SNMP), upon which many centralized network management tools rely. However, Mac OS 8.5 now includes an SNMP client as an optional installer, and a new release of the Apple Network Administrator Toolkit provides remote install services, screen sharing, and other services for tracking and configuring remote Macs via AppleTalk or IP.

Compatibility. Only Macs run AppleTalk as a default protocol, and for administrators of UNIX or Windows networks, AppleTalk represents an additional protocol to support. Then, there is the matter of Windows NT Server using Microsoft-only variations of protocols and authentication methods, which have been implemented on the Mac only with Open Transport 2.0. On Novell networks, the Mac OS has been subject to limited support. Recently, however, ProSoft Engineering has taken over Mac client development, which has led to recent updates to Mac NetWare services. Chapter 4 covers these and other Mac network compatibility issues.

Interface. While not as complicated as configuring a UNIX system for network access, the various versions of the Mac OS sport a variety of control panels and extensions related to network configuration. The purpose of each of these may be confusing to the uninitiated. The next section explains the why and how of each of these control panels.

Table 3-1 contains links to resources and references relevant to the pros and cons of Mac networking.

CONFIGURING MAC NETWORKING

Here we discuss the Mac OS control panels related to networking. Refer to this section when connecting your Mac to a local-area network or a dial-up connection. Some of the options become available when you install Apple Remote Access (ARA) client software, which allows you to dial into AppleTalk networks and use your computer as if it were at the remote site. If your network connection is working properly, please use caution when changing any network settings.

Table 3-2 contains pointers to sources of information on the extensions needed and additional networking options.

AppleTalk

The AppleTalk control panel has two basic options: connection port and zone selection. By default, you can connect to an AppleTalk network via

Table 3-1. Mac OS Networking Pros and Cons

Description	Location
AppleShare IP file sharing performance	*www.apple.com/appleshareip/text/performance.html*
Installing the Mac OS 8.5 SNMP client	*www.apple.com/macos/8.5/start/nt/pgs/ntadsnmp.htm*
Apple Network Administrator Toolkit	*www.apple.com/networking/anat*
"Apple's Net Future"	*NetProfessional Magazine,* July/August 1998. *www.netprolive.com*
NetWare 5 for Macintosh, from ProSoft Engineering	*www.prosofteng.com/NetWare.htm*

Configuring Mac Networking

Table 3-2. Networking Control Panels and Extensions

Description	Location
The Complete Conflict Compendium is an on-line collection of Mac OS applications, control panels, and extensions that can interfere with one another.	*www.mac-conflicts.com*
Conflict Catcher, commercial software by Casady & Greene, for detecting extensions and control panels that don't play well together	*www.casadyg.com/products/conflictcatcher*
FreePPP, freeware for dial-up PPP connections	*www.rockstar.com/ppp.shtml*
InformINIT, an invaluable shareware reference by Dan Frakes on Apple and third-party control panels and extensions	*www.informinit.com*
Internet Config, freeware from Stairways Software	*www.stairways.com*
MacPPP, freeware from the MacBel group	*ink2.ink.org/docs/software/mac/ppp/readme.html*
MacSLIP, a commercial package from Hyde Park Software for older-style SLIP connections (updates only)	*www.zilker.net/~hydepark/updaters.html*
PPP Menu adds a system for managing PPP connections and Internet applications.	*www.rockstar.com/Products/Other/plugins.html*

Ethernet, Modem Port, or Printer Port. As a rule of thumb, this option should be set to the port to which your network cables are connected. If you have ARA installed, you will see a Remote Only option for dial-up connections.

Once you are connected to an AppleTalk network, you can select the zone, or section of an AppleTalk network, to which you belong. Zones help organize the computers and printers on the network into more convenient and manageable groups. With the Configurations... menu option, you can save several configurations, useful for traveling PowerBooks, for example.

AppleTalk addresses are usually defined automatically, so the basic AppleTalk control panel, shown in Figure 3-1, is very simple. Choose the Get Info... menu option to see your AppleTalk addresses and AppleTalk software versions, as in Figure 3-2. Figure 3-2 also shows the control panel's advanced and password-protected administration modes (select Edit: User Mode...), which allow network managers to configure the AppleTalk settings for the computer. Average users shouldn't have to change the advanced settings.

Configuration Manager

When you install Microsoft Internet Explorer, the Configuration Manager control panel is also installed. Here you can set not only your preferences for Internet Explorer, but also virtually all of your Internet-related preferences, from firewalls and proxies to your default home page. Except for the Internet Explorer settings, these preferences can also be set via the public domain Internet Config application and, in Mac OS 8.5, the Internet control panel.

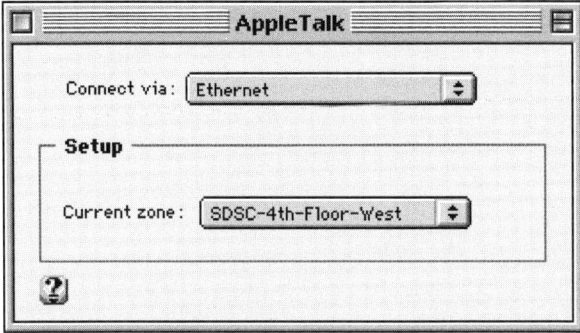

Figure 3-1. Basic AppleTalk control panel

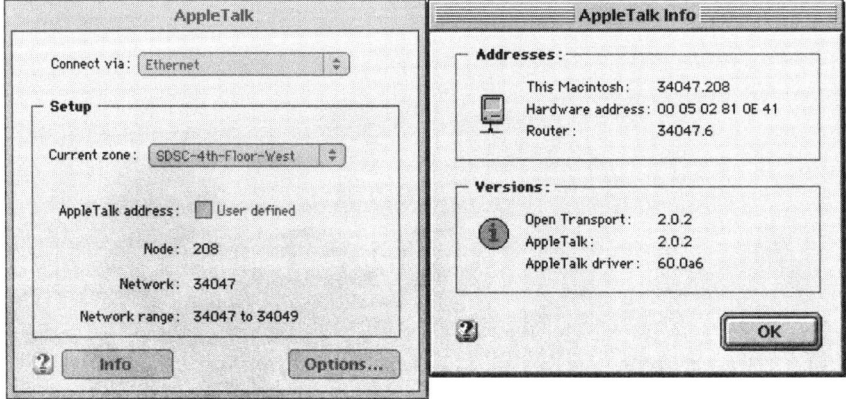

Figure 3-2. Advanced AppleTalk settings and info

DialAssist

If you use ARA and the number you have to dial is anything more complicated than a seven-digit local number, DialAssist lets you specify country codes, area codes, outside-line prefix, long-distance carrier prefix, and a calling card or credit card suffix. Unfortunately, this handy control panel comes only with the ARA client and not with other dial-up options, such as the default PPP control panel.

Infrared

This control panel sets the protocol used on a PowerBook's infrared port. Most PowerBooks support IRTalk (AppleTalk over the infrared port) or IrDA, a cross-platform standard for infrared connections that is supported by Palm Pilots and other devices.

Internet

This Mac OS 8.5 control panel, shown in Figure 3-3, lets you configure system-wide settings for your on-line identity and e-mail, Web, and news services. These settings (and others) can also be configured with Internet Config and the Configuration Manager control panel. All three of these options use the *same* Internet Preferences file in the Preferences folder, so making a change in one is reflected in the other two.

Internet Config

Although technically not a control panel, you might see this small application on your hard drive. It may have been installed with Netscape Communicator, for example. As described with the Configuration Manager and Internet control panels, this public domain tool from Stairways Software brings together all your Internet-related settings into one place, through a straightforward interface shown in Figure 3-4. Credit should go to Stairways Software for realizing as early as 1994 that it would be incredibly handy for all your Internet applications to have these preferences in one place.

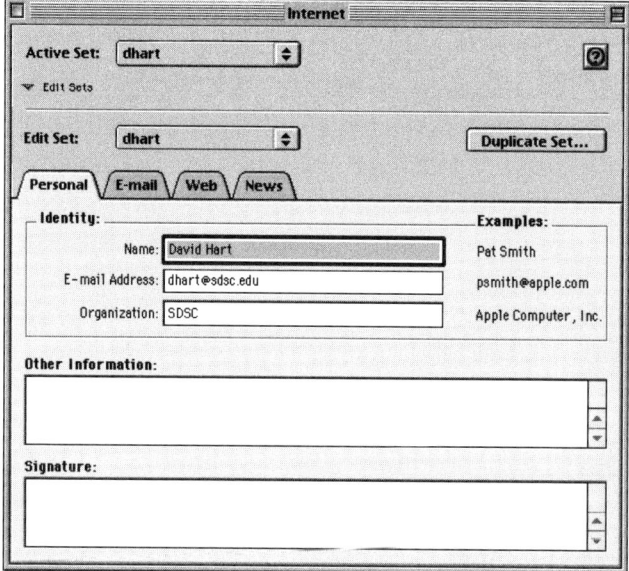

Figure 3-3. Mac OS 8.5 Internet control panel

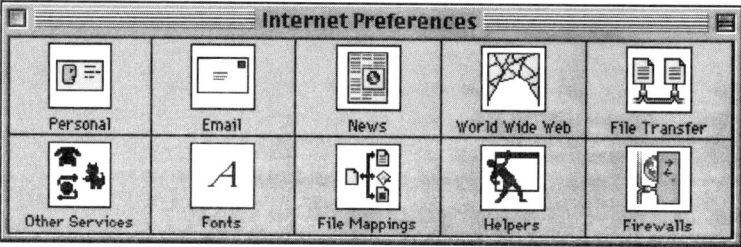

Figure 3-4. Internet Config

Location Manager

On PowerBooks, the Location Manager control panel allows you to save settings, including network configurations, that change depending on the location at which you're using your PowerBook. For example, when you move the computer from your office to your home, you can change all the relevant control panels and network settings at once, as shown in Figure 3-5.

Configuring Mac Networking

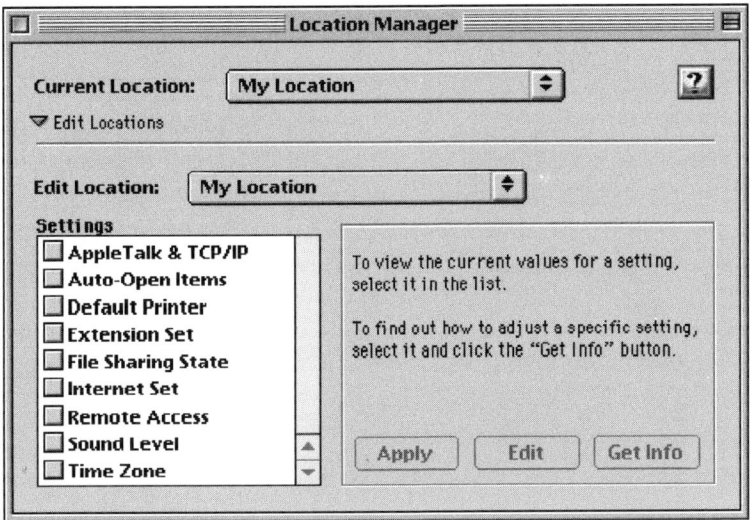

Figure 3-5. Location Manager control panel

MacTCP

For Mac OS versions 7.5 and earlier, prior to Open Transport, this was the control panel used to configure TCP/IP settings. Again, if you have this control panel, you should look into upgrade options.

Modem

The Modem control panel tells your Mac how to communicate via its modem if you are not using ARA. Your modem is most likely connected via the modem port, the "Modem" option specifies the make and model of your modem, and the "Dialing" option, for most people, is Tone. You can also turn off (or on) the melodious sounds of two modems making a connection. If you do not use a modem to connect to a network, you can disable this control panel (with the Extensions Manager, for example).

Network

If you have the Network control panel, you are using version 7.5.2 or earlier of the Mac OS. This control panel lets you switch between different types of networks; it was superseded by the AppleTalk control panel and the Open Transport architecture.

PPP

The Open Transport PPP control panel, shown in Figure 3-6, lets your Mac dial into an Internet Service Provider (ISP) to access the Internet. The PPP, or Point-to-Point Protocol, control panel comes with the Mac OS. If you install the ARA 3.0 client software, the Remote Access control panel supersedes this control panel. The basic settings let you specify your user name, password, and phone number of your dial-up service.

If you use PPP to connect, your TCP/IP control panel must be set to connect via PPP and configure using the PPP server. With the Options... button of the PPP panel, you can automate redialing or record the commands you must type for a command-line host. You can use the Configurations... option to save settings for several different Internet Service Providers.

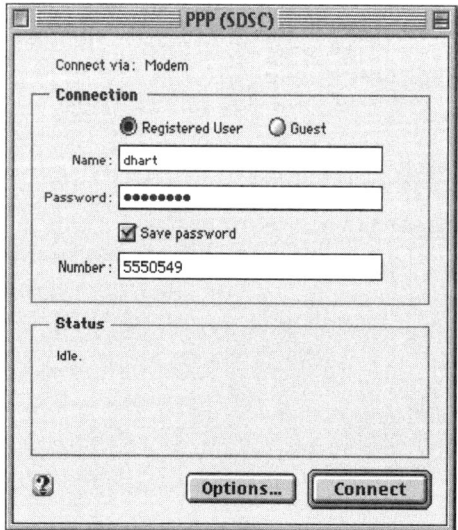

Figure 3-6. Open Transport PPP control panel

Configuring Mac Networking

Remote Access

If you are using ARA 3.0, this control panel, shown in Figure 3-7, replaces both the Remote Access Setup and PPP control panels. It consolidates the interface and configuration for accessing both PPP and ARA networks. ARA 3.0 also allows you to establish AppleTalk and PPP connections over the same dial-up line.

Remote Access Setup

The Remote Access Setup control panel lets you configure modem settings for using the ARA 2.1 software. ARA lets you dial into an AppleTalk network and use network services such as printing and file sharing as if your computer were on the network. The settings here are very similar to those in the Modem control panel.

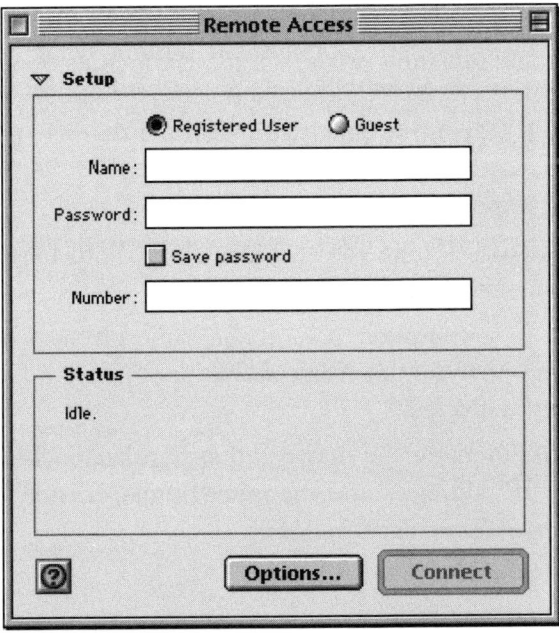

Figure 3-7. Remote Access control panel

TCP/IP

The TCP/IP control panel contains your Mac's settings for, of course, its connection to a TCP/IP network. We won't go into great detail on the settings, because the information needed to configure this control panel will come from your network administrator. *Once your network connection is working, you should not change the information in this control panel without consulting your administrator or your ISP.* This control panel, like the AppleTalk control panel, can be password protected.

In most cases, you can connect via one of the following:
- "AppleTalk (MacIP)" lets you connect to a TCP/IP network over an AppleTalk connection. This is more likely on older Macs without built-in Ethernet.
- "Ethernet" is for the Mac's built-in Ethernet.
- "PPP" is for connecting to a TCP/IP connection over a dial-up (modem) connection. See the PPP control panel.
- If the control panel shows another "Connect via" option, your Mac may have an expansion card and you will probably use this option.

Figure 3-8 shows the TCP/IP control panel with typical Ethernet settings, configured manually.
- The *IP address* is your computer's Internet identification.
- The *subnet mask* is a network setting too technical to go into here; it typically looks something like 255.255.255.0.
- If you send a message to a computer not on the same physical network, the message goes first to the *router address* specified, and the router makes sure it gets delivered.
- The *name servers* are computers on the network that translate back and forth between numeric IP addresses and the more human-friendly *domain names*, such as *www.apple.com* or *t90.sdsc.edu*.

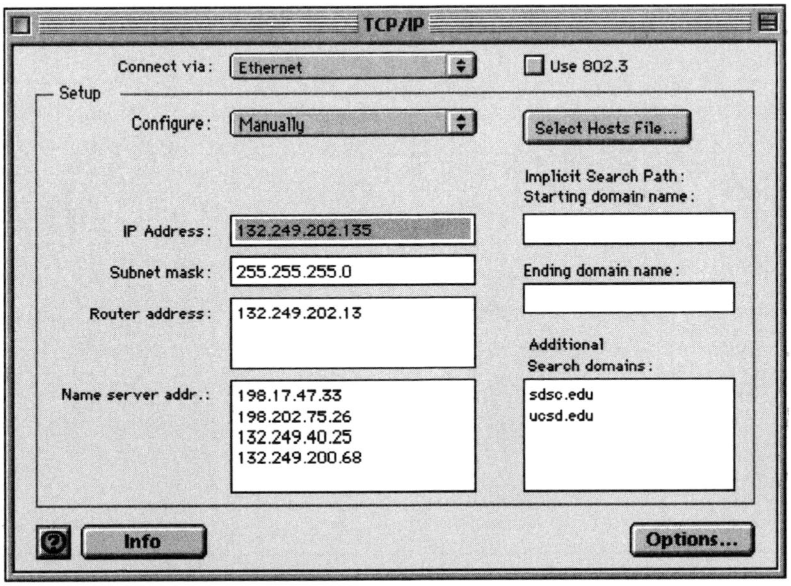

Figure 3-8. TCP/IP control panel

In the column on the right are several optional settings that help your computer find other computers on the network. None of these settings are required. You might ask your network administrator if he or she recommends any.

The TCP/IP control panel also offers three other "Configure" options besides manual: BootP, DHCP, and RARP. As described in the Appendix, these protocols allow your computer to request a temporary IP address from a network server each time your computer connects to the network. This is fine if you're just reading e-mail or surfing the Web. However, if you want to use your computer to host a Web site, for example, you may want to get a permanent IP address. (See Chapter 5.)

HIGH-PERFORMANCE MAC NETWORKING

All current Macintosh computers, including the iMac, come with built-in Ethernet and Fast Ethernet for networking at 10 megabits per second (Mb/s) and 100 Mb/s, respectively. But those are not the only high-speed networking options available for Macs.

- The *Fiber Distributed-Data Interface,* or FDDI (pronounced "fiddy"), is a standard for communicating on fiber optic cable at 100 Mb/s.
- *Asynchronous Transfer Mode* (ATM) supports communication at 155 Mb/s or 622 Mb/s. (Not to be confused with your bank's automated teller machines.)
- *Gigabit Ethernet* is a standard for transmitting data at 1,000 Mb/s (or 1 gigabit per second).

Table 3-3 lists makers of network interface cards for high-speed standards, as well as vendors who produce Ethernet and Fast Ethernet network interface cards for older Macs (with NuBus or PCI architectures). If your network administrators say the Mac can't support any of these standards, tell them about these companies.

Table 3-3. High-Speed Mac Networking

Fast Ethernet (100 Mb/s)	
Apple Computer	*www.apple.com*
Asanté Technologies	*www.asante.com*
Farallon Communications	*www.farallon.com*
Kingston Technology	*www.kingston.com*
Sonic Systems	*www.sonicsys.com*
Team ASA	*www.teamasa.com*
FDDI (100 Mb/s)	
Team ASA Stallion adapter series	*www.teamasa.com*
ATM (155 Mb/s)	
3CX	*www.3cx.com*
Fore Systems (ForeRunner LE and 200E adapters)	*www.fore.com*
Interphase 5575 ATM adapter	*www.iphase.com*
Gigabit Ethernet (1,000 Mb/s)	
Farallon Communications	*www.farallon.com*
Publishing Solutions/Packet Engines	*www.pubsol.com*
Team ASA Stallion-GE adapters	*www.teamasa.com*

Note that with versions of Open Transport prior to 2.0, regardless of the networking interface used, a Mac probably won't see major performance gains beyond the performance seen at 10 Mb/s. In addition, using AppleTalk, especially the low-level protocols, will also hinder performance. Newer Apple products such as AppleShare IP use faster low-level TCP/IP protocols.

NETWORKING SUMMARY

As a networking platform, the Mac OS has had to overcome a reputation from years ago as an under-performing network neighbor. To use your Mac in a cross-platform environment, the following are the key points to consider.

- Upgrade to the newest version of the Mac OS that your Mac will run. Mac OS 8.6 is better than Mac OS 8.1, which is better than any version of Mac OS 7.
- Upgrade to the latest version of the Open Transport networking software. You can compare the version shown by the Get Info… option of your Mac's AppleTalk or TCP/IP control panels with the latest version available from the Apple Software Updates site. Newer versions of the Mac OS have newer versions of Open Transport.
- Once your Mac is connected to and working properly on your organization's network, you should not change the settings in the networking control panels without consulting your network administrator. If you must change settings, be sure to save the working state with the Configurations… option of the relevant control panel so you can recover if you make a mistake.

CHAPTER 4

Local-Area Networks

*N*ow that you've got the software for working with files between platforms, you want to smooth out the cross-platform bumps between you and your co-workers on the local-area network in your office. As a Mac user on that network, you want to be sure that your Mac can connect with the appropriate Mac OS, Windows NT, or UNIX servers that your network administrators support. On the other hand, if you're a network administrator, you want all of the Mac, Windows, or UNIX systems to be able to access your file servers.

So, in this chapter we're going to cover a lot of ground. We will cover Mac OS, Windows NT, Novell NetWare, and UNIX servers, in turn, and describe how a Mac OS client can access those servers. And for all those network administrators who want to provide file services from a Mac OS-based server, we will also cover how Windows and UNIX clients can access Mac file servers. (We'll assume that those of you running Windows NT, NetWare, or UNIX servers know about providing services to those three platforms.)

Finally, before we move on, we'll discuss some of the basics of network administration. To keep this from getting out of hand, we'll talk mainly about the issues from a client Mac perspective: the software and configuration settings you need so that your network administrator stays happy. We'll also highlight some of the software and resources for Mac-based network administrators.

For the record, we'll be talking a lot about the AppleTalk Filing Protocol (AFP) in this chapter. AFP is the network protocol in the AppleTalk family (see the Appendix) that lets you share folders and files on other networked Macs via the Chooser, and access them as if they were directly connected to your computer. This is very handy, and it makes file sharing a snap. It's important in this chapter because AFP support is closely tied to support for Macs. File sharing isn't the only LAN service, but it's a major one.

MAC SERVERS

If you're running a Mac OS-based file server, you are almost certainly running a version of AppleShare, Apple's flagship file and print server package. At the time of writing, AppleShare IP 6.1 was the latest release, and it is the version discussed here. (Apple has since released version 6.2, optimized for Mac OS 8.6.) There are several reasons to consider an upgrade:

- *Performance.* AppleShare IP runs AFP over the more efficient IP protocols where possible to get better performance, but it can use AppleTalk if that's the only protocol available. AppleShare IP 6.1 and Mac OS 8.5 can compete head-to-head with Windows NT Server for file sharing performance.

- *Native Windows client support.* To a Windows 95/98/NT client, AppleShare IP 6 looks and feels like a Windows NT server, using the Windows Server Message Block (SMB) protocol and appearing as part of the client's Network Neighborhood.

- *Internet and e-mail support.* In addition to AFP and SMB sharing, AppleShare IP supports the Internet's FTP protocol, the primary file sharing method for UNIX machines. You can also use it to run a Web server. For e-mail, AppleShare supports the POP3, SMTP, and IMAP protocols.
- *LPR and AppleTalk printing.* Besides supporting traditional Mac printing, AppleShare IP allows you to establish UNIX-standard LPR print queues.

AppleShare IP probably handles most of the cross-platform issues you might encounter for file, e-mail, and print serving. Figure 4-1 shows the AppleShare IP Manager status window for these services. It is not the purpose of this book to provide a manual for AppleShare IP, so I won't write one here. I'll skip over how to run AppleShare IP as a file and print server for Macs, because that's not a cross-platform issue. Also, I won't discuss the Web server or e-mail features of AppleShare IP here for the same reason (but see Chapter 5). However, I will go into some detail on a few specific areas: AppleTalk Filing Protocol (AFP) over TCP/IP networks, Windows and UNIX file sharing, and printing.

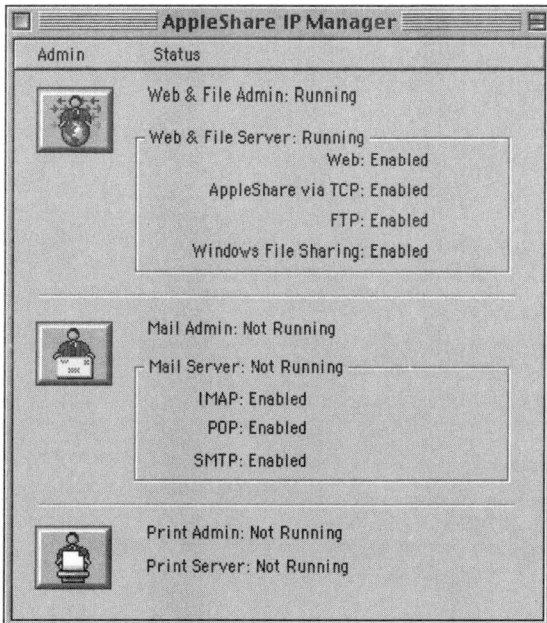

Figure 4-1. AppleShare IP Manager

Sharing over TCP/IP Networks

If you run an older networked Mac environment, you may be facing the decision of whether to have both AppleTalk and TCP/IP protocols on your network. If you're a Mac user, your network administrators may be making this choice for you. In any case, it's not necessarily a bad situation. The low-level IP protocol is more efficient than DDP, its AppleTalk counterpart. And because both the AppleTalk and TCP/IP protocols were designed in layers, Apple and third-party software developers have created software to provide the AppleTalk functions you know and love while taking advantage of the performance of IP.

Here, I'm only giving the basic steps for migrating from AppleTalk to IP networks. A more detailed plan is laid out at the Open Door Networks Web site and in the July/August 1998 *NetProfessional* magazine (see Table 4-1).

1. First, run both AppleTalk and IP over the network. Pockets of older Macs can be connected via gateways. The Vicomsoft Internet Gateway software can route traffic between LocalTalk and MacIP networks and IP networks through a single IP connection.
2. Split your AppleTalk network into AppleTalk pockets connected by the IP network. Services between pockets can be maintained with AppleTalk-to-IP gateways. Apple's AppleShare IP and ShareWay IP from Open Door Networks provide AppleTalk connectivity over IP networks.

Table 4-1. AppleTalk over IP Networks

Description	Location
AppleTalk-to-IP migration plan from Open Door Networks	*www.opendoor.com/migration/migrationpicture.html*
"Migrating Macintosh Networks to Internet Protocols"	*NetProfessional*, July-August 1998 *www.netprolive.com*
ShareWay IP Professional from Open Door Networks	*www.opendoor.com/shareway*
Vicomsoft Internet Gateway	*www.vicomsoft.com/vig*

Mac Servers

3. Provide AppleTalk-over-IP capability on individual Macs in each pocket. The newest AppleShare client software from Apple uses IP protocols if they are available, and ShareWay IP will connect any Mac with an IP connection (see Figure 4-2).

Another advantage of running AppleTalk over an IP network is the flexibility it gives to remote, dial-up users. Apple Remote Access (ARA) software from Apple allows dial-up access to an AppleTalk network, but perhaps your small Mac-based office doesn't want to support dial-up access, so your staff connects from home or on the road via an ISP of their choice. With an AppleTalk-over-IP gateway on the Mac file server in the office, remote users can enter the server's IP address into the Chooser and mount shared folders or even run applications on the file server as if they were in the office. Of course, there is still the performance bottleneck of a modem connection.

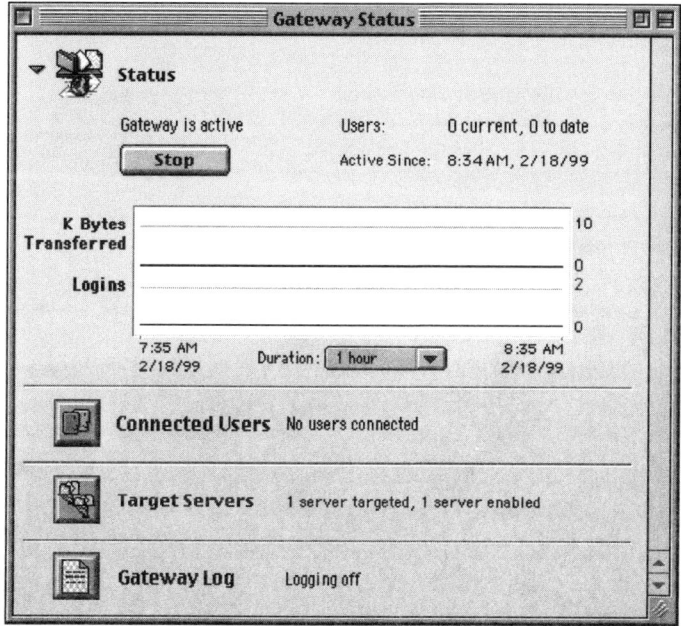

Figure 4-2. ShareWay IP Professional, courtesy Open Door Networks, Inc.

Sharing with Windows and UNIX

Now let's say you're running an AppleShare IP file server, and for some reason you need to run a UNIX or Windows 95/98/NT machine on your network. You don't want to migrate away from your AppleShare server, obviously, and you don't have to. There are a couple of options for you, which are summarized in Table 4-2.

First, this may be a good time to upgrade to AppleShare IP 6 (or the latest version available when you read this). AppleShare IP supports not only AFP, but also the Server Message Block (SMB) sharing of Windows and file transfer protocol (FTP) for UNIX. Figure 4-3 shows the panel for setting up AppleShare IP for Windows file sharing. Once you've set this up, the server will appear in the Windows Network Neighborhood. Figure 4-4 shows the configuration panel for sharing a folder—the same settings apply to users connecting from Mac, Windows, and UNIX clients via AFP, SMB, and FTP. Shared folders are automatically shared via all protocols that you've enabled.

Table 4-2. Mac File and Print Server Resources

Description	Location
AppleShare IP	*www.apple.com/appleshareip*
TSSTalk, AppleShare client for Windows 95/98/NT formerly known as COPSTalk, from Thursby Software	*www.thursby.com*
K-FS, AppleShare client software for UNIX from Xinet	*www.xinet.com/npg/kfs.html*
netatalk implementation of AppleTalk for UNIX systems	*www.umich.edu/~rsug/netatalk*
PC MACLAN, AppleTalk client software for Windows 95/98/NT	*www.miramarsys.com/products*
ShareWay IP Gateway from Open Door Networks makes any AFP server accessible over IP	*www.opendoor.com/gateway*
Tkchooser2, a preliminary implementation of the Mac OS Chooser for UNIX	*www.cs.columbia.edu/~etgold/-software/tkchooser2*

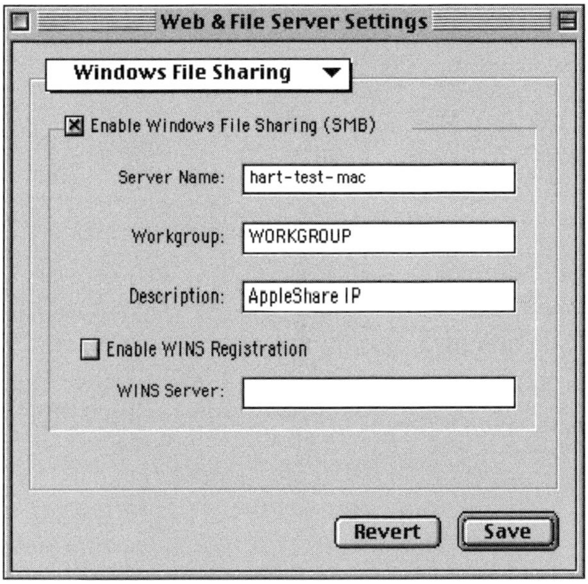

Mac Servers

Figure 4-3. AppleShare IP Windows file sharing set-up

Figure 4-4. Sharing a folder with AppleShare IP

Second, if you don't want to upgrade AppleShare, you can install AppleTalk clients for your Windows systems. PC MACLAN from Miramar Systems and COPSTalk from COPS can help turn a Windows system into a virtual Macintosh for the purposes of file sharing and printing with AppleShare IP or ShareWay IP servers.

PC MACLAN. PC MACLAN allows cross-platform file sharing across an Ethernet network. Using the Network Neighborhood interface, any Windows machine can access Macs or AFP servers on the network, as shown in Figure 4-5. At the same time, Macs can mount files, volumes, and drives from the PC MACLAN machine via the Chooser. Note that PC MACLAN is not designed to turn a Windows machine into a full-fledged file server, but rather a full-featured client on a Mac-centric or Mac-friendly network.

TSSTalk. The TSSTalk software from Thursby Software, formerly COPSTalk, lets a Windows 95/NT (or even Windows 3.1 or DOS) machine communicate via AppleTalk. The Windows client can see AppleShare file servers, Macs with personal file sharing turned on, and AppleTalk printers as if they were part of a Windows network. However, Macs cannot see or connect to the TSSTalk-linked Windows machine since TSSTalk does not publish the Windows device on the network.

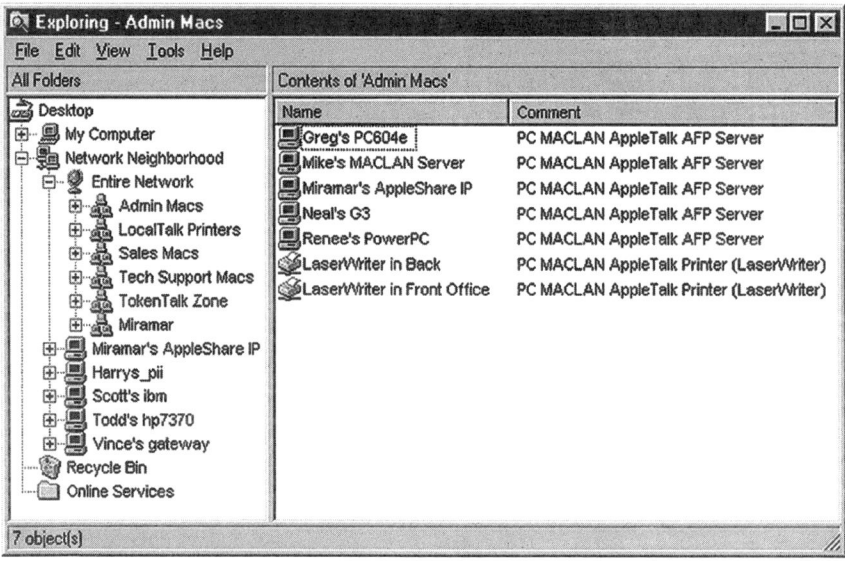

Figure 4-5. PC MACLAN sharing, courtesy Miramar Systems, Inc.

UNIX. Finally, the choices for adding a UNIX client to a Mac network and sharing from a Mac-based file server are more limited. Xinet, Inc., does produce a UNIX AppleShare client called K-FS, shown in Figure 4-6. The only other implementation is the tkchooser2 interface by Ethan Gold, which was only in alpha-testing at the time of writing. K-FS and, in theory, tkchooser2 give UNIX clients a Mac OS Chooser-like graphical interface for accessing AppleShare volumes. (Tkchooser2 also intends to include Windows SMB shared volumes.)

A more common UNIX alternative is to use FTP sharing, either with AppleShare IP or another Mac OS FTP server. For more on FTP, see Chapter 5.

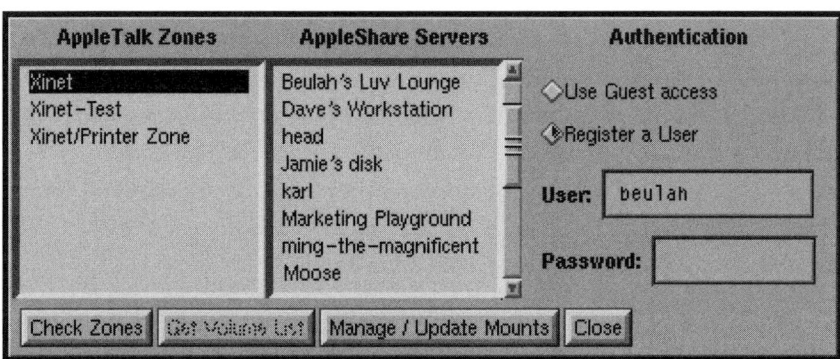

Figure 4-6. K-FS, a UNIX AppleShare client, courtesy Xinet, Inc.

Printing

Whether you're running an AppleShare, Windows, or UNIX server, printing to a shared printer from a combination of Mac, Windows, and UNIX clients remains more complicated than sharing files. Macs have support for network printing built in, but Windows has no built-in services for network printing without a print server or additional printing software. AppleShare IP does not support native Windows printing as it does native file sharing for Windows clients. However, AppleShare IP can receive LPR/LPD print jobs, which is the UNIX standard and which Windows understands.

For client-side options, both the PC MACLAN and TSSTalk clients allow Windows systems to print to AppleTalk-connected printers. PC MACLAN, for example, even gives Windows the print-job status messages that Macintosh users see. For UNIX, the netatalk suite provides the *pap* utility for printing to AppleTalk-connected printers.

MAC OS X SERVER

Apple's Mac OS X Server falls somewhere in between a Mac OS-based server and a UNIX server. As you might expect, Mac OS X Server is ready, willing, and able to share files with Mac OS clients. From the perspective of a Mac client, a Mac OS X Server provides Apple File Services that make it appear to be another AppleShare server. So technically, I don't need to say much else here.

But I will. The performance numbers for Mac OS X Server show that it may become a force to be reckoned with; however, from a cross-platform perspective, Mac OS X Server lacks one element: native SMB file sharing for Windows-based clients. (UNIX clients, on the other hand, actually experience a big step forward since Mac OS X Server can share volumes via the Network File System.) For details, see *www.apple.com/macosx/server*.

This is not to say that Windows clients cannot access a Mac OS X Server at all. It just means that Windows clients must have an AppleShare client, such as PC MACLAN or TSSTalk, installed so they can see the server. Please refer to the previous section for further information.

WINDOWS NT SERVERS

If you have a Windows NT server in your network neighborhood, you have several options to help your server play nice with the Macintosh neighbors. The immediate option is the Services for Macintosh (SFM) component built into Windows NT Server. Your server administrator must install the SFM package, which is included with the NT Server software. Here are the basic instructions for installing SFM on Windows NT Server:

1. Place the NT Server CD-ROM into the NT Server.
2. Open the Network control panel.
3. Select the Services tab, and press the Add button.

4. Select "Services for Macintosh" from the dialog box, as shown in Figure 4-7, and click OK.
5. You can configure Services for Macintosh, which may include using the NT Server as the AppleTalk seed router.
6. Close the Network control panel and reboot.

Once SFM is turned on, as shown in Figure 4-7, it is straightforward to define Mac volumes on the server. From your Mac client, the NT Server looks just like any other AppleShare server in the Chooser.

SFM has two major limitations. The first is that SFM makes only a one-way connection. Macs can see the NT Server, but Macs cannot see other Windows clients, and Windows machines cannot access the Macs. The second is printing. Although Macs can send print jobs to NT Server queues and on to printers, SFM's printing support is limited to 300 dpi, and color printing is not permitted. High-end printing remains a sticking point.

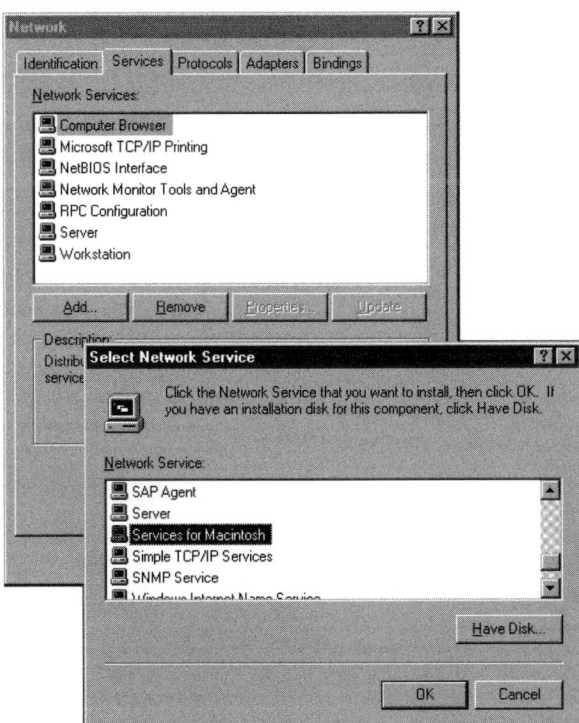

Figure 4-7. Installing Windows NT Services for Macintosh

MacServer IP. MacServer IP, developed by Germany's cyan Software and distributed in North America by Team ASA, provides another Windows NT option on the server side. Running alone or alongside SFM, MacServer IP provides Mac-style file sharing for Windows NT Workstation, as well as NT Server. MacServer IP supports AFP-over-IP sharing (giving it a performance edge over SFM), sharing drives that are not NTFS formatted, and remote administration. This product can be purchased in several configurations, ranging from 10 simultaneous clients up to unlimited simultaneous clients, so it may be cost-effective for small workgroups not already running NT Server.

DAVE. In the worst case scenario, let's say your network administrator refuses to turn on NT Server's Services for Macintosh, leaving your trusty Mac high and dry. Even if you have an Internet connection, you might not be able to share files conveniently with your co-workers. Time to call on DAVE. In much the same way that PC MACLAN turns a Windows machine into a virtual Mac, Thursby Software's DAVE will turn a Mac into a virtual Windows machine, at least as far as communicating with other machines on the network goes.

DAVE has three major advantages over SFM. First, nothing needs to be changed on the NT Server, which should make the server administrator happy. Second, you can see every Windows machine on the network, and all the Windows machines can see your Mac. Finally, DAVE also lets you print to PC-connected printers. Some of DAVE's windows are shown in Figure 4-8.

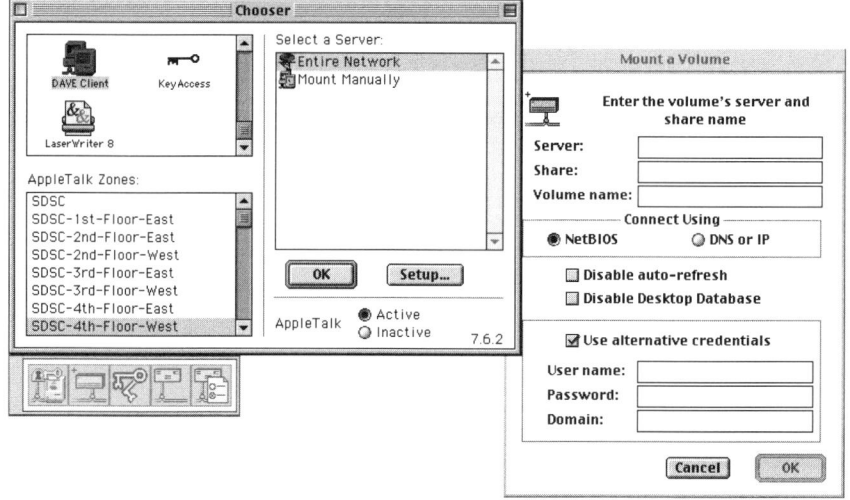

Figure 4-8. DAVE file and printer sharing, courtesy Thursby Software Systems, Inc.

One final note: Microsoft offers a free administration utility, Windows NT Server Web Administration 2.0, that lets any Internet client, whether it's a Mac, UNIX, or NT Workstation, use a Netscape or Microsoft browser to administer the server. The software is available through the Microsoft Web site.

Table 4-3 lists Web sites for the software to let Macs communicate with Windows NT-based servers.

NETWARE SERVERS

Macintoshes have been second-class citizens on Novell Networks for the past few years. The NetWare client software had not been updated for two years, there were lingering bugs, and NetWare 5 shipped without NetWare for Macintosh, a NetWare Loadable Module (NLM) for the server that lets Macintosh users share server files without additional client software. However, things are looking up. Table 4-4 has links to NetWare information for Macintosh.

NetWare for Macintosh Client. In mid-1998, Novell licensed Prosoft Engineering to develop and support all future NetWare for Macintosh products. Early 1999 saw the first results, the release of NetWare Client 5.12 for Macintosh. According to Prosoft, the client has a number of significant new features and bug fixes. The NetWare client takes advantage of performance improvements in the latest versions of the Mac OS and allows Macs to access all NetWare shared drives and print queues via the Mac OS Chooser, as shown in Figure 4-9. Among

Table 4-3. Macs and NT Servers

Description	Location
DAVE from Thursby Software lets a Mac share with Windows neighbors.	*www.thursby.com/DAVE2*
MacServer IP from Germany's cyan Software, distributed by Team ASA	*www.teamasa.com*
Services for Macintosh information from Microsoft	*microsoft.com/Mac/msmacproducts/ntsmac.htm*
Web Administration 2.0 for Windows NT Server	*www.microsoft.com/ntserver/management*

the more than 100 bugs fixed, according to Prosoft, are longstanding problems with the Mac client's reporting of file sizes and available volume space.

The client also has a new Mac-like installer, which can be installed over the network. The basic install will place one new control panel (MacIPX) and several extensions, identified by names that include either "NetWare" or "MacIPX." From your Mac's perspective, the new client connects to your NetWare network in a familiar Mac fashion. You connect to shared files and printers through the Chooser in the same way you do on AppleTalk networks. Your network administrator gets a more stable network client.

Table 4-4. NetWare for Macintosh Resources

Description	Location
Prosoft Engineering, licensed developers of NetWare products for Mac OS	*www.prosofteng.com/nw4mac*
Basic instructions for installing Netware for Macintosh NLMs—search for TID 2929686	*support.novell.com/search/kb_index.htm*
Novell NetWare documentation	*www.novell.com/documentation*

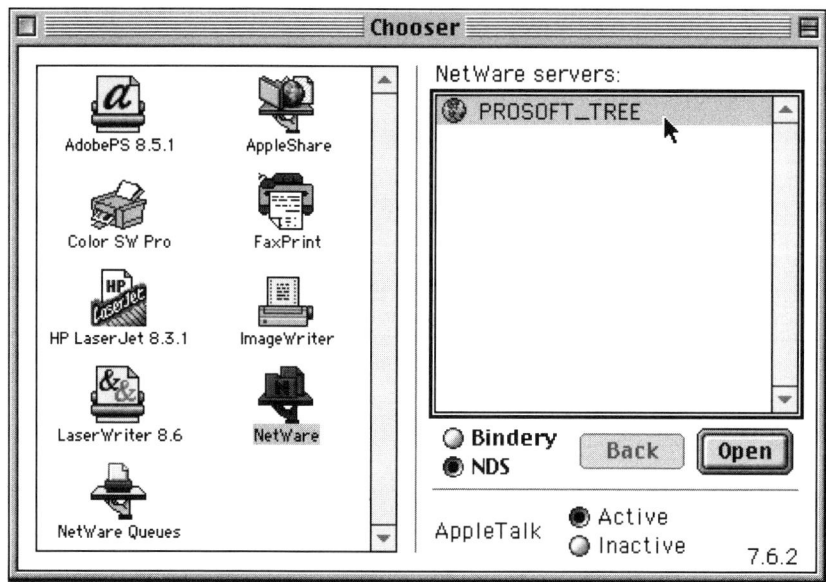

Figure 4-9. NetWare extensions for the Chooser, courtesy Prosoft Engineering, Inc.

NetWare 5 Services for AppleShare. At the time of writing, Prosoft was close to releasing the NetWare 5 Services for AppleShare NLMs. They should be available by the time you read this or soon thereafter. These modules turn a NetWare server into a virtual AppleShare server for those Macs without the NetWare client software, as well as provide greater access to the NetWare network environment for Mac clients. In other words, the NetWare client for Macintosh lets a Mac connect to NetWare servers, but the server-side NLMs allow any number of Mac clients to access file services.

The high-level steps for installing the Macintosh NLMs are similar to the steps for NetWare 4. More detailed instructions are available from Novell's on-line support area or with the NLM software distribution.

1. Install the Macintosh NLMs using NWCONFIG.NLM. (This was called INSTALL.NLM in NetWare 4.)
2. LOAD APPLETLK to add AppleTalk support.
3. LOAD XXXXXXX.LAN Int=X Port=XXX frame=Ethernet_Snap name=SNAP. The exact values of these parameters depend on your current NetWare configuration.
4. BIND Appletlk to SNAP.
5. LOAD AFP (AppleTalk Filing Protocol) to enable Mac file sharing.

NetWare over IP for Macs. Prosoft Engineering is also producing software to allow Macs to access NetWare-over-IP networks. The company is developing a native IP NetWare client for the Mac OS and AppleShare IP NLMs for the server. Both were scheduled for release by the time you read this.

UNIX SERVERS

This was an odd section. In researching the available software that allowed Mac clients to connect to a UNIX server, I queried the various Web search engines for "UNIX and Macintosh," and I turned up a few sites on the UNIX variants that run on Macs. Searching for "UNIX and AppleTalk," I turned up only the free Columbia AppleTalk Package (CAP) from the University of Melbourne and netatalk from the University of Michigan.

About the same time I was writing this though, the SDSC desktop systems group was trying out an alternative to CAP called K-AShare from Xinet, Inc. Xinet targets the printing and pre-press environment, long a Mac stronghold. Xinet also turns up in a Web search of "UNIX and AppleShare." And through the Xinet site I found references to several other commercial server options. These options are listed in Table 4-5.

In other words, there's no real reason why, if you use a UNIX as your server workhorse, you can't accommodate plenty of Mac clients. The Xinet Web site also includes helpful information about setting up balanced and reliable UNIX-Mac networks. CAP and netatalk provide free options, while the commercial packages offer a wider range of services, performance, and integration.

Table 4-5. UNIX Server, Mac Client Resources

Description	Location
Columbia AppleTalk Package (CAP) from the University of Melbourne	*www.cs.mu.oz.au/appletalk/cap.html*
EtherShare, UNIX-based AppleShare server from Helios Software GmbH	*www.helios.com/products/produktES.html*
Intragy from Ascend (formerly Intercon's NFS/Share)	*www.ascend.com/2400.html*
K-AShare from Xinet, Inc.	*www.xinet.com/npg/kashare.html*
MacNFS, commercial Mac NFS client, from Thursby Software Systems	*www.thursby.com/products/macnfs.htm*
netatalk AppleTalk suite for UNIX, from the University of Michigan Research Systems UNIX Group	*www.umich.edu/~rsug/netatalk*
PC-Enterprise from Platinum Technology	*www.platinum.com/products/sysman/-pcent_ps.htm*
TotalNET Advanced Server from Syntax, Inc.	*www.syntax.com/totalnet/totalnet53.htm*
Information from Xinet on setting up UNIX server, Macintosh client workgroups	*www.xinet.com/benchmarks*
More AppleTalk software from the University of Melbourne	*www.cs.mu.oz.au/appletalk*

At SDSC, Xinet's K-AShare was installed to provide Chooser-based and faster access for Macs to the center's UNIX file servers. Although CAP had previously been available, its performance limited its usefulness for frequent file exchange. In my case, I regularly update pages on the center's Web site, and an FTP client proved a much faster option. CAP was favored by fewer Mac users; often those who could accept the performance limitations to avoid learning to navigate the FTP hierarchy. Because of its greater performance, however, K-AShare and the ease of the Mac Finder interface may offer stronger competition to FTP.

Network File System. The native shared file system for UNIX is known as the Network File System (NFS), and for some time Macs have been excluded from accessing NFS files, while Samba (*www.samba.org*) provides NFS access to Windows systems. However, a Mac client option, MacNFS, is on the way from Thursby Software Systems, scheduled for release in late 1999. MacNFS will let an NFS-mounted volume function like a local disk.

The obvious benefit of MacNFS for network administrators is that they can choose the most sensible option—a server-side solution if they have lots of Mac clients or a client-side option for a smaller number of Macs.

Printing. The UNIX options in Table 4-5 also support cross-platform printing for Macintosh and often Windows clients. K-AShare, EtherShare, CAP, and netatalk offer printing to AppleTalk printers. PC Enterprise and TotalNET Advanced Server support both Macintosh and Windows printing, while Intragy supports LPR printing.

NETWORK ADMINISTRATION

Up front, I'd like to say that I don't intend to insult anyone's intelligence and pretend to cover the complex subject of network administration in one section of a chapter. Instead, the point of this section is to briefly talk about administration from both the network client and central administrator perspective. First, I'll talk about SNMP for Mac clients, and then I'll mention a few tools for administrators who want to use a Mac for day-to-day tasks or those who manage Mac clients.

Simple Network Management Protocol

The Simple Network Management Protocol, or SNMP, is the standard protocol of network management, with which network administrators are able to monitor network devices and their functions. Network management with SNMP requires two pieces of software: an SNMP agent on each computer to be managed and a central management application, called a console, for collecting and analyzing information. The SNMP agent software collects information, called variables, and relays this information to the central console. The variables managed by an SNMP agent are defined in a database called a MIB (Management Information Base), which specifies what each variable does and whether it can be modified.

With Mac OS 8.5, Apple re-introduced the SNMP architecture as part of Open Transport. A custom Mac OS 8.5 install option will let you install an extension, Open Transport SNMP; a shared library, OpenTptSNMPLib; preferences file, SNMP Preferences; and an SNMP Administrator application. With SNMP support, any network administration tool that uses the SNMP standard can be used to monitor and collect information from Mac clients.

Table 4-6 provides some pointers to information about SNMP in general and specifically for the Mac OS. Even though SNMP is a standard, I should point out that some network management tools may require their own software or extensions to be installed on each networked computer.

Tools for Network Administration

Once you have the SNMP agent software installed on all the computers on your network, the next question becomes how to collect and analyze all that information. You may also want to distribute a standard set of software to every com-

Table 4-6. Macintosh SNMP Information

Description	Location
Definition of SNMP	*whatis.com/snmp.htm*
Instructions for installing Open Transport SNMP in Mac OS 8.5	*www.dartmouth.edu/netsoftware/snmpwatcher/Agents/*
Apple Technical Information Library on Open Transport SNMP	*til.info.apple.com/techinfo.nsf/artnum/n58128*

Network Administration

puter or manage software licenses from a central repository. In this section, I've listed a few of the central console tools that run on the Mac OS. Network administrators who would rather use a Mac, whether they manage all-Mac or multi-platform networks, may want to look into some of the products described here and listed in Table 4-7.

Many of the companies whose products are listed in this section develop other tools related to network and system management. If you're managing a network of Macintosh or mixed-platform clients and your favorite administration tool is not mentioned here, please visit the book's Web site and post your tools and advice there.

Apple Network Administrator Toolkit. The Apple Network Administrator Toolkit is a collection of programs for managing a network of Macs. Using the toolkit, administrators control the network from a single workstation. The toolkit includes Apple Network Assistant and At Ease for Workgroups, which allows control over computer access.

Apple Network Assistant. Apple Network Assistant helps manage networks of Macs by providing remote assistance, system profiling and configuration, and software distribution. Network Assistant supports TCP/IP and AppleTalk networks, and even text and voice communications.

Table 4-7. Network Administration Tools and Resources

Description	Location
Apple Network Administrator Toolkit and Apple Network Assistant from Apple	*www.apple.com/networking*
FileWave and Asset Trustee from Wave Research	*www.waveresearch.com/filewave*
InformUser from Advanced Ideas	*www.advancedideas.com*
KeyServer from Sassafras Software	*www.sassafras.com*
LANsurveyor from Neon Software	*www.neon.com/LANsurveyor.html*
MacAdministrator from Hi Resolution	*www.hi-resolution.com/MacAdministrator*
NetOctopus from Netopia	*www.timbuktupro.com/netoctopus*
SNMP Watcher from Dartmouth College	*www.dartmouth.edu/netsoftware/snmpwatcher*
Timbuktu Pro from Netopia	*www.timbuktupro.com*

FileWave and Asset Trustee. FileWave from Wave Research provides automated, centralized software and configuration management for Mac-based networks. An agent on each workstation checks the server for new files, downloads them, and continuously maintains the integrity of the installation on the client side. Asset Trustee automatically scans the system software and applications on your Mac OS and Windows clients and updates a central database.

InformUser. InformUser from Advanced Ideas allows a system administrator to broadcast messages to all users without the users being logged into a server. For instance, if a server goes down, the administrator can broadcast a message to all Macintosh and Windows users indicating the status.

KeyServer. Sassafras Software's KeyServer is a network tool to manage software licenses for Windows and Macintosh computers. The KeyServer, which can run on a Mac or Windows machine, meters licenses of local and remote software launches throughout a network.

LANsurveyor. Neon Software's LANsurveyor helps map out the structure of an AppleTalk network. LANsurveyor displays computers, printers, routers, and other nodes and uses SNMP to profile and monitor network devices. LANsurveyor can also gather information for hardware, system, and software profiles, generate software inventory reports, automate file distribution, and allow remote control and management.

MacAdministrator. For greater control, MacAdministrator from Hi Resolution lets an administrator control, monitor, and audit a group of Mac clients. Users are required to log in to client Macs, as in a school computer lab, and users see their "own" computer no matter which machine they log in to. MacAdministrator allows you to control printing, software distribution, and other services.

NetOctopus. A system administration tool, netOctopus from Netopia supports remote software installation, system configuration, and comprehensive inventories. NetOctopus lets you "see" every Mac and Windows workstation on the network from a central administrative Mac workstation. NetOctopus can collect and report more than 300 hardware and system software details, active software, installed software, active fonts, and all AppleTalk network devices.

SNMP Watcher. SNMP Watcher from Dartmouth College displays SNMP information for AppleTalk and IP devices. SNMP Watcher 1.0 includes the Macintosh management information bases (MIBs) that ship as part of Open

Transport 2.0 (Mac OS 8.5). For a properly configured Mac OS machine, these MIBs allow you to see the applications, control panels, and extensions that are installed on the computer.

Timbuktu Pro. Timbuktu Pro from Netopia is a cross-platform remote administration tool. For example, with Timbuktu on an NT server and Mac clients, the one can be used to control the other. So a network administrator might change server configurations from a Mac client or use Timbuktu Pro's file synchronization features to update files on the clients. Timbuktu Pro works with network administration software from many vendors, including Platinum Technology, Computer Associates, and Tivoli Systems.

SDSC's Cross-Platform Installation

For a real-world example, I asked SDSC's Support Services group to describe the setup used to link the center's approximately 500 UNIX, Windows NT, and Macintosh computers, as well as several dozen AppleTalk and IP printers. With a few key pieces of hardware and software, all the systems are able to share files and print to the same set of printers.

AppleTalk

In addition to supporting a wide variety of computers, the center's networking is also charged with providing a secure environment. Desktop systems are connected to a number of IP subnets. The two Macintosh subnets also route AppleTalk traffic. NT workstations are on another subnet, while UNIX workstations are on several other subnets.

While IP traffic passes across all subnets, security and management concerns have limited AppleTalk traffic to the Macintosh subnets and SMB traffic to the NT subnet. The center's printers are connected to the AppleTalk subnets.

File Sharing

While seamless Mac/NT/UNIX file sharing remains a future goal, a few key pieces of hardware and software make it possible to share files between Mac and Windows, Mac and UNIX, and Windows and UNIX systems. Mac-to-Mac,

UNIX-to-UNIX, and NT-to-NT file sharing is accomplished through the mechanisms native to each platform. I should also add that many smaller files are exchanged as e-mail attachments.

Exchanging files from a Mac to a Windows machine is accomplished via a Windows NT Server that has Services for Macintosh running. The Macs and NT workstations can all view the entire shared area of the file system. Initially, the Macs shared files through a Mac-only area of the NT Server, but now Macs and NT workstations share all of the same folders and files. Files moving from a Windows NT workstation to a Macintosh also go through the NT Server. (For the truly technical-minded, the current NT Server setup at SDSC is being modified to use a primary NT Server as a "domain controller" for a suite of file, print, application, and video servers.)

Moving files from a Mac to the UNIX systems is often accomplished via FTP for many day-to-day activities. A designated "scratch" area on the center's NFS file server volume can be accessed by all UNIX machines, and Macs can access these same areas with FTP client software through a number of general-purpose workstations. The center at one time provided access to the UNIX server via the free Columbia AppleTalk Package (CAP), but I, for one, found FTP to be much faster. However, the center has since begun using Xinet's K-AShare software to allow Macs to access the UNIX file system, and performance has improved substantially. For the record, Windows workstations access the same areas of the NFS file system with the Samba package (*www.samba.org*).

In the opposite direction, files must be moved from a UNIX system to a Mac or an NT workstation. This is possible through Xinet's K-AShare, but more often than not, the UNIX file is placed in an accessible location on the NFS server, and the Mac or NT systems must get the file with an FTP client.

Printing

I'd like to state here for the record that the Support Services group has outdone itself in supporting network printing at SDSC. As I noted earlier, all printers are connected to one of the two Macintosh subnets. As a result, Mac users can essentially use the Chooser to print to any of the AppleTalk printers in the building. UNIX workstations access the printers via a Xinet print spooler on a UNIX system. This same UNIX spooler allows the Macs to print to a number of high-speed IP-only printers.

The NT workstations follow a slightly less direct route through an NT Server-based print server that sends jobs through the UNIX spooler to the AppleTalk and IP printers. (Inserting the NT Server into the picture offers the advantage of PostScript translation. Non-PostScript print jobs can be sent to PostScript printers, and PostScript jobs can be sent to non-PostScript printers.)

LAN Summary

In short, there's no reason why Macintosh, Windows, and UNIX clients can't exist on the same local-area network, regardless of the type of server.

For a Mac server, AppleShare IP provides the means for Mac, Windows, and UNIX clients to connect via AFP, SMB, and FTP, respectively.

For a Windows NT Server, Microsoft's Services for Macintosh will let Mac clients share files with their Windows counterparts. MacServer IP offers even better performance by running AFP over IP protocols, alongside or instead of Services for Macintosh.

For a UNIX server, Xinet's K-AShare and similar products will let Mac clients connect to the server. MacNFS from Thursby Software Systems is a client-side solution to let Macs access the UNIX-standard Network File System.

CHAPTER 5

The Internet

*T*he Internet is, in many ways, the ultimate cross-platform environment. As long as you have the appropriate software installed on your Macintosh, no one really needs to know or care what operating system your computer runs. After a quick introduction to the Internet, this chapter points you to software that can make your Macintosh a full Internet citizen.

This chapter is going to cover a lot of ground very quickly, but you can make it easier on yourself by keeping in mind your Internet needs and goals. You don't need a detailed on-line strategy, but you can ask yourself which of the following best describes your situation:

- You want to use the Internet for occasional file sharing or a minimal Web site.
- You're running a file server and want to add Internet capabilities.
- You want to be the next Yahoo!, Lycos, or Amazon.com.

For most basic needs, it should take you a matter of minutes to set up your Mac to share files over the Internet.

INTERNET BASICS

For the sake of sanity, I'll start by defining what I mean by "the Internet." Here, *the Internet* is the global set of connected networks communicating in the language of the TCP/IP protocol stack. Whether this definition is completely comprehensive can be debated at length around your dinner table. Table 5-1 also provides resources for additional Internet information not covered here. At the moment, I'm more concerned with what it means as far as getting your Mac on the Internet, and aside from the software discussed in the rest of this chapter, there are two essential elements.

- **TCP/IP networking software.** The Mac OS comes with the Open Transport architecture, as described in Chapter 3 and the Appendix, which provides TCP/IP communications. If your Mac does not have Open Transport, I strongly recommend that you upgrade your Mac OS to the latest version your system will support, whether that is Mac OS 7.6, 8.1, or 8.5.

- **An IP address.** An IP, or Internet Protocol, address uniquely identifies your computer in Internet messages, in much the same way your home address uniquely identifies where you receive mail from the U.S. Postal Service. An IP address can be permanent or temporary. A permanent IP address is assigned once by a network administrator, while a temporary IP address might be assigned automatically from a pool of available addresses each time you start your computer.

Internet Basics

Table 5-1. Internet Information

Description	Location
A short definition from whatis.com	*whatis.com/internet.htm*
The Internet Society, the Internet governing body	*www.isoc.org*
The Internet Engineering Task Force	*www.ietf.org*
Mac OS 8 Web Server Cookbook	*www.sdsc.edu/Cookbook/Mac*
Internet Relay Chat information	*www.newircusers.com*
Introduction to USENET newsgroups	*www.pbs.org/uti/guide/usenet.html*

Clients and Servers

A discussion of the Internet also requires that you understand the concept of *client-server* computing. Computers at the beginning and the end of an Internet transaction are either clients or servers. The terms *client* and *server* don't describe a type of physical computer, but a type of behavior. A client requests information from servers, and a server supplies information in response to requests from clients. Your Macintosh might therefore be both a client and a server, depending on the circumstance.

Aside from the fact that this chapter is organized according to client and server software, the client and server concepts relate in a practical way to your computer's IP address. In practice, a computer used primarily as a client can use either a temporary or permanent address, while a computer used as a server needs a permanent IP address. Think of it this way: If you (the client) wanted to send a Christmas card (a request) to your aunt in Peoria (the server), you would have a hard time getting the card to her if she moved around a lot (had a dynamically changing address).

In other words, if you want to use your Mac as an Internet server, it's easier if you have a permanent IP address. As part of a large organization, you might be able to request one from your network administrators. As an individual or small business, many Internet Service Providers (ISPs) offer the ability to register a domain name and permanent IP address as a premium or business-oriented service.

As an alternative, several companies provide services that map a permanent domain name to a computer with a dynamic IP address. The services, ranging in cost from free to around $40 per year, will alias your machine's dynamic address to a permanent domain name. If you're interested, check the sites listed in Table 5-2. All of these sites support Mac customers. If you plan to use the Internet as a regular and substantial way to share files, I still suggest a full-time connection for your Mac—at least a dedicated phone line or a cable modem—unless you really enjoy annoying Web surfers with "server is not responding" messages.

As we discuss the Macintosh software for Internet clients and servers, we will assume that you have a permanent IP address if you decide to install and use the server options.

Table 5-2. Domain Name Services for Dynamic IP Addresses

Description	Location
Dynamic DNS Network Services free aliasing services	www.dyndns.org
DynIP Internet Name Service, starting at $36 per year	www.dynip.com
DynDNS.com dynamic DNS service, starting at $25 per year	www.dyndns.com
TZO Internet Naming Service, starting at $25 per year	www.tzo.com

Internet Services

The connections and common TCP/IP language of the Internet have spawned a wide array of services that allow computers and their users to communicate. Therefore, you can also think of the Internet as the total of all the services or applications—such as the World Wide Web—that the Internet makes possible. It is not technically accurate, although quite common, to equate the Web and the Internet; the Web is one of many possible ways of exchanging information over the Internet.

The Web, e-mail, and FTP are three of the most common Internet services, and we will cover them in this chapter. If you are interested in more detail on using your Macintosh as a Web, e-mail, and FTP server, you should check out the *Mac OS 8 Web Server Cookbook* (Prentice Hall/PTR) by Phil Bourne and yours truly, David Hart. Other Internet services include Internet Relay Chat (IRC) for real-time chatting with other users, USENET newsgroups for subject-specific electronic bulletin boards, and M-bone for Internet broadcasts.

Using Internet Config

When you install Internet software, particularly client software, you are bound to see a small public domain application called Internet Config from Stairways Software (*www.stairways.com*). You may have several copies already. Internet Config provides a centralized registry for many of your Internet-related settings, from e-mail signature and servers to your preferred Web home page to mappings between file types and helper applications.

The main interface for Internet Config is straightforward and was shown in Figure 3-4. Figure 5-1 shows the interface for customizing file mappings—the application assigned to handle a particular file type. Now you have no excuse for being surprised when you come across Internet Config on your Mac or in the rest of this chapter (and book).

Figure 5-1. Internet Config file mappings interface

THE WORLD WIDE WEB

If you have not yet heard of or used the Web, we need to talk. In practical terms, the World Wide Web—or simply, the Web—is an Internet service for exchanging information. In networking terms, the Web is a collection of servers and clients communicating via the hypertext transfer protocol (HTTP), which is itself an application protocol built on the TCP/IP protocol stack.

While the workhorse files of the Web are text files that have been annotated with the HyperText Markup Language (HTML), Web servers can make any type of file available for downloading to clients. And because Web protocols are defined in platform-independent terms, the Web is a powerful tool for cross-platform file exchange. On the Web, no one needs to know that you're serving or requesting files from a Mac.

As a quick Web lesson, I'll describe a typical Web interaction between client and server:

1. A client user—someone looking for information—enters a Web address in a client application, usually a Web browser.

2. The address usually takes the form of a Uniform Resource Locator (URL), such as *"http://www.a-company.com/folder1/folder2/file.html."* The "http://" identifies the protocol to be used, "www.a-company.com" identifies the Web server to which the request is directed, and "/folder1/folder2/file.xyz" gives the path on the server to the specific file, file.xyz.

3. The Web browser sends the URL onto the Internet (along with other information, including a return address), and the network of Internet routers and name servers finds the machine that answers to "www.a-company.com" and delivers the request.

4. The server application at www.a-company.com intercepts the request, sees that it has been asked for file.xyz, which is in folder2 inside folder1, and sends that file back to the return address. The client application can then display or save the file as appropriate.

There are two points to note here. First, a Web request requires http software on both the client and server machines. Either or both machines can be Macs, and the rest of this section will discuss browser and server software for the

The World Wide Web

Mac. Second, files exchanged on the Web do not need to be text-only HTML files. "File.xyz" could be a TIFF image (file.tiff), a Microsoft Word document (file.doc), or a BinHexed Stuffit archive (file.sit.hqx). This section will describe the Web in terms of file exchange only. For a lengthier discussion of Web possibilities, such as serving Java applets, database contents, and dynamic HTML, you should check out the *Mac OS 8 Web Server Cookbook*. Table 5-3 provides pointers to additional Web information.

Web Browsers

You will likely have one of two Web browsers on your Macintosh—Netscape Navigator (as a stand-alone browser or part of Netscape Communicator) or Microsoft Internet Explorer. Because these are the predominant browsers, I will describe them briefly here, but I would also like to mention that they are not the only game in town. Table 5-4 lists Web references not only for Navigator and Internet Explorer but also for several alternative Web browsers, including iCab, WannaBe, and MacLynx, all of which were in beta testing when this was written.

Table 5-3. General Web Information

Description	Location
Definitions of World Wide Web and HTTP from Whatis.com	*whatis.com/www.htm*
	whatis.com/http.htm
The World Wide Web Consortium	*www.w3.org*
Mac OS 8 Web Server Cookbook	*www.sdsc.edu/Cookbook/Mac*

Table 5-4. Macintosh Web Browsers

Description	Location
iCab, a graphical Web browser from Germany, notable for being small and having Web ad filters	*www.icab.de*
MacLynx, a Mac port of the Lynx text-only browser	*www.lirmm.fr/~gutkneco/maclynx*
Microsoft Internet Explorer	*www.microsoft.com/mac/ie*
Netscape Communicator	*www.netscape.com/download*
WannaBe Web Browser, a text-only browser by David Pierson	*mindstory.com/wb2*

Web browsers such as Netscape Navigator and Microsoft Internet Explorer also allow you to download files from FTP servers; however, they will not suffice for all situations, since they only support anonymous FTP access. (See the FTP section of this chapter for more details.)

Netscape Communicator

Netscape produces a Web browser, called Navigator, which can be installed by itself or as part of the Communicator package—which also includes Composer, for creating Web pages, and Messenger, for e-mail and newsgroups. Once you have installed Navigator for viewing Web sites, you can use it to download files from Web servers.

A link on a Web page usually points to another Web page, but it may also point to files or directories (folders) of files that you can download. For example, a directory with no HTML pages might, by default, display a list of the files or subdirectories in it, as shown in Figure 5-2. To save a file, first click-and-hold with the mouse while pointing to its link or file name. (You can also "control-click"—hold down the Control key on the keyboard and click the mouse button.) This will bring up a menu with the option to "Save this link as…" a file on your computer. In the Save dialog box, select the Source option from the Format menu.

If the Web server is configured properly, it will specify a MIME type for many common file formats. A Multipurpose Internet Mail Extension, or MIME, type tells the Web browser which file format to expect. By default, Navigator recognizes many MIME types, and you can add others or customize how Navigator handles particular file and MIME types in the Preferences dialog, as shown in Figure 5-3. By selecting "Edit…" you can specify whether Navigator should view the MIME type with a plug-in, open it in a "helper" application, or save the file to disk.

A disadvantage of using Netscape Communicator is that it does not use all of the settings that you may have specified in Internet Config. For example, even if you specify a mail reader program such as Eudora Pro to handle "mailto:" URLs, Communicator will still use the built-in Messenger component. The file mappings you specify in Internet Config must also be entered separately in Communicator. (The Navigator stand-alone application is somewhat better at using Internet Config settings.)

The World Wide Web

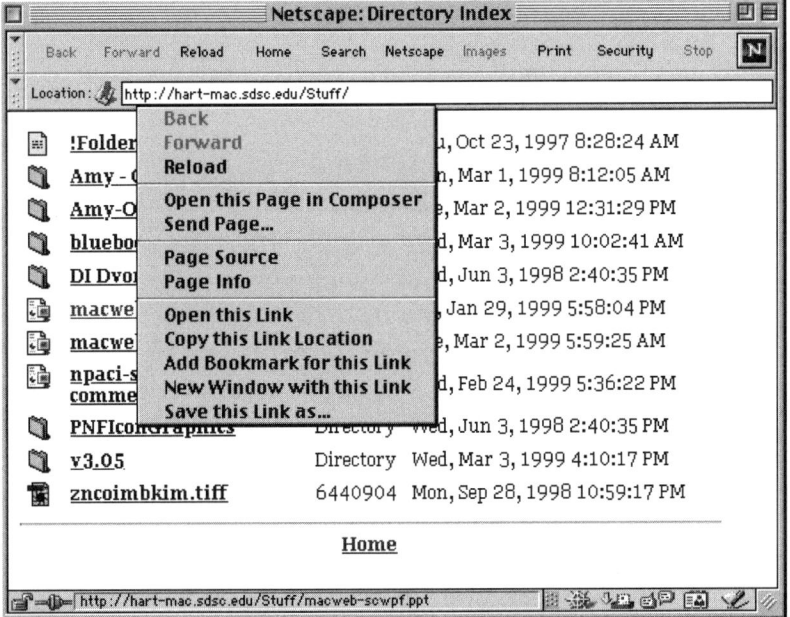

Figure 5-2. Saving files with Netscape Navigator

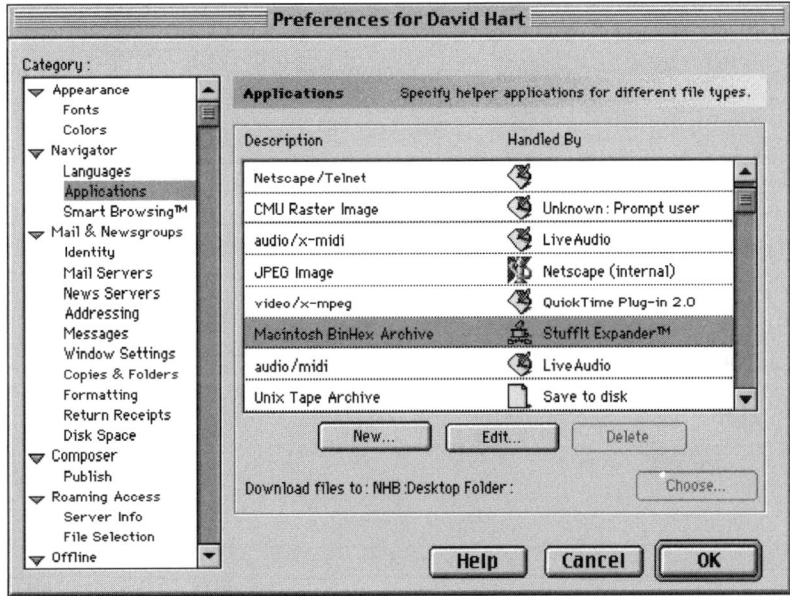

Figure 5-3. Configuring Navigator helper applications

Microsoft Internet Explorer

Microsoft Internet Explorer provides many of the same functions as Netscape Navigator. In addition to browsing Web sites, you can download files from Web servers. Figure 5-4 shows Internet Explorer displaying a folder of files available from a Web server. To save a file, first click-and-hold with the mouse while pointing to its link or file name. (You can also "control-click"—hold down the Control key on the keyboard and click the mouse button.) This will bring up a menu with the option to "Download Link to Disk" as a file on your computer. In the Save dialog box, select the Source option from the Format menu.

As with Communicator, you can customize how Internet Explorer handles files based on their MIME types. Internet Explorer uses the file mappings saved by Internet Config, but also provides its own interface for changing them. The installation for Internet Explorer also installs a control panel called Configuration Manager, which can be started from the Control Panels menu or by selecting the Preferences menu option in Internet Explorer. Therefore, you should not be surprised that Configuration Manager also lets you set Internet Explorer preferences, in addition to customizing the file mappings as shown in Figure 5-5.

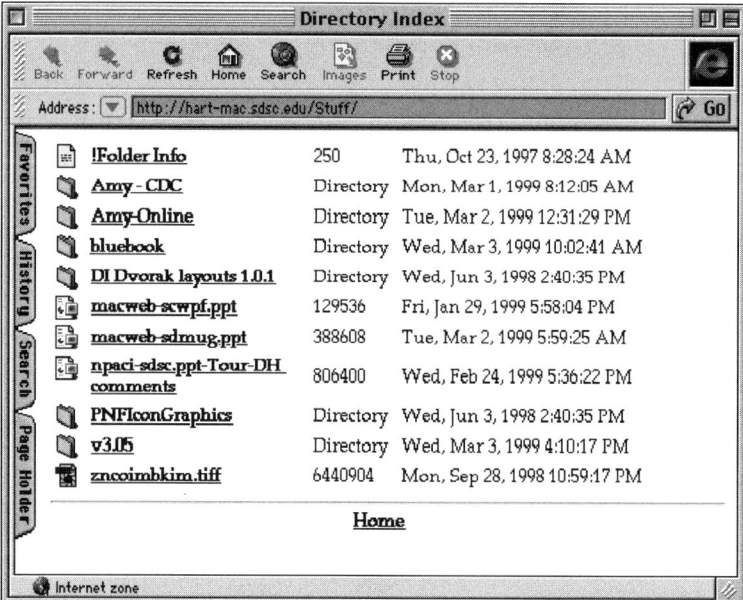

Figure 5-4. Downloading files with Microsoft Internet Explorer

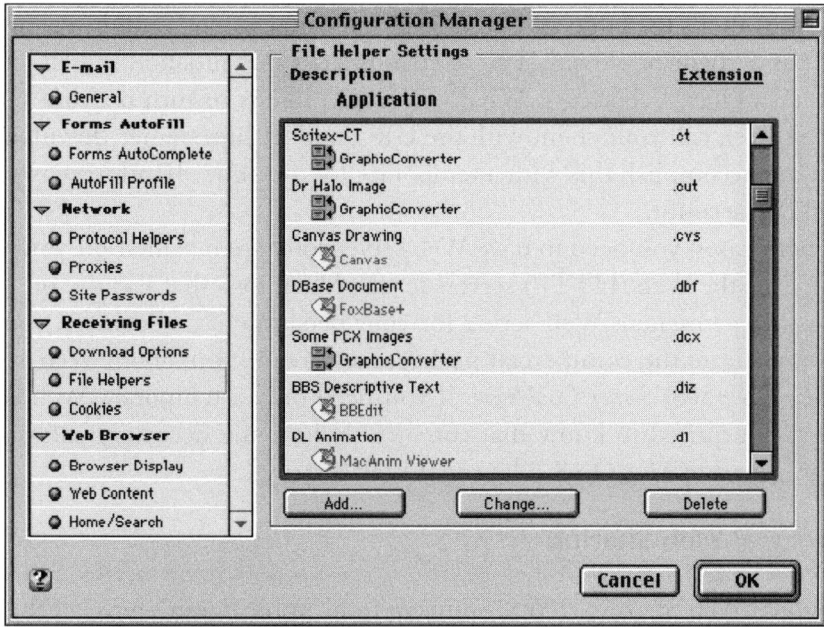

Figure 5-5. Configuration Manager

Web Servers

You may find that you need to share files with users across the Internet. These users may be on a variety of platforms or, ideally, you don't even want to know what kind of computer they're using. In such a case, you want to turn your Mac into a Web server from which they can download the files.

To allow users to connect to your Web server with their Navigator or Internet Explorer client software, you must be able to give them a URL that identifies your computer. You have a choice at this point, and the choice depends on whether your Web file sharing is an occasional need or a permanent solution.

For a Web server that's available 24 hours a day, possibly with your own clever domain name—*www.bobsleds-r-us.com* perhaps—you need to have either a permanent IP address or a service that maps your dynamic IP address to a permanent domain name, as described in the Clients and Servers section. (The Appendix has more detail on IP addresses.)

On the other hand, let's say you have a business client across the country who needs a scanned photograph in TIFF format for a marketing brochure. You have the file but it's too large to send as an e-mail attachment, and the client can't use FTP as a client or server. (I have encountered this situation myself.) However, the client has Web access. What you would like is to turn on your temporary Web server, call your client with the URL, and let him or her download the file. You can accomplish this with a temporary (or dynamic) IP address as part of a normal ISP account.

In both cases, you need to have Web server software installed on your Mac. Table 5-5 lists the Web (HTTP) servers for the Macintosh that I know of. If you want to run a permanent Web server for your department or business, you may want to investigate the commercial packages and read more about Web serving in the *Mac OS 8 Web Server Cookbook*. If you need only a temporary Web server, you may be surprised to know that you already have the necessary software on your Mac as part of Mac OS 8—Personal Web Sharing.

Personal Web Sharing

The Personal Web Sharing (PWS) software from Apple doesn't have all the bells and whistles of the larger commercial packages, but it is perfect for sharing files. PWS has two parts—a system extension and a control panel. (The basic installation also creates a folder called "Web Pages" on your hard drive.) Here's how to start your Web server. Hold on!

1. If you aren't already connected to the Internet (via your ISP or otherwise), do that now.
2. Open the Web Sharing control panel, which is shown in Figure 5-6.
3. Choose your Web folder, the folder holding the files that you want to share. You probably do not want to share your entire hard drive or your System Folder, even though users will have read-only access.
4. PWS may automatically ask you to choose a Home Page. If not, click the second PWS "Select..." button now. You can choose an HTML file (in your Web folder) to serve up by default, or you can choose "None." If you choose None, PWS will simply display the names of all the files and folders in the Web folder—very handy for sharing files.

Table 5-5. Macintosh Web Servers

Web Server	Location
AppleShare IP from Apple	www.apple.com/appleshareip
EasyServe, freeware by Jason Linhart	summary.net/soft/easyserve.html
First Class Intranet Server, commercial software by SoftArc	www.softarc.com
httpd4Mac, freeware by Bill Melotti	sodium.ch.man.ac.uk/pages/httpd4Mac
MacCommon LISP Server, freeware by John C. Mallery	www.ai.mit.edu/projects/iiip/doc/cl-http
MacHTTP, shareware from StarNine	www.starnine.com/machttp
NetPresenz, Web, FTP, and gopher server shareware from Stairways Software	www.stairways.com/netpresenz
Personal Web Sharing, commercial software from Apple, part of Mac OS 8	www.apple.com
Quid Pro Quo, freeware and commercial software from possibly defunct Social Engineering	www.socialeng.com
TeleFinder, commercial software from Spider Island Software	www.spiderisland.com
Web Server 4D, commercial Web and database server from MDG Computer Services	www.mdg.com
Webink and Webink Pro, commercial Web and database servers from Webink	www.webink.com
WebSTAR, commercial software from StarNine	www.starnine.com/webstar
WebTen, commercial software from Tenon Intersystems	www.tenon.com/products/webten

5. Choose either to "Give everyone read-only access" or "Use File Sharing to control user access." If you don't know, choose the first option.
6. Click on the "Start" button to turn on Web sharing. (The Start button turns into a Stop button.) You're now running a Web server.
7. Take a break. I know you must be exhausted.

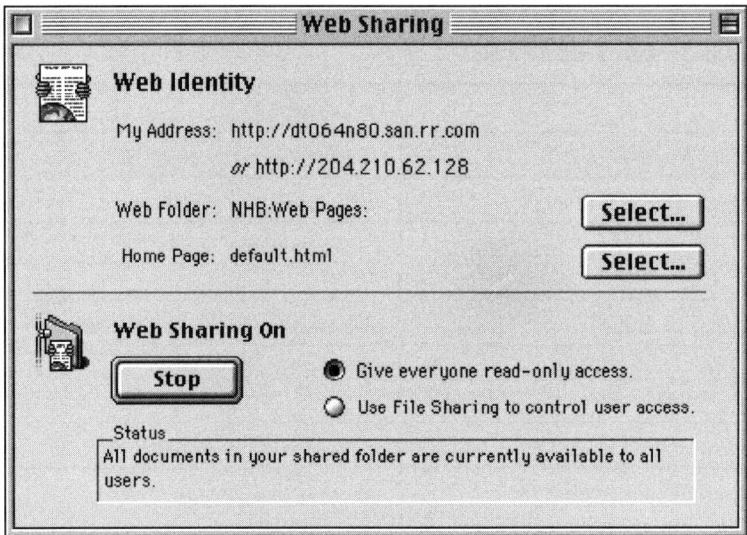

Figure 5-6. Mac OS 8 Personal Web Sharing

8. The Web Sharing control panel now displays the URL at which your Web server can be reached from the Internet. It may show only the IP address form (*http://204.210.62.128*) or a domain name (*http://dt064n80.san.rr.com*), which may be just as forgettable. **If you have a temporary IP address, it is important to remember that this URL can change each time you start your computer.**

To share a file or a folder, simply drag it into the Web folder you have specified. Clients can point their Web browsers at your URL and see that file or folder. So there you have a basic Web server. If you want to run a Web server with CGI scripts and forms, server plug-ins, database access, or other advanced Web server functions, PWS can do some of this, but you should explore some of the options in Table 5-5.

FILE TRANSFER PROTOCOL

The File Transfer Protocol (FTP), as you might guess from the name, was designed for transferring files between networked computers. As such, it has a few features that make it a more convenient option than a Web server for sharing files. For example, it supports both text and binary file transfers, it is more efficient (particularly for large files), and it can transfer entire folders at a time, including all files and subfolders.

File sharing with FTP can be either anonymous or password-protected. Anonymous FTP is similar to Guest access in Macintosh File Sharing. Anonymous FTP allows clients to log in to an FTP server using a default username—usually "guest," "anonymous," or "ftp"—and no password or their e-mail address. Since it is relatively open, anonymous FTP also implies restricted access. Often anonymous access is read-only, although a write-only "drop box" can allow anonymous users to deposit files on the server.

If your main cross-platform interest is exchanging files over the Internet, you should be prepared to retrieve files with an FTP client and make files available as an FTP server.

FTP Clients

As I mentioned in the Web browser section above, you can use Netscape Navigator or Microsoft Internet Explorer to download files with an anonymous FTP connection. This suffices for downloading most software applications, for example. However, if you need to get access to files that a business customer would rather not make publicly accessible, you will need to have a general-purpose FTP client application so you can log in with a username and password. And if you download lots of files from FTP servers, these clients are generally faster. Furthermore, the FTP clients have the advantage of being much smaller applications.

Table 5-6 lists the major Mac FTP clients. Again, as with the Web browsers, you may find other applications with FTP functions built in, including some Web site management programs such as Adobe GoLive.

With all the FTP clients, the interfaces look different from one to another, and each client offers a unique set of advanced features. However, at the minimum, they all offer two basic functions: first, logging into an FTP server, and second, downloading and uploading files. Here I'll show the basic idea using the windows in the Fetch client.

Table 5-6. Macintosh FTP Clients

Description	Location
Anarchie Pro, shareware from Stairways Software	*www.stairways.com/anarchie*
Download Deputy, shareware from ilesa Software	*www.ilesa.com/software/deputy.html*
Fetch, shareware from Dartmouth College	*www.dartmouth.edu/pages/softdev/fetch.html*
NetFinder, shareware by Peter Li and Vincent Tan	*www.ozemail.com.au/~pli/netfinder*
Networkz, batch file transfer freeware by James Andrews	*www.catbase.com/networkz*
Transmit Pro, shareware from Panic Software	*www.panic.com/transmit*
Vicomsoft FTP client, shareware and commercial software from Vicomsoft	*www.vicomsoft.com/ftp.software.html*

Figure 5-7 shows the basic FTP connection window. At minimum, you need to provide a server (host) name. If you leave the username and password fields blank, Fetch will attempt an anonymous FTP connection.

Once you have logged in to the FTP server, either anonymously or with your username and password, the FTP client will display the contents of the directory you specify. If you leave the directory field blank, it will display the contents of the default directory. Figure 5-8 shows the default directory for anonymous access to my Mac's FTP server. At this point, you can put (upload) or get (download) files from the FTP server. In Fetch, you can do this using the Put and Get buttons, or by dragging and dropping files to and from the Fetch window.

Those are the basics of FTP client access. As I noted, each FTP client has its own strengths and unique features, so you may want to evaluate several before choosing.

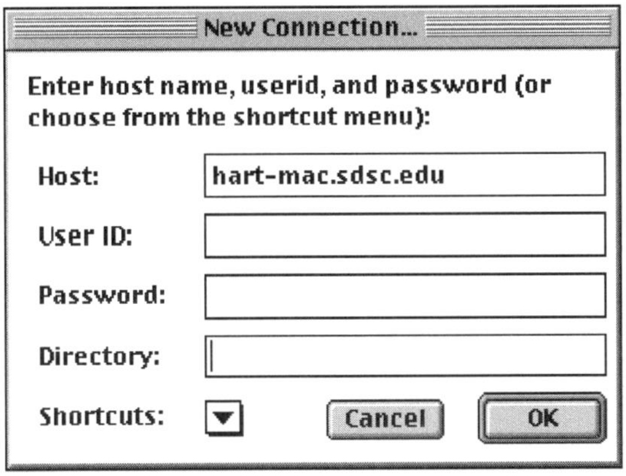

File Transfer Protocol   79

Figure 5-7. Making an FTP connection with Fetch

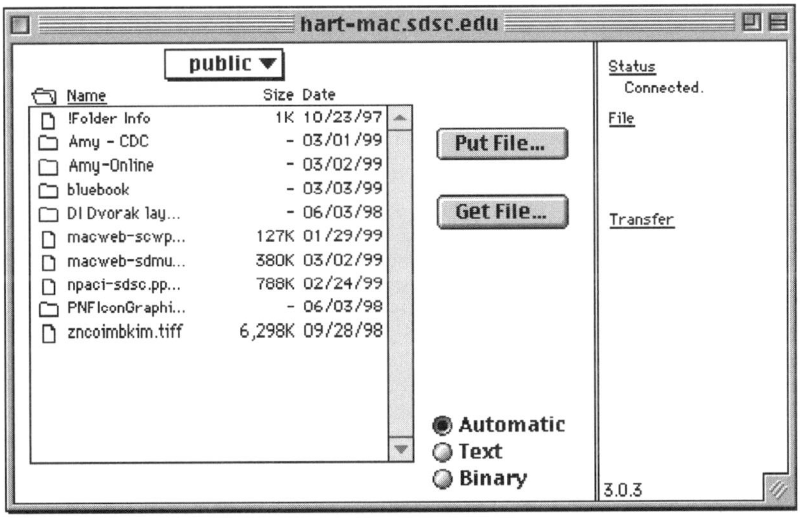

Figure 5-8. Exchanging files with Fetch

FTP Servers

Now, if your goal is to let other users come to your Mac and either get files from you or give files to you, then you need to consider running an FTP server on your Mac. Here, I will describe the NetPresenz shareware, but there are several options for Macintosh FTP servers, shown in Table 5-7. Note that StarNine's WebSTAR and Tenon's WebTen Web servers can also function as FTP servers (see Table 5-4). In general, NetPresenz may be a little slower than some Mac FTP servers because it needs Mac OS File Sharing to be turned on. If you plan to run a heavily used FTP service, it may be worth investigating other alternatives.

Configuring NetPresenz as your FTP server involves five basic steps.

1. Use the File Sharing control panel to turn on file sharing. In the Mac OS Finder, identify the folders to be shared by Everyone (anonymous FTP) and by specific users. NetPresenz uses the preferences set in the Finder and the passwords and users created with the Users and Groups control panel. Note that if you have already set up a folder for sharing files with "Guests," you should plan to use this folder for anonymous FTP access.
2. Run the NetPresenz Setup program, which displays a panel with six options, as shown in Figure 5-9. Choose FTP Setup from this panel and set the access privileges for you (the Owner), named users (as listed in the Users and Groups list), and Guests (anonymous FTP clients).
3. Choose FTP Users from NetPresenz Setup and choose the default login directory for Owner, Users, and Guests. Named users can each be assigned a unique default directory as long as that folder can be shared by the user.
4. Choose Summary from NetPresenz Setup to see if everything is set properly. If it says "You must fix this!" anywhere, you should fix it.

Table 5-7. Macintosh FTP Servers

FTP server	Location
AppleShare IP, file server software from Apple	*www.apple.com/appleshareip*
Core FTP Server, commercial software from Core Technologies	*www.coretechnologies.net*
NetPresenz, FTP (and Web and Gopher) server shareware by Stairways Software	*www.stairways.com/netpresenz*
Rumpus, commercial software by Maxum Development	*www.maxum.com/Rumpus*

E-mail

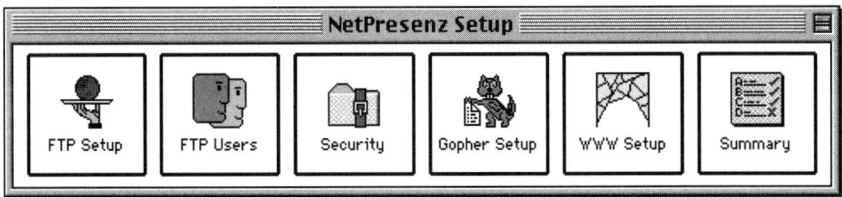

Figure 5-9. NetPresenz Setup

5. Quit NetPresenz Setup and double-click the NetPresenz icon to turn on your FTP server.

Other FTP servers require similar setup steps—defining which folders to share, defining users with access greater than that permitted by anonymous FTP, and running the server software. Once you have NetPresenz running, UNIX users can access your shared folders with the FTP services built in to UNIX. Windows users have their own choice of FTP clients with which they can access your shared files.

E-MAIL

In most people's on-line life, e-mail ranks right up there with the Web as an essential Internet application. From the client side, you need to be able to read e-mail messages and keep up to date on essential Internet humor and hoaxes. In addition, you want to be able to accept and open *attachments*—files enclosed with an e-mail message.

From the server side, you have several possibilities that you may need to support, depending on your cross-platform needs.

1. You may want to deliver *incoming* e-mail to users, either via the Post Office Protocol version 3 (POP3) or Internet Mail Access Protocol (IMAP).
2. You may want to send *outgoing* e-mail that is bound for addresses across the Internet via the Simple Mail Transfer Protocol (SMTP).
3. You may want to manage mailing lists with a list server that accepts incoming messages and redistributes them to a list of subscriber e-mail addresses.

4. You may want to automatically send files, as e-mail attachments, back to users who send e-mail requests. This is particularly useful if a significant chunk of your audience only has e-mail access (but not Web or FTP) to the Internet.

Maintaining the full spectrum of e-mail server functions can be a more time-consuming activity than providing Web (HTTP) and FTP services. In the following sections, I'll discuss e-mail clients, introduce e-mail server functions, and provide some examples of list server and e-mail file server functions.

The Most Common E-mail Problem

In researching cross-platform difficulties for particular applications (see Chapter 6), I found that a common source of trouble was not with the applications themselves but with sharing the files as e-mail attachments.

When an e-mail client sends an attached file across the Internet, the software at both ends performs steps that aren't visible to the user. Specifically, the attached file must first be "encoded" on the sender's machine, and on the receiver's machine the encoded file must be "decoded" so that the recipient can use it. The reason for encoding is that the e-mail protocols expect data in a certain form, and binary attachments are not in that form. The same limitation of the e-mail protocols often leads to problems in the translation of special characters such as curly quotes (" ") or accented letters (é, ü).

Problems arise because there are different types of encoding, which not all e-mail clients can decode. For example, Eudora Pro on the Mac can encode files as AppleDouble, AppleSingle, BinHex, and Uuencode data fork, as shown in Figure 5-10. (You can also change the encoding method for an individual message with the encoding button in the message window.)

I'll give you two guesses to determine which two encoding methods you might use mainly for Mac recipients. On the other hand, Outlook Express 4.5 for the Mac cannot use AppleSingle, but it does understand AppleDouble, MIME (Base64), Uuencode, and BinHex. BinHex is more widely accepted, but if all else fails, you can use the older standard of Uuencoding. In contrast, the Windows version of Eudora permits encoding via MIME, BinHex, and Uuencode, while Outlook Express permits MIME and Uuencode.

E-mail

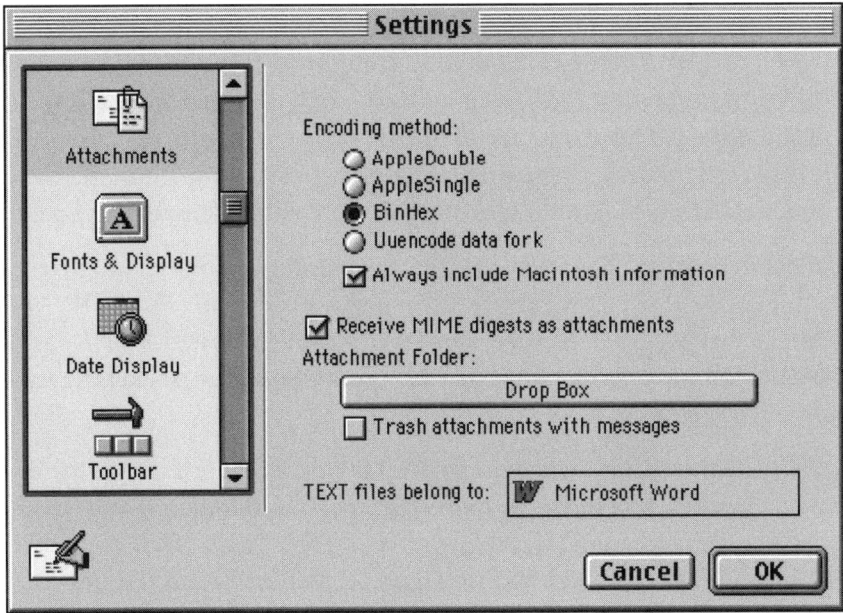

Figure 5-10. Eudora Pro attachment settings

The Mac Eudora settings window also points out another potential problem—the checkbox "Always send Macintosh information." Again, if you exchange files regularly with non-Mac users, you may want to disable this option so that Windows or UNIX clients aren't confused by the information in the Mac file's resource fork.

E-mail Clients

If you think you're limited to Qualcomm's Eudora Pro or Microsoft's Outlook Express for your e-mail client, have a look at Table 5-8. And the list doesn't include Claris Emailer, discontinued by Apple, but which you might find available for download, and which, according to persistent rumors, might be resurrected.

In practice, there are a few features that may help you decide which e-mail client best suits your needs.

POP3 or IMAP. You need to determine which protocol your e-mail provider supports, and select an e-mail client that can speak the appropriate protocol. With POP3, your e-mail software downloads all your e-mail messages from the server to your computer. You then read, reply, and save your messages on your Mac. You might set messages to remain on the server for several days, but for the most part, your e-mail is on your computer. With IMAP, on the other hand, your e-mail stays on the server, and you read, reply to, and save your messages on the server. The advantage of IMAP is that you can use any computer with an IMAP client and a network connection to read your e-mail. No matter where you are, your e-mail messages and folders will be there when you log in.

Password security. Your network administrator may choose a higher level of security than plain-text passwords for accessing your e-mail. For POP, you may need a client that supports Kerberos or APOP (authenticated POP) passwords. For IMAP, you may need a client that supports the secure sockets layer (SSL) used by secure Web forms.

Off-line features. If you have a dial-up connection to the Internet or use a laptop while you're away from the network, you should look for an e-mail client that supports off-line reading, writing, and saving of e-mail. Most do. Some have additional features such as holding messages for delivery until the next time you go on-line.

Table 5-8. Macintosh E-mail Clients

Description	Location
Macintosh E-mail Resource Page	*www.macemail.com*
CommuniGator from Stalker Software	*www.stalker.com/CommuniGate/CLIENT*
eMail inChorus, multimedia e-mail from Softlink	*www.inchorus.com*
Eudora Pro and Eudora Light from Qualcomm	*www.eudora.com*
MailSmith from Bare Bones Software	*www.barebones.com*
MailStrom from Tree Star, Inc. (available, but no longer supported)	*www.treestar.com/mailstrom*
Messenger, part of Netscape Communicator	*www.netscape.com*
Mulberry (IMAP-only e-mail) from Cyrusoft International	*www.cyrusoft.com/mulberry*
Musashi from Sono Software (Japanese and English versions)	*www.sonosoft.com/musashi*
Outlook Express from Microsoft	*www.microsoft.com/mac/oe*
PowerMail from CTM Development	*www.ctmdev.com*

E-mail

Attachments. Since we are considering e-mail in terms of a cross-platform working environment, you want to be sure your e-mail client accepts and sends attached files. Again, most do. Extra features that you may want to look for include automatic compression of outgoing attachments.

Beyond these considerations, you should select an e-mail client that you feel comfortable using, ranging from the 500-kilobyte download of Musashi to the 5.5-megabyte PowerMail to the 10 megabyte Eudora Pro demo download. To get started with any client, you need the same basic set of configuration information, which is shown in Figure 5-11. The figure shows the e-mail settings panel from Internet Config, instead of a particular e-mail client. You need to know, at minimum:

- Your e-mail address, of the form *username@your-company.com*, to which other Internet users should direct their messages to you.
- Your e-mail account, the username on the server that stores your incoming e-mail. With POP accounts, the server often, but not always, has "pop" in the name. Your e-mail account may or may not be the same as your e-mail address.

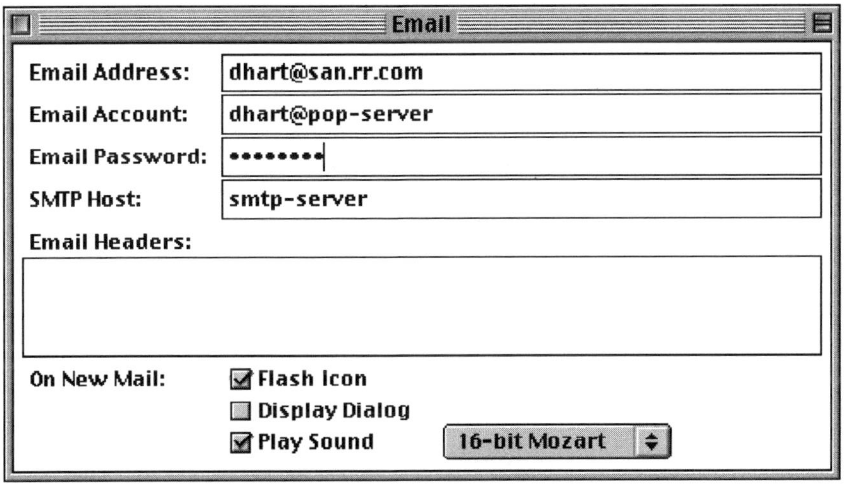

Figure 5-11. Internet Config basic e-mail settings

- Your e-mail password.
- Your SMTP host, the name of the server that handles your outgoing mail. The SMTP server often has "smtp" in the name, but it can also be the same as the POP server. For example, *post-office.your-company.com* may handle both incoming and outgoing mail.

E-mail Servers

While using an e-mail client is a virtual necessity in the Internet world, running an e-mail server is a major commitment. If you run a POP3 or IMAP server, you must manage accounts for all users for whom you accept incoming mail. In the case of IMAP, you must ensure that you have enough disk space for the volume of e-mail traffic to your users. An SMTP server is more straightforward—all users send mail through the same SMTP server.

For the purposes of operating in a cross-platform environment, your e-mail server may run on a Macintosh, UNIX, or Windows machine. If you need to manage the e-mail accounts for a set of users, Table 5-9 lists the available e-mail servers for the Mac. I've also included whether the server supports SMTP, POP3, IMAP, or HTTP. (In this table, HTTP support means the server allows users to read e-mail through a Web browser.)

In solving a cross-platform file exchange problem, a more likely need for an e-mail server may be to support subscriber mailing lists or automatic file distribution. For such applications, discussed in the next section, an e-mail server may be a prerequisite. In such a case, perhaps the Eudora Internet Mail Server or Stalker Internet Mail Server, both free, will suffice. Note that several e-mail servers also include list server capabilities.

Mailing List Servers

You probably belong to one or more Internet mailing lists, so you may know how they work. For those of you who don't, here's the basic idea. A mailing list comprises a collection of e-mail addresses belonging to subscribers. Messages are sent, or posted, to the mailing list as if the list were a single user, and *list server*

E-mail

Table 5-9. Macintosh E-mail Servers

Description	Protocols	Location
AppleShare IP from Apple	SMTP, POP3, IMAP	*www.apple.com/appleshareip*
CommuniGate from Stalker Software with list server	SMTP, POP3, IMAP, HTTP	*www.stalker.com/CommuniGate*
Eudora Internet Mail Server (EIMS) from Qualcomm	SMTP, POP3	*eudora.qualcomm.com/free/servers.html*
First Class Intranet Server from SoftArc with list server	SMTP, POP3, IMAP, HTTP	*www.softarc.com*
RingTwice4Mail from Building4Media with list server	SMTP, POP	*www.b4m.com/rt4m.html*
Stalker Internet Mail Server (SIMS) from Stalker Software	SMTP, POP3	*www.stalker.com/SIMS*
TeleFinder Server from Spider Island Software	SMTP, POP3	*www.spiderisland.com/product*

software at the receiving end redistributes the message to all subscribers. Within this framework, there are a number of options.

- **Subscriptions.** A list may allow users to subscribe or unsubscribe their own e-mail addresses, or the list may have access limited to a predefined group.
- **Messages or digest.** Instead of receiving each message to the list, some subscribers may want to receive the information as digests—typically a day's worth of messages collected into one message. Digests keep the mailing list from swamping their mailbox.
- **Closed, moderated, or open.** With an open list, any subscriber, or possibly even non-subscribers, can post messages to the list. For a moderated list, each submitted message goes first to a human moderator, who weeds out the off-topic or redundant messages. A closed list allows postings only from a fixed group of people. Closed lists can be used for announcements and newsletters, for example.

- **Autoreply.** You can also use some list servers as a means to share files. Besides understanding subscribe and unsubscribe commands, these servers recognize requests for files and will automatically return the file to the requestor as an attachment. If you need to share a small number of files that don't change often with a large number of users, you might use a list server for this. Some examples of files you might want to share in this fashion are product data sheets, brochures, or FAQ (frequently asked questions) lists.

For mailing lists, these options imply that you must manage subscriber lists and options for each list you support. Much of this is done automatically, but creating new lists and handling special requests or moderated lists entails human intervention. If you distribute files via e-mail requests, you must manage where those files are stored.

Another requirement is that you must be able to create e-mail accounts. You generally need one account to accept list server commands, such as requests to subscribe or unsubscribe. For example, *macjordomo@your-company.com* is common if you are using the Macjordomo list. You also need one account per mailing list to which subscribers post their contributions. If you run an e-mail server, you create the accounts. If you use the e-mail server provided by your ISP or company, you may need to ask (and possibly pay) to have them created.

Table 5-10 lists the list servers available for the Macintosh. List servers can be distinguished by whether they are based on POP or SMTP e-mail servers. You can use a POP-based list server even if you don't control the e-mail server. A POP list server, such as Macjordomo, behaves like another e-mail user. It watches for incoming mail, downloads the mail from the server, and redistributes it accordingly. An SMTP list server, on the other hand, is more closely tied to the SMTP e-mail server. So closely tied, that the software may have an SMTP server built-in.

Because list servers vary widely in the features they support and the interface they use to set up and manage lists, I will not attempt to describe how to install and use them here. With the spread of the Web and FTP, e-mail file distribution has also become less vital for cross-platform operation. Furthermore, auto-reply services are not designed as a general file-sharing tool. You must know which files you want to share and make sure you configure your auto-reply software to share them.

An Internet Recap

Table 5-10. Macintosh List Servers

List Server	Location
AutoShare, freeware SMTP list server by Mikael Hansen. Requires Eudora or Stalker Internet Mail Server. (Auto-reply text and files)	*www.dnai.com/~meh/autoshare*
CommuniGate list server software by Stalker Software. Requires CommuniGate Server.	*www.stalker.com/CommuniGate/LIST*
FireShare, shareware by Jerry Stratton. Created for auto-reply file exchange via e-mail. Requires EIMS or SIMS.	*www.hoboes.com/html/NetLife/Nspace/-FireShare*
First Class Intranet Server from SoftArc.	*www.softarc.com*
LetterRip, POP and SMTP list server by Fog City Software. (Auto-reply text)	*www.fogcity.com*
ListSTAR, POP and SMTP list server by StarNine Corporation. (Auto-reply text and files)	*www.starnine.com/liststar*
Macjordomo, freeware POP list server by Michele Fuortes. (Auto-reply text)	*leuca.med.cornell.edu/Macjordomo*
RingTwice4Mail from Building4Media, includes e-mail server and list server.	*www.b4m.com/rt4m.html*

AN INTERNET RECAP

At this point you have either way too much information about Internet serving and file sharing or not enough. If you're in the "not enough" category, I'd like to suggest the *Mac OS 8 Web Server Cookbook,* which covers all of the above topics and more.

On the other hand, if your head is swimming in Internet details, here's where I boil it down to the bare necessities.

As an Internet client, you need three main tools: a Web browser, an FTP client, and an e-mail program. Choose the software that works best for you.

As an Internet server, you have a slightly more complicated decision. First, let's go back to the question posed at the start of the chapter. Which of the following best describes your situation?

- You want to use the Internet for occasional file sharing or a minimal Web site.
- You're running an AppleShare IP file server and want to add Internet capabilities.
- You want to be the next Yahoo!, Lycos, or Amazon.com.

If you're in Category 1, your best bet is to stick with Apple's Personal Web Sharing and NetPresenz from Stairways Software. You don't need a separate computer or even a permanent IP address. You just have to tell those with whom you're sharing files your new Internet address each time. And I wouldn't worry about e-mail servers at this point. But if you want to run a mailing list, I recommend Macjordomo, a freeware POP mailing list server. This entire setup, great for casual use, will cost you $10 for NetPresenz and whatever it costs you for two (at least) e-mail accounts through your ISP.

For those of you in Category 2, I suggest you look into the Web, FTP, and e-mail capabilities of AppleShare IP. If you haven't yet, this may be another reason to upgrade to the latest version. In starting out, AppleShare IP should give you all of the Web functions and horsepower you need. If you also want to manage mailing lists from your AppleShare IP server, you should consider one of the free or commercial POP list servers. (You can't run two SMTP servers on the same machine.)

Category 3 is where the fun begins. Before choosing software, you first need a permanent IP address and preferably a high-speed connection through your ISP. Then you need a separate Macintosh dedicated to Internet serving. If you're really aiming high, you might want three Macs, one for Web, one for FTP, and one for e-mail. And don't scrimp on the software. You'll want to evaluate the high-end packages to see which provides the full range of performance and features you need. That goes for the Web server, FTP server, e-mail server, and list server. Does that sound like a lot of work? It is. Be prepared to devote more human resources than you might expect to Internet serving—at least part of a person's time to start, and an entire person as your site grows.

But now I'm digressing from the point of this chapter, which is to share files between platforms across the Internet. For that purpose, you should start with Category 1 or Category 2 and see how things go for you. In any event, as you start and as you expand, you can handle your Internet needs with the Macintosh on your desk.

CHAPTER 6

Applications, File Formats, and Web Standards

*I*n an ideal world, you would contentedly edit your reports in whichever word processor you like on your Mac, save it, and send it off to electronic colleagues across the Internet. On your colleagues' machines, whether they use Windows or UNIX systems, the report would open in their favorite word processor with no trouble at all. You can imagine the same scenario with image files, presentations, magazine layouts, Web pages, and spreadsheets.

Too bad we all live in the real world. Even though you can send the same stream of bits across the Internet, it's tough to guarantee that your Windows- and UNIX-bound colleagues will see a file exactly the same way that you see it on your Mac. In theory, you'd think that if you create, for example, a Microsoft Word 98 document on your Mac, you would have no problem exchanging that document back and forth with a Windows user who has Microsoft Word 97. Also in theory, pigs can fly if you strap them to a hang-glider.

IT SHOULD WORK JUST FINE...

Okay, so perhaps the flying pigs crack is a bit harsh on Microsoft and software developers in general, not to mention the pigs. In practice, most applications are getting better at understanding the language of their cross-platform siblings or using the same language. And most cross-platform standards are just that, provided certain developers haven't taken it upon themselves to "enhance" the standards with platform- and software-specific additions.

As a general rule, you can make your cross-platform experience less painful by sticking to the basic features of applications and standards. Even better, you may want to view your documents or files on both Mac and Windows throughout the creation process, so you can identify problems as they crop up instead of after you've invested a lot of effort. This compromise approach means you may not be able to get the full benefit of these tools. What's a Mac user to do?

This chapter covers several variations on this theme. First, we'll check out some major applications that have cross-platform versions and see how easy it is to work across platforms. Next, we'll look at a few cross-platform file formats, which were developed independently of platform or expressly as cross-platform, and see how well they live up to their billing. Finally, we'll look at some Web standards and how you can best take advantage of them on your Mac.

APPLICATIONS

In the context of cross-platform operation, we can talk about two types of issues. First, there are the universal issues that crop up in lots of different applications, and then there are the unique surprises that individual applications throw at you. Here we're going to talk a little about both. We'll start with the universal and work our way to the individual.

E-mail File Exchange

Sending an e-mail attachment is a common way to exchange files between two computers. It's faster and more convenient than a disk as long as the file size doesn't exceed the limits of the e-mail server. However, sending files by e-mail introduces a translation problem, discussed in the E-mail section of Chapter 5.

Files must be encoded and decoded by e-mail clients of both the sender and receiver, and all encoding methods are not created equal. As a result, you may find yourself exchanging files between e-mail clients with incompatible encoding methods, even if both machines are Macs. If you run into a situation in which an attachment appears to be corrupted on another machine, you should first try sending it with a different encoding method.

Windows (and Web) File Names

File names are the source of another general problem in exchanging files between Mac and Windows applications, as described in detail in the File Conversion section of Chapter 2. The important point here is that Windows file names require a three-character extension to identify the file type and help the operating system determine which applications can open it.

If you plan to exchange files with Windows machines—or on the Web, which also uses file extensions to determine how to deal with files—you will want to learn, or make a handy list of, the Windows (and Web) extensions for the file types you use most often. This chapter includes the Windows file extension for the appropriate file types. (For completeness, I've also included the relevant Mac Creator and Type codes.)

You should note also that, since the Mac OS doesn't use file name extensions, it's quite possible to append, for example, a *.gif* extension to a file but forget to "save as" a GIF file type. This mismatch will cause problems when a Windows user (or a Web browser) tries to open the file. A number of Mac applications now automatically add the correct extension, but a little diligence is required for those that don't.

As a quick reference, Table 6-1 summarizes the Windows file extensions and the Mac Creator and Type codes for the applications and file formats in this chapter.

Table 6-1. Common File Extensions and Types

Application and File Type	Windows File Extension	Mac Creator	Mac Type(s)
AppleWorks (formerly ClarisWorks) word processing, spreadsheet, database, and graphics files	.cwk	BOBO	CWWP, CWSS, CWDB, CWGR
Adobe Acrobat (PDF) document	.pdf	CARO	PDF
Adobe Illustrator 8 EPS	.eps	ART5	EPSF
Adobe Photoshop 5 document	.psd	8BIM	8BPS
FileMaker Pro 3 or 4 database	.fp3	FMP3	FMP3
GIF image	.gif	(*various*)	GIFf
JPEG image	.jpg	(*various*)	JPEG
Microsoft Excel 98 spreadsheet (template)	.xls (.xlt)	XCEL	XLS8 (sLS8)
Microsoft PowerPoint 98 presentation (template)	.ppt (.pot)	PPT3	SLD8 (PPOT)
Microsoft Word 98 document (template)	.doc (.dot)	MSWD	W8BN (W8TN)
PostScript file	.ps	vgrd	TEXT
QuarkXPress document	.qxd	XPR3	XDOC
Quicken data file	.qdf (.qdb, .qdt)	INTU	BDAT
Rich Text Format file	.rtf	(*various*)	RTF
Text file	.txt	(*various*)	TEXT
TIFF image	.tif	(*various*)	TIFF

The Font Problem

One common issue causes problems for many cross-platform applications: fonts. A font is a set of text characters in a particular style and size. The cross-platform problem is that no two machines are guaranteed to have the same set of fonts. In fact, it's difficult to guarantee that any two Macintoshes will have the same set of fonts.

Font substitution. As a result, files created with text in a particular font on one machine may look very strange on a machine with a different font set. That's because if an application opens a file that uses an unknown font, the application will substitute another font. Font substitution prevents you from being presented with a blank page; however, the substitute font may be completely different, or it may be only slightly different. Both situations present problems.

If the substitute font is way off base, the document may be unreadable. This could happen if, for example, you're using a decorative font with mini images instead of letters. Suddenly your arrows and shapes become letters scattered throughout the file. And if the document depends on precise positioning for its layout, the substitute font almost certainly will ruin the look you had worked so hard to achieve.

If the substitute font is similar to but not exactly the same as the original, you might be faced with more insidious problems. At a quick glance, the document will look virtually identical to the original. However, if you examine it more closely, you might notice that page breaks happen in the wrong places, columns of text might wind up a line shorter or longer, producing orphans and widows, or special characters are replaced by unexpected substitutes. Carefully positioned text may also move slightly out of place.

TrueType vs. Type 1. Another variation on the font problem is the ongoing battle between Apple's TrueType and Adobe Type 1 fonts (also called PostScript fonts). Macintosh and Windows computers these days use TrueType fonts as the primary fonts for screen display and printing. However, graphic designers and other printing professionals often use Adobe Type 1 fonts for high-end printing tasks. (UNIX systems, in general, use Type 1 fonts only.) Substituting a Type 1 font for a TrueType font or vice versa, even if they share the same name and style, can lead to the second type of font problem—small changes that are difficult to spot at first glance.

Special Characters. Refer to the "Plain" Text part of the File Formats section later in this chapter for a discussion of why special characters—em dashes, curly quotes, and accented letters—turn into gibberish when files move between Mac and Windows machines.

A Font Solution?

I wish I could provide a universal fix for the font issue. There isn't one as far as I know. The best solution is to limit your choice of fonts in documents that must be shared. This suggestion applies even if you are sharing documents with other Macintosh users. Even though you are infatuated with, for example, the TrueType font Latin725 BT (one of my personal favorites), you can't expect all users to have it on their systems.

On the Macintosh, the basic set of fonts installed by Mac OS 8.1 includes Charcoal, Chicago, Courier, Geneva, Helvetica, Monaco, New York, Palatino, Symbol, and Times. Mac OS 8.5 adds a few more fonts to the mix: Capitals, Gadget, Techno, Textile, and Sand.

By comparison, a basic Windows installation includes the fonts—at least for Windows NT Server—Arial, Courier, Courier New, Lucida, Modem, MS Sans Serif, MS Serif, Roman, Script, Small Fonts, Symbol, Times New Roman, and Wingdings.

Clearly, there's not a lot of guaranteed font overlap between a Mac OS and a Windows machine. On the other hand, if you work with a limited set of colleagues, you may be able to work out a larger set of fonts that everyone has. With the advent of the Web, and in particular the wide distribution of Microsoft Office and Microsoft Internet Explorer, there is another possibility in the Microsoft Web Font Pack.

Sometimes it seems as if it's almost impossible to prevent Internet Explorer from being installed on your Macintosh. Whether you're installing the Mac OS system, installing Microsoft Office, or visiting the Microsoft Web site, there are plenty of opportunities to download and install Internet Explorer. If you do so, Microsoft kindly installs the 11 fonts in the Microsoft Web Font Pack. And since virtually every Windows machine also has Internet Explorer installed, you can almost guarantee these fonts are on most Macintosh and Windows machines. The Web font pack includes eleven TrueType fonts: Andale Mono, Arial, Arial Black, Comic Sans, Courier New, Georgia, Impact, Times New Roman, Trebuchet MS, Verdana, and WebDings.

Table 6-2. Font Resources

Description	Location
A definition of font, typeface, and typeface family	*whatis.com/font.htm*
TrueType Typography	*www.truetype.demon.co.uk*
Microsoft Web font pack	*www.microsoft.com/typography/fontpack*
Font sites all over the Web. Try your favorite search engine, perhaps Yahoo!	*search.yahoo.com/bin/search?p=fonts*

Even though the Web fonts are designed for optimal viewing on the screen, they are TrueType fonts and can be used in any word processor, spreadsheet, or non-Web application. While you may have to forego the personalization and panache that comes from typing a marketing report in Baker Signet MT, you will make life easier on yourself and your co-authors on the report. Table 6-2 has some resources on fonts and how to get Microsoft's Web fonts *without* installing Internet Explorer.

Specific Applications

This is the section where I will probably disappoint some software development companies. Let me apologize by saying that this is neither a reflection on the companies omitted nor necessarily a recommendation of the software included. I simply cannot produce an exhaustive cross-platform comparison of every application that comes in Macintosh and Windows flavors. There is neither time in my schedule or space in a single book.

That having been said, I applied highly non-scientific criteria to select the applications listed here. First, I chose well-known, widely available software that I knew came in cross-platform versions. Second, the software had to have a fairly wide Mac user base. Finally, it also helped if I used it in my day job. The results are what you see here. If you have cross-platform experience with these or other applications, please visit the book's Web site and contribute your insights.

A Note on UNIX: In general, this chapter will be concerned with crossing between Macintosh and Windows systems, and not UNIX or Linux systems. I do not mean to slight the various flavors of UNIX or Linux, but in practical terms, the set of applications available for the Mac OS, Windows, UNIX, *and*

Linux is almost vanishingly small. This is primarily a testament to the different purposes and audiences of each platform. There are a few exceptions. Corel WordPerfect has Mac, Windows, and Linux versions; and some Adobe applications have UNIX versions, but these are no longer as current as the Mac OS and Windows versions. Therefore, in the interest of keeping this chapter short, I will mention UNIX on occasion, but for the most part, the focus will be on Macintosh and Windows applications.

Adobe PhotoShop

Most Adobe products are created for both Mac and Windows, and as a rule the versions have identical feature sets and binary-compatible file formats for both platforms. (A recent exception to the rule was the first release of Adobe Acrobat 4.0, in which the Mac OS version lacked a few features found in the Windows version.)

A search through the various Photoshop on-line support options, shown in Table 6-3, turned up very few cross-platform issues. The main problems once again arise indirectly in file naming and e-mail attachments.

Plug-ins are a more likely source of cross-platform discrepancies. Adobe PhotoShop, for example, is designed so that third-party developers can extend the program's functions with application pieces called plug-ins. A plug-in may be Mac-only or Windows-only, so you cannot assume that a co-worker will have access to the same plug-in features. On the other hand, plug-ins should not change the final file format, so the files can still be read and manipulated by other users.

Table 6-3. Resources for Adobe Photoshop and Other Adobe Products

Description	Location
Adobe products page	*www.adobe.com/prodindex*
Adobe customer support	*www.adobe.com/supportservice/custsupport*
Adobe's Customer Forums	*www.adobe.com/supportservice/custsupport/forums.html*
Photoshop mailing lists	*onelist.com/subscribe.cgi/photoshop*
	www.sc.edu/deis/PHOTOSHP
Adobe newsgroups	*news:comp.graphics.apps.photoshop*
	news:alt.graphics.illustrator

AppleWorks

AppleWorks, formerly known as ClarisWorks, is bundled with iMac and also available for Windows, so I've included it here. AppleWorks provides much of the same functionality as Microsoft Office on a much smaller and more manageable scale for users who don't need the more extensive features, the more expensive cost, and more memory-intensive bulk of Microsoft's offering.

My experience with AppleWorks is less comprehensive than with Microsoft Office. However, I can add a few points. First of all, AppleWorks files are binary compatible between the Macintosh and Windows versions. If you save a file in one version, it should pop open in the other without a hitch.

Based on messages posted to the help forums listed in Table 6-4, AppleWorks and ClarisWorks users have few problems moving files back and forth between platforms. There are two additional points worth mentioning.

First, you should avoid using the Subscribe and Publish functions, which link files into a document, because of the fundamental differences in the Macintosh and Windows operating systems.

Second, remember to add the Windows file extension ".cwk" to files you intend to open on a Windows machine. Table 6-1 lists the common Mac Creator and Type codes.

FileMaker Pro

FileMaker Pro from FileMaker, Inc.—the software house formerly known as Claris—is one of the more popular database applications available for Mac and Windows because it is easy to use, inexpensive, and Web-ready. It is also designed for cross-platform environments. If you need to transfer FileMaker Pro databases from Windows to Mac, the database files are platform independent.

Even better, you can open a FileMaker Pro database on one machine, regardless of the platform, and both Mac and Windows users on the network can view and update the database. (Of course, you can set passwords and permissions for various levels of network sharing.) Both Mac and Windows versions of FileMaker Pro permit multi-user sharing that is independent of file servers or

Table 6-4. AppleWorks Information

Description	Location
AppleWorks product page from Apple	*www.apple.com/appleworks*
ClarisWorks User Group	*www.cwug.org*
ClarisWorks moderated discussion list	*listserv.temple.edu/archives/claris-works.html*

protocols on the network. In other words, even if your network has a Windows NT file server and is dominated by Windows machines, you can host a database on a Macintosh and share it with Windows FileMaker Pro users without any additional software.

FileMaker provides a guide, listed in Table 6-5 along with other FileMaker Pro resources, to help developers ensure that their databases work well in cross-platform environments. Once again, file names and fonts come into play, and if you're not careful, they could be more than just an annoyance.

Windows file names. As long as the FileMaker Pro (version 3 or 4) database file name ends in *.fp3*, it can be opened on both platforms. The file name issue arises not only in moving individual files between platforms but also in complex applications with relationships defined between multiple databases. The relationships depend on file names, and the relationships are not automatically updated if you later need to change the database names because you moved the database from Mac to Windows. So if there's any possibility that the application may be moved to a Windows system, it's best to start with Windows-safe file names.

Fonts and display. Since much of the FileMaker interface is on-screen, instead of printed, the font problem shows up in the interfaces to cross-platform applications. A screen layout designed on and for a Mac can be awkward or, at worst, unreadable on Windows computers, if the designer doesn't allow for Windows fonts consuming more screen space than their Mac counterparts. FileMaker Pro will substitute fonts, but the substitution can alter the carefully crafted look of the interface.

Table 6-5. FileMaker Pro Resources

Description	Location
FileMaker Pro product page	*www.filemaker.com*
FileMaker support page	*www.filemaker.com/support*
FileMaker Pro mailing lists	*www.filemaker.com/support/mailing.html*
FileMaker Pro newsgroup	*news:comp.databases.filemaker*
FileMaker Tech Info. Search for article number 102453 on cross-platform databases.	*www.filemaker.com/support/techinfosearch.htm*

One option for Mac developers is to design a compromise interface, using common fonts (such as the Microsoft Web fonts) and leaving room in the layout to account for the larger appearance of Windows fonts. The downside of a compromise, of course, is that the interface does not look its best on either platform.

If screen appearance is worth a little extra effort, FileMaker Pro gives designers another option. You can design two layouts—one Mac-specific, one Windows-specific—and use the Status(CurrentPlatform) script function to select the appropriate one. See the FileMaker Tech Info article, listed in Table 6-5, on cross-platform databases for details.

Microsoft Office

I would be remiss to overlook Microsoft Office 98, which is the standard in many offices, for better or for worse. On the positive side for Mac users, Microsoft Office is widely used and has a Mac version for Microsoft Word, Excel, and PowerPoint. Therefore, for employees who perform many of their job duties with a word processor, spreadsheet, or presentation maker, Microsoft Office gives the Mac, if not equity, then at least a solid foothold on the desktop.

On the negative side, Microsoft Office for Windows includes the Microsoft Access database software. With the importance of databases, the lack of a Mac version of Access can present a serious problem for Mac users. The best solution available to Mac users is FileMaker Pro, which in version 4.1 provides, at the time of writing, a preview release of an ODBC (Open Database Connectivity) interface. ODBC is a standard for allowing a program (in this case, FileMaker Pro) to access a database created by a different database program. Microsoft has also released an Office 98/FileMaker Pro importer to bring database information into Word 98 and Excel 98 documents.

However, this chapter isn't here to bemoan the absence of a database application in Office 98. We want to know how well Word 97 or Word 2000—the Windows versions—deals with Word 98 files from the Mac, and vice versa. The same comparison can be made for Excel and PowerPoint.

On the whole, the applications work well between platforms for the vast majority of features. The files are binary compatible, meaning the Mac applications will open a Windows-saved file, and Windows applications will open Mac files without complaint. On the other hand, you may encounter some minor compatibility issues. Table 6-6 lists some resources for more information about

Microsoft Office 98 and Windows compatibility. Here are the problems I've encountered in going between platforms.

Windows file name extensions. Table 6-1 has a quick run-down of Windows file extensions and the Mac file creators and types for the applications in Microsoft Office. You can almost sense the logic in the Windows extensions, but don't ask me to explain the Mac file type codes.

Macro virus protection. This difference actually works in the Mac's favor. Word, Excel, and PowerPoint files allow you to attach macros—instructions to run some commands automatically when a file is opened—to Office documents. Sometimes this is handy, but this same feature has also led to the spread of macro viruses, good macros gone bad. Every Office application has the option to "Enable macro virus protection," which displays an alert box and lets you choose *not* to run any attached macros. On the Mac, this option is by default turned on; on Windows, it's turned off, which means a Windows user may never know he or she has just launched a macro virus. As a rule, you should never open a macro-enabled file from *anyone* else, even someone you know, because macros are so rarely used. A safer route is to let that person know he or she just sent a file with a macro attached. You may find out the macro is safe, but your colleague's system may also be infected with a macro virus.

Table 6-6. Microsoft Office 98 Information

Description	Location
Microsoft Office 98 product page	*www.microsoft.com/macoffice*
Microsoft Office 98 and Microsoft Office 2000 compatibility page	*www.microsoft.com/mac/office2000*
Microsoft Office 98/FileMaker Pro importer	*www.microsoft.com/mac/fmtools.htm*
Office 98 user area, with downloads, support pages, and other information	*www.microsoft.com/macoffice/users.htm*
Woody's Office Watch, a weekly e-mail bulletin	*www.mcc.com.au/wow/index.htm*
Microsoft Office newsgroup	*news:microsoft.public.office.misc*
MacCentral Help Forums	*www.maccentral.com/help*

Applications

Font substitution. The font problem, of course, also rears its serif head when exchanging files. If you don't have the fonts originally specified for a document, Microsoft Word will substitute fonts without letting you know. Oddly enough, the document will retain the original typeface name but substitute an available font. Until you realize you don't have the font Signet Mealworm on your machine, you're none the wiser. If precise positioning is important, you should be aware of this. To determine what fonts Word substituted, choose Preferences from the Tools menu, select the Compatibility tab, and then click the Font Substitution button, as in Figure 6-1. Simple! In Excel, the application will substitute fonts, but there's no way to change the substitution. In fact, the substitute font may always be Geneva. In PowerPoint, the application will substitute fonts, and you can change the substitution with the Replace Font option in the Format menu.

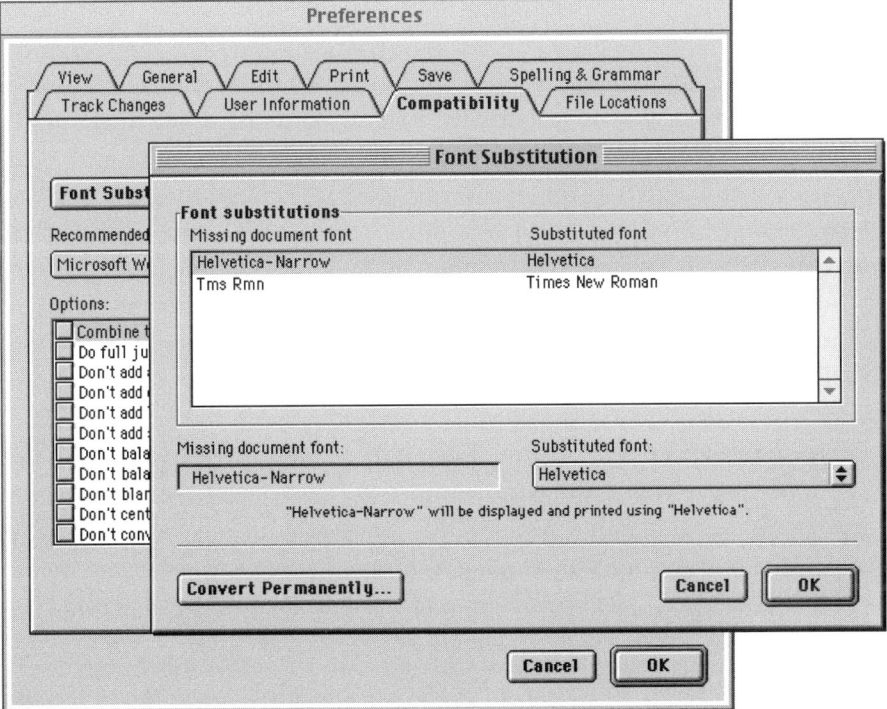

Figure 6-1. Microsoft Word font substitution

Embedded TrueType fonts. Word does, however, offer a possible way around the font problem that may or may not work for you. If you know that you're using fonts that your co-workers don't have, Word has the option to embed TrueType fonts in the document, so that they can be displayed and printed by users who don't have the fonts. (Type 1 fonts cannot be embedded.) A terrific idea, perhaps too good to be true. The MS Word Help states, "Note that TrueType font vendors determine the licensing rights for embedding fonts. For example, some fonts can't be embedded, and other embedded fonts can be viewed and printed but not modified."

So you need to experiment with *your* fonts to determine if embedding fonts will solve your cross-platform problem. I had mixed results, successfully preserving the view and printing of an embedded font in one of three tries. You should also be aware that embedding fonts rapidly increases the file size—a 20-kilobyte file might balloon to 400 kilobytes with a few embedded fonts.

Neither Excel nor PowerPoint has the option of embedding fonts.

Images and movies. Microsoft Office is more proficient with some image formats than others. I have experienced some difficulty when exchanging files containing Encapsulated PostScript (EPS) images between Macs and Windows machines. An embedded image in a Mac document printed fine, but printed as if it were screen-resolution from a Windows machine. The workaround was to transfer the EPS file and re-insert the file on the Windows machine.

For movies, the basic Mac format—QuickTime—is not the default Windows format—Microsoft AVI files. PowerPoint for Windows 98 and Windows NT will play QuickTime movies if QuickTime is installed on the Windows machine. It's not easy, but it is possible; you should consult the Microsoft Web site for more information. In a nutshell, though, you must delete the QuickTime movie from and re-insert the movie into the PowerPoint slide. I encountered similar problems with sound files, so this work-around may apply to all media files—movies and sound. Therefore, you must be sure to transfer any media files along with PowerPoint documents because, unlike images, PowerPoint does not embed media files in the document, only pointers to the files.

Saving as HTML. All Microsoft Office applications have the option of saving documents as HTML files, which is handy if you're looking for a simple route to the Web. However, I have consistently encountered problems when saving long Word documents or PowerPoint presentations with lots of images as HTML. The application will convert part of the document or presentation, but then report an "out of memory" error and stop. And yes, I increased the amount of memory assigned to the application. I gave the Word and PowerPoint gobs of memory, 80 megabytes and more. On this particular issue, I have to admit I wound up using a Windows machine to convert the files to HTML. It is theoretically possible to break up large documents or presentations into smaller chunks; however, for PowerPoint in particular, you will wind up with multiple sets of HTML files named sld001.htm through sld020.htm, or some such. Getting the links between chunks and file names straightened out can be a headache.

More Excel Differences. In the Microsoft Excel 98 Help, use the Help Index to look up "Windows-based files" and select Show Topics. One of the topics should be "Differences between Microsoft Excel 98 for Macintosh and Excel 97 for Windows." The Help indicates that the Mac and Windows versions have differences in converting files and retrieving external data; the graphics and movie formats the application can import; publishing, linking, and embedding; some minor differences in add-in programs and on-line user assistance; and some features of macros and Visual Basic. You may never run into the Excel differences, but it's nice to know your limitations. The Help files for Word and PowerPoint do not have such convenient summaries.

QuarkXPress

QuarkXPress is not an entry-level program, but it's the leading professional desktop publishing software for Mac and Windows, the impact of Adobe's upstart InDesign notwithstanding. QuarkXPress documents are binary-compatible, so you can move Quark documents between Macs and Windows platforms without generating any pesky errors.

However, because QuarkXPress documents—and desktop publishing documents in general—almost always require very precise positioning for layouts and printing, the font problem can become a font nightmare. In desktop publishing terms, the font problem can cause unwanted "reflow," meaning different fonts can cause text to flow out of the position you wanted and into the position where the font will fit. To keep text from reflowing, you must not only use the same fonts on both machines, but also use *identical versions* of the fonts on both systems. The Quark Web site gives a detailed description of this potential issue (see Table 6-7), but in short, fonts are identical if they have the same font metrics, which specify the character spacing and size of a font.

Table 6-7 QuarkXPress Resources

Description	Location
QuarkXPress product page	*www.quark.com/quarkxpress*
Support for Quark products	*www.quark.com/tech*
Tech notes for Quark products	*www.quark.com/tech/technotes.html*
Quark's explanation of the font problem	*www.quark.com/tech/technotes/tn006.html*
Quark user forums	*www.quark.com/tech/techforums.html*

Another potential problem arises from the graphics included in a Quark document. Some formats are better understood by both platforms than others. In particular, TIFF and EPS graphics are generally safe for both the Mac OS and Windows. On the other hand, PICT, BMP, and PCX, for example, are native to one platform or the other and could lead to difficulties in cross-platform situations.

Finally, you must also use the Windows file name extensions in cross-platform situations. The Mac Creator code for Quark is XPR3, and the type code for a QuarkXPress document is XDOC. In Windows, Quark documents are identified by the extension *.qxd*, and Quark templates by the extension *.qxt*. The Quark Web site lists other file name extensions for Windows.

Quicken

Intuit's Quicken financial management software is included here because it is bundled with the iMac and because it is one of the most popular finance programs, with good reason, for both Macintosh and Windows. I have found Quicken overall to be a great way to keep tabs on our household's money. With any luck, however, you won't be exchanging a lot of Quicken data between platforms because Quicken is *not* designed to work well between platforms.

For example, let's say you want to transfer your Quicken data from a Windows machine to a Mac. (I've done this.) First, you're confronted with a list of restrictions for the types of characters and names you cannot use in the cross-platform version. Making sure that you don't violate one of these restrictions could involve going through every transaction you plan to transfer.

Next, you have to export all your Quicken data into a "QIF" interchange file. Theoretically, according to the application help, you should be able to import the Windows file into the Mac version of Quicken. But in transferring, depending on your software versions, you might get an error such as "Invalid transaction in account: xxxx." When you finally get to the Intuit Web site to search for help, you find the "Frequently Asked Question" on this very subject at the Intuit Web site. Here you are told you need to delete *manually* a line from *every* transaction in the QIF file. What a joy that is.

If you use Quicken to track your finances and MacInTax to do your taxes, both on a Macintosh, you may have also discovered that you need to export and import data between the programs. Perhaps I'm just spoiled from using Microsoft Office between platforms, but this just wasn't worth the effort. Or perhaps I was dissuaded by my previous experience with Quicken QIF files.

In any event, let me stress that it *is* possible to transfer Quicken data between platforms. Just be prepared for a little more effort than you might have hoped for. Table 6-8 has pointers to additional information on Quicken.

Table 6-8. Intuit Quicken Resources

Description	Location
Quicken product page	*www.intuit.com/quicken98*
Intuit's Quicken support network	*www.intuit.com/support/quicken*
Resolving the "Invalid transaction in account: xxxx" error when importing a Windows QIF file	*www.intuit.com/support/quicken/faqs/mac/2269.html*
Quicken newsgroup	*news:alt.comp.software.financial.quicken*

FILE FORMATS

So, maybe you refuse to submit to the Microsoft juggernaut, and you choose to use another of the fine word processors available for the Macintosh, such as Nisus Writer (*www.nisus.com*) or Mariner Write (*www.marinersoft.com*). Or maybe you simply can't afford to lay out the cash necessary for high-end software such as Microsoft Office, QuarkXPress, or PhotoShop. That's all well and good, but what happens if you need to exchange a report or other document with a Windows user or even another Mac user? In another scenario, a Windows rebel using Lotus WordPro wants to send you a file. What's the best format to use to retain as much formatting as possible?

Chapter 2 presented some file conversion tools, such as MacLinkPlus, for the Macintosh. That's one option, but as a rule you can expect most files of any complexity to lose some formatting in the translation to another format. Another option is to exchange the information in a software-independent or cross-platform format. This section covers some of the major formats that might meet your needs.

"Plain" Text

You might think that the guaranteed solution for exchanging information between platforms would be to choose the "plain text" or "text only" option for saving files from your application. The file can then be read properly on any computer that understands standard text. This will *usually* work, but not if you use special characters such as accented letters (é, ä, ñ) or typesetting characters such as curly quotes (" ") or em dashes (—). You've seen this problem yourself, if you've encountered text that looks like this:

> ÒWeÕre committed to keeping the national research community at the leading edge of high-performance computing,Ó said André Lacièle, the centerÕs director. ÒBy combining our expertiseÑin research and supercomputing technologyÑwe can provide scientists with the advanced tools necessary to achieve significant advances in computational science and engineering.Ó

"Plain text" isn't as plain as you might think. Virtually every computer uses the standard character set known as ASCII (American Standard Code for Information Interchange). ASCII is a seven-bit code that defines 128 unique characters, numbered 0 to 127. ASCII characters include the uppercase and lowercase letters of the Roman alphabet, numerals, and common punctuation, along with some non-displaying control characters such as tab and carriage return. However, with only seven bits, ASCII does not have enough codes to represent special characters, which computer designers have worked around by defining "extended ASCII" character sets that use eight bits to produce 256 characters.

Extended ASCII variations. In fact, at least four extended ASCII variations, which have even more names, are used to assign characters to codes from 128 to 255.

The Mac OS has its own extended ASCII set. Computers using MS-DOS have another set (also known as IBM extended ASCII), which is recognizable for having characters that are useful for drawing lines and boxes on screen. And the most common extended ASCII set, used by Windows 3.1/95/98 and UNIX, is called the Windows, ANSI, UNIX, or ISO 8859-1 set, depending on who you ask. Windows NT uses an entirely different code, called Unicode, which can have a maximum of 65,356 different characters—room for the letters in all of the world's alphabets.

Here's a note for HTML page creators. It is possible to display extended ASCII characters in HTML pages using the notation *°* to insert ASCII code 176. Mac Web browsers will translate these ASCII character codes with the ISO 8859-1 character tables, even though other applications may use the Mac OS character tables.

I found it unbelievably difficult to track down a Web page that listed the differences between the character codes used by the Mac OS and Windows. I finally found some useful resources by Eric-Paul Rebel and Wolfgang Husmann, which are listed along with additional references in Table 6-9.

Table 6-9. Character Code Sets

Description	Location
ASCII Converter shareware by Marco Bambini	*www.geocities.com/SiliconValley/Network/7185/software.html*
Pages of IBM, Mac, Windows, ISO Latin, and other character sets, by Eric-Paul Rebel	*utopia.knoware.nl/users/eprebel/Communication/CharacterSets*
High ASCII glyphs to HTML entities, by Wolfgang Husmann	*home.rhein-zeitung.de/~husmenschen/cgi-bin/highascii/userfrontend.pl*
Numeric codes for special characters in HTML pages	*www.zdnet.com/devhead/resources/href/ascii.html*
The ISO Latin-1 or 8859-1 standard	*ppewww.ph.gla.ac.uk/~flavell/iso8859/iso8859-pointers.html czyborra.com/charsets/iso8859.html*
The Unicode standard	*www.unicode.org*

Plain text solutions. What does all this mean to cross-platform users? To avoid problems with incompatible special characters, you have a few options. The easiest and probably least helpful solution is to use no special characters. This is great when it works, but terrible when you need to send your résumé to Otto Schönbein *mañana*.

As a second option, many applications provide ways to convert or adjust special characters so that they are cross-platform friendly. The Eudora Pro e-mail program, for example, provides an 18-page document explaining character sets. For example, the "Fix curly quotes" preference setting tells Eudora to convert curly quotes, em and en dashes, and the bullet (option-8) characters to ASCII substitutes. Eudora can also use "quoted-printable" encoding, which converts special characters to a three-character code—*é* becomes =E9, for example—that the receiving e-mail program will translate back to the special character, if the e-mail client is MIME-capable.

As another application example, Microsoft Word 98 offers three (count 'em) "text only" file formats—text only, MS-DOS text only, and Unicode text. If you know with whom you need to share a text file, you can save the appropriate text format. All three formats are equivalent if you don't use any special characters except for curly quotes (" "), which Word appears to convert to ASCII straight quotes ("). If you do have special characters, use "text only" to exchange files with other Macs, "MS-DOS text only" to send files from a Mac to older MS-DOS machines, and "Unicode text" to send Mac files to Windows NT. Saving a text file as HTML also preserves special characters, but not all word processors can interpret the HTML tags. (Saving files as regular Word documents also preserves special characters between cross-platform versions of Microsoft Word.)

One final option is the helpful shareware utility, ASCII Converter by Marco Bambini. ASCII Converter can translate text files between Windows and Mac formats. According to Bambini, ASCII Converter converts between the Mac and Windows ASCII tables.

To be completely technical. Mac and Windows plain ASCII text files also differ in the carriage return character, which is one character on the Mac (ASCII code 13), but two characters on Windows—code 13 and the ASCII line feed character, code 10. Therefore, a text originally created on Windows may show an extra character after each carriage return on the Mac, while Mac text may not wrap properly in some Windows editors. The line feed character can be added or removed on the Mac by searching in Word for "Manual Line Break."

File Formats   111

Rich Text Format

Rich Text Format (RTF) is a widely used standard, originally developed by Microsoft, to preserve formatting when documents are exchanged between otherwise incompatible programs. It almost goes without saying, but using RTF requires that the creating and receiving applications have RTF translators. Most word processors, and many other applications, support RTF as an application-independent document format. If your word processor does not support RTF, then you need a translator such as MacLinkPlus from DataViz (see Chapter 2).

Creating an RTF file is a matter of selecting the "Save As" option in an application and choosing the Rich Text Format file type. To exchange the resulting file with a Windows machine, you should use the *.rtf* file extension. Viewing an RTF file requires opening it in an application that understands RTF, such as just about any word processor.

An RTF file is a text file, except that most of the file is devoted to describing the formatting of the document. If you were to "read" an RTF file, it would begin something like this:

```
{\rtf1\mac\ansicpg10000\uc1
\deff0\deflang1033\deflangfe1033{\upr{\fonttbl{\f0\fnil\fcharset256\fprq2
{\*\panose 02020603050405020304}Times New
Roman;}{\f4\fnil\fcharset256\fprq2{\*\panose
02000500000000000000}Times;}
{\f20\fnil\fcharset256\fprq2{\*\panose
02000500000000000000}Palatino;}}{\*\ud{\fonttbl{\f0\fnil\fcharset256\fpr
q2{\*\panose 02020603050405020304}Times New Ro-
man;}{\f4\fnil\fcharset256\fprq2{\*\panose 02000500000000000000}Times;}
...
```

As a rule, I tend to use RTF as a last resort. If it is possible to avoid the intermediate RTF stage, for example, by saving a Word 98 document directly as a Word 5.1 file, then do so. RTF will preserve *most* formatting, such as headings, indents, character styles, and paragraph alignment, but you should not expect an RTF file to duplicate exactly the precise typography and layout of a document, as PDF or PostScript will (see the following sections). On the other hand, RTF works well with straightforward formatting, and you can edit the contents of an RTF file after opening it in a word processor, unlike PDF or PostScript formats.

For example, the font problem can arise if your collaborator does not have the fonts specified in the RTF file. And no matter how accurately an RTF file records the formatting of a document, RTF won't enable a basic text editor to access document features created on a full-featured word processor. For example, you can save Microsoft Word 98 paragraph styles in an RTF document, but you won't be able to edit those styles with a text editor that does not support paragraph styles.

The Microsoft Word 98 Help also points out that RTF files can be substantially larger than the equivalent native word processor document. Graphics in particular contribute to the size increase; JPEG and PNG images embedded in a Word 98 document are converted to bitmaps, which can be up to 10 times larger. Table 6-10 points to some additional RTF resources.

Portable Document Format

The Portable Document Format (PDF) was developed by Adobe to capture all the elements of a printed document—the fonts, formatting, colors, and graphics—in an electronic version that you can view, navigate, print, or send to someone else. PDF files are especially useful for documents such as magazine articles, brochures, or flyers for which the original graphic appearance is a key feature.

Viewing a PDF document requires that you have the Adobe Acrobat Reader software, a free utility available for the Mac, the various forms of Windows, most flavors of UNIX, Linux, and OS/2. To retain the document's appearance, PDF files can embed fonts so that they're available to any viewer. They can also include interactive elements, such as buttons for forms entry and for triggering sound and QuickTime movies. You can navigate a PDF file not only by paging forward and backward, but also with links to document sections or to external Web sites.

Table 6-10. Rich Text Format Resources

Description	Location
RTF definition	*whatis.com/rtf.htm*
The RTF 1.14 specification	*www.sunpack.com/RTF/RTF114.html*
RTFtoHTML utility	*www.sunpack.com/RTF*
RichReader by Michael Arena lets Palm Computers read RTF files	*www.erols.com/arenakm/palm/RichReader.html*

On the other hand, creating or editing PDF files requires additional software, usually the full Adobe Acrobat software or plug-ins to other applications. Many of the tools listed at the PDF Zone Web site are Acrobat plug-ins or utilities. In general, you create the document in an appropriate application—QuarkXPress or Microsoft Word 98, for example—and then use Acrobat's Adobe Distiller or PDFWriter components to "print" a PDF version. To add Acrobat-specific features, such as the table of contents or Web links, you use Adobe Exchange to edit and optimize the PDF file.

Regarding cross-platform issues, PDF files work rather well. With the release of Acrobat 4.0, while this book was being written, Adobe broke from its normal practice of cross-platform equality and provided Web capture and digital signature features initially for Windows only. Plans called for soon thereafter releasing the Macintosh versions of the relevant Acrobat plug-ins, which were in beta release as the book went to press. (The Web Capture plug-in requires Mac OS 8.6.) However, the PDF files created by both the Mac and Windows versions are readable on all platforms.

If requiring the Acrobat Reader software is too restrictive, the new Adobe Document Server (ADS) will let almost anyone with a Web browser view PDF files. ADS serves PDF files by converting them to Web-viewable JPEG images for the screen, and it can convert files to text so they can be read by screen-reading programs. While this makes PDF files even more accessible, at the time of writing ADS is available only for Windows NT and Solaris, and only through third-party developers. Table 6-11 contains links to some PDF resources.

Table 6-11. Portable Document Format Resources

Definition	Location
PDF definition	*whatis.com/pdf.htm*
Adobe PDF information	*www.adobe.com/prodindex/acrobat/adobepdf.html*
Adobe Acrobat, software for creating, editing, and reading PDF documents. Acrobat Reader is free.	*www.adobe.com/prodindex/acrobat*
The PDF Zone, an independent site of PDF information, user forums, and PDF software.	*www.pdfzone.com*
PDF newsgroup	*news:comp.text.pdf*

PostScript

PostScript is a page definition language, developed by Adobe in 1985, used to describe the appearance of a printed page. Most high-end laser printers understand PostScript, and most professional printing houses use PostScript to create pages for printing. In other words, it's a widely used standard, and PostScript files can be identified by their *.ps* suffix.

PostScript files are primarily intended to be printed, although it is possible to view them on-screen with software utilities. Contrast this to PDF files, which are primarily intended to be displayed on-screen, although they can be printed. However, PostScript files, like PDF files, are designed to be printed or simulate a printed document. They are not easily edited, which for documents that you don't want your readers to edit can be an advantage.

PostScript files, like RTF files, are text files in which the bulk of the text comprises page layout commands. For example, in producing this book, Chapter 6 was a 152-kilobyte Microsoft Word 98 document with no figures, which became a 2.7-megabyte PostScript file.

A PostScript file begins like this:

```
%!PS-Adobe-3.0
%%Title: Microsoft Word - psb.doc
%%Creator: Windows NT 4.0
%%CreationDate: 16:8 9/23/1997
%%Pages: (atend)
%%BoundingBox: 12 15 599 782
%%LanguageLevel: 2
%%DocumentNeededFonts: (atend)
%%DocumentSuppliedFonts: (atend)
%%EndComments
%%BeginProlog
...
```

From there, it gets complicated, but I can assure you—it's a real page-turner. On the Macintosh, you have several courses of action when you encounter a PostScript file.

- Print it to a PostScript-capable printer. Apple LaserWriters that understand PostScript generally have "PS" in their names, such as the LaserWriter 16/600 PS. This is probably the most straightforward option.

File Formats   115

- Convert it to a PDF file with Adobe Acrobat Distiller. Obviously, this requires that you have the full version of Acrobat.
- View it with the Macintosh version of the freeware GhostScript utility, listed in Table 6-12.
- If you know it's an image, convert it to an Encapsulated PostScript (EPS) image with Adobe Illustrator or other image creation software.
- Try to get the original file from which the PostScript file was generated. If the file came from a UNIX user, the original is usually a TeX or LaTeX file. There are tools to convert LaTeX to easier-to-edit formats such as RTF. See Gary Gray's Macintosh TeX and LaTeX Web Site, listed in Table 6-12.

On the other hand, if you need to create a PostScript file, the steps are fairly straightforward. The only software you need is the LaserWriter printer driver that comes with the Mac OS; make sure that the LaserWriter extension is in the Extensions folder. Even if you don't have a LaserWriter printer, the following steps will work.

1. Open the Chooser, and select the LaserWriter icon to set your default printer.
2. Close the Chooser, and click OK if a dialog box appears warning you that you have changed your default printer.

Table 6-12. PostScript Resources

Description	Location
Definition of PostScript	*whatis.com/postscri.htm*
Adobe PostScript overview	*www.adobe.com/prodindex/postscript*
A First Guide to PostScript	*www.cs.indiana.edu/docproject/programming/-postscript/postscript.html*
GhostScript, PostScript interpreter and viewer for Macintosh	*www.cs.wisc.edu/~ghost/mac*
PostScript newsgroup	*news:comp.lang.postscript*
LaTeX/TeX resources for Macintosh compiled by Gary Gray	*www.esm.psu.edu/mac-tex*

3. Print, either by typing Command-P or selecting Print… from the File menu, the document from which you want to create a PostScript file. The LaserWriter dialog appears.
4. In the upper right-hand corner, set the Destination to "File." You'll notice that the Print button becomes a Save button.
5. In the "Background Printing" settings, set it to Foreground Printing.
6. In the "Save as File" settings, set the Format to PostScript job, PostScript level to Level 1 Compatible, and Data Format to ASCII. (These are the defaults.) To make sure everything prints properly, set the Font Inclusion to "All."
7. Click Save. The document will be printed to the location and file name you enter in the Save dialog box.

You can print or exchange the generated PostScript file as you would any other file, but for long documents, you should be prepared to deal with large files. A 100-kilobyte word processing document, without images, might balloon to 500 kilobytes.

Spreadsheets and Databases

With spreadsheets and databases, your file exchange options are relatively straightforward. First, you're in luck if your application has cross-platform versions, such as Microsoft Excel or FileMaker Pro. In such cases, you can probably exchange the file as is.

Your second option is to convert the file to the format used by a common spreadsheet or database application. For spreadsheets, you might save the spreadsheet in Lotus 1-2-3 (.wk1) or Microsoft Excel (.xls) format, for example.

Finally, the option that will give you the greatest cross-platform compatibility—at the sacrifice of some formatting or application-specific features, of course—is to save the spreadsheet or database in a generic, text-based format understood by virtually all spreadsheet and database applications. In this regard you have two main choices, a comma-separated values (CSV) file or a tab-delimited file. In both cases, the rows of your spreadsheet or records in the database are exported to a plain text file. One line of the text file corresponds to one row of the spreadsheet or one record of the database. The column or field values are enclosed in quotes and separated either by commas or tabs.

File Formats

Most spreadsheet and database applications have "Save As" options for creating CSV or tab-delimited files. You should use the *.csv* file name extension for CSV files and either *.tab* or *.txt* for tab-delimited files. For viewing these files, most applications automatically recognize the CSV or tab-delimited format, although some require you to specify the format when you open the file.

Microsoft Excel, for example, can save files in three different types of CSV files, corresponding to the several "plain text" standards, Mac, Windows, or MS-DOS. Excel also recognizes and opens these formats automatically.

ODBC. For databases, there is one other alternative, but not for the faint of heart or non-programmers. The Open Database Connectivity (ODBC) standard allows applications to communicate with a variety of databases. Both the client application on your Mac and the database application must have ODBC support enabled. Microsoft Office 98, for example, has ODBC support available as an optional component. Put in the Office 98 CD-ROM, open the Value Pack folder, and start the Value Pack installer. Check the "Data Access" box to install the ODBC tools.

For a more general solution, Augsoft's ODBC Router provides connectivity from Macs and Windows clients to any ODBC-compliant database through an NT-based proxy server and universal client software. Table 6-13 lists some additional ODBC resources.

Graphics

With graphics files, as with spreadsheets and databases, your first choice for exchanging files should be in the native format of a cross-platform application, such as Adobe PhotoShop. Using the native format will preserve the most information and make it easier to work with others on an image.

Table 6-13. ODBC Resources

Description	Location
ODBC definition	*whatis.com/odbc.htm*
Augsoft's ODBC Router and Mac ODBC info	*www.augsoft.com*
FileMaker Pro ODBC preview	*www.filemaker.com/products/odbc/preview.html*
Microsoft Universal Data Access page	*www.eu.microsoft.com/data/odbc*

Second, as mentioned in Chapter 2, you might want to invest in the Graphic Converter shareware from Lemke Software. This will let you open just about any graphic format file you receive, including native Windows (*.bmp*), SGI (*.rgb*), or Sun (*.rs*) formats, not to mention formats that originated on Amiga or Atari computers.

On the other hand, let's say you don't need to edit the images and you're mainly concerned that the images can be viewed as easily as possible by just about anyone. In this case, you should choose a format based on the ultimate use of the image—in particular, whether the image will be viewed on-screen or professionally printed. For the screen, GIF and JPEG images are the best options. For high-quality printing (as in magazines or brochures), TIFF, EPS, and to a lesser extent PNG, files work better. We'll cover each in turn, and Table 6-14 summarizes the characteristics of each format. At the end of the section, Table 6-15 lists sources of more information.

Table 6-14. Common Graphics Formats

Format	Color Depth	Compression	Best For	Comments
EPS	24-bit	Vector-based	High-resolution printing	The benefits of vector-based images are lost if the image is converted to a bit-mapped image.
GIF	8-bit (256 colors)	LZW	On-screen graphics, logos, line art	Variations allow transparent images and animations. First Web standard.
JPEG	24-bit true color	4:1 to 20:1	Photographic art	High compression for small images. Compression is "lossy" and unpredictable.
PNG	1-8 bit palette 1-16 bit gray-scale 24-, 48-bit	Lossless, 10-30% smaller than GIF	All GIF uses, some TIFF uses	The latest versions of Adobe PhotoShop and Illustrator produce PNG images. More built-in PNG support is coming.
TIFF	24-bit true color	LZW	High-resolution images, printing	Not viewable in a Web browser, but useful for cross-platform exchanges.

EPS (Encapsulated PostScript) files differ from the other formats here in that they are a vector image format, as opposed to a raster (or bit-mapped) image. An EPS file (file extension *.eps*) and other vector-based formats, such as Scalable Vector Graphics, store images not as colored pixels, but as colored lines and regions. The upshot of using EPS files is that they are written in PostScript, the native language of printing, and they can be scaled more accurately. EPS is not the best format for easy, general, cross-platform viewing of images, however.

GIF (Graphics Interchange Format) files are recognized by all Web browsers. The major drawback of the GIF format (file extension *.gif*) is that it only supports 256 colors, which may be insufficient to provide the richness needed for some images. GIF was developed in 1987 for use with 8-bit color displays by the CompuServe on-line service. Extensions to the original standard, notably GIF89A, include support for more colors. Most current Web browsers recognize other GIF89A enhancements, such as GIF animations and transparent images.

The GIF format works best for line drawings and other images with few colors or color gradations. However, photographs and complex images quickly degrade as GIFs.

JPEG (Joint Photographic Expert Group) format has higher resolution and more colors than GIFs while generally offering better compression than GIFs. Thus, JPEG (file extension *.jpg*) can create smaller, high-resolution images. On the other hand, JPEG uses a "lossy" compression scheme—the quality of an image can be degraded in color or detail when it is compressed.

When exchanging files, JPEG files work best for photography or very detailed artwork with rich color. JPEG files are easily viewed in most Web browsers, but because of the lossy compression, they are not the best choice for printing.

PNG (Portable Network Graphics) is an emerging Web graphics format, supported by a recommendation from the World Wide Web Consortium, designed to supplant GIF. GIF has certain limitations on image quality, and since 1995, GIF patent holders have demanded royalties on programs that produce GIF images.

PNG is an extensible, patent-free file format (file extension *.png*) for the storage of indexed-color, grayscale, and true color raster (bit-mapped) images. PNG is a portable format that compresses well without loss. PNG is also the native format of Macromedia's Fireworks application, for example. PNG is designed for on-line viewing, but because of the lossless compression is slightly better than JPEG for higher-resolution tasks such as printing.

TIFF (Tagged Image File Format), designed by Microsoft and Aldus, is the format produced by most scanners (file extension *.tif* or *.tiff*). This high-quality format is readable by most image-processing applications, such as Photoshop and Illustrator, but not within most Web browsers. TIFF is commonly used to exchange high-resolution images across platforms.

Table 6-15. Graphics Format Resources

Description	Location
GIF	*whatis.com/gif.htm*
	dir.yahoo.com/arts/visual_arts/animation/-computer_animation/animated_gifs
JPEG	*www.jpeg.org*
	www.faqs.org/faqs/jpeg-faq
PNG	*whatis.com/png.htm*
	www.cdrom.com/pub/png
TIFF	*whatis.com/tiff.htm*
	home.earthlink.net/~ritter/tiff
Graphics File Format Page	*www.dcs.ed.ac.uk/~mxr/gfx*
FAQs from graphics-related newsgroups	*www.faqs.org/faqs/graphics*

WEB STANDARDS

As described in Chapter 5, the Web was designed as a computer-independent means of exchanging information. As such, Web pages generally work well for exchanging information, but they still suffer from the occasional cross-platform hiccup as you include fancier and more complicated techniques in your pages.

Several of these standards are programming languages, and you may encounter them only if you are a programmer or operating a Web server. Because this is a more limited audience than the book intends to cover, I'll limit the discussion here to high-level issues and point you to sources of more detailed information.

HTML

The HyperText Markup Language (HTML) is the language of the platform-independent Web. Because there are Web browsers available for just about every computer platform, HTML files can be a convenient way to exchange documents. If you send someone an HTML file, they almost certainly will be able to read it by opening it in a Web browser. However, that's about the only guarantee you can make about basic HTML files.

In case you're not familiar with HTML, here's a little background. An HTML file comprises plain ASCII text interspersed with tags that define how the text is to be formatted. For example, a first-level header is enclosed by <H1> and </H1> tags, while a plain body paragraph is enclosed by <P> and </P> tags. HTML deals with ASCII special characters by inserting the Unicode values; for example, the character *ä* can be written as *ä* in an HTML file.

As far as the look and layout of a document goes, sharing HTML files introduces all of the issues related to the font problem. You can't guarantee a user will have a font specified in the HTML file, and you can't control precise document layout between the various Mac and Windows versions of all the different Web browsers. On top of that, you can't even be sure that every browser supports every HTML tag or Web standard in exactly the same way.

Editing HTML files is yet another issue. If you're working with someone who doesn't mind getting his or her hands dirty with a little HTML markup, then that person can edit the file with any text editor. If that person doesn't know how to write HTML, then you need to be sure that the other person has an application that can edit HTML files while hiding the gory markup details. On the plus side, such programs are becoming much more common. Aside from the growing number of what-you-see-is-what-you-get HTML page editors, many general applications, such as Microsoft Word 98, are acquiring HTML smarts.

Of course, HTML documents can include links to images and other documents or Web pages. That's what makes the Web so useful and visually appealing. If you decide to share files with a Web server (see Chapter 5), you will probably share at least some information as HTML pages.

Now that I've waffled back and forth, let me say that, for sharing documents, HTML files work great as long as your most important concerns are being able to view and read the content, and possibly to link to images or other Web pages. For editing or precise look and feel, you may want to consider a format such as RTF. Table 6-16 points you to some additional sources of HTML information.

Beyond HTML

In addition to making a world of information accessible after a seemingly interminable wait of ten seconds, the Web has also been responsible for a rapid proliferation of acronyms—DHTML, CSS, CGI, VRML, XML, XSL—and associated terms such as Java, JavaScript, and Perl. It's enough to make your head spin.

How do all these rapidly emerging standards affect you as a Mac user trying to function in a cross-platform world? I can unequivocally answer that question: It depends. If you're trying to earn your keep as a Web guru, then you had better get out your sextant and star chart and try to predict the direction of the Web's prevailing winds. Chances are many of today's hottest technologies will fall by the wayside as we enter the next century. (Anyone remember Web channels?)

On the other hand, if you're just a casual Mac surfer of the Web, all I can say is: Hang on. Typically, your best bet is to keep up with the major Web browser upgrades from Netscape or Microsoft. When the Big Two go to the trouble of incorporating a feature into the browser, it may be around for a while. Or it might not. Either way, as a user, you haven't invested too much time and energy.

Table 6-16. HTML Resources

Description	Location
W3 Consortium HTML page	*www.w3.org/MarkUp*
High ASCII glyphs to HTML entities, by Wolfgang Husmann	*home.rhein-zeitung.de/~husmenschen/cgi-bin/-highascii/userfrontend.pl*
Numeric codes for special characters in HTML pages	*www.zdnet.com/devhead/resources/href/ascii.html*
HTML Goodies	*www.htmlgoodies.com*
HTML Help by the Web Design Group	*www.htmlhelp.com*
Webmonkey HTML collection	*www.hotwired.com/webmonkey/html*

Web Standards

The other point to realize here is that not all Web browsers are created equal. There may be features of today's greatest Web standard in the latest Netscape Navigator that don't work correctly in Microsoft's Internet Explorer, or vice versa. At the same time, some plug-ins or browser features may not be available for the Mac at the very beginning. RealPlayer G2 from Real Networks, for example, took its sweet time showing up on the Mac OS.

Because the Web is in a constant state of flux, it doesn't makes sense for this book to go to great lengths to tease out the differences, minor or major, in Mac, Windows, or UNIX implementations of the various Web standards. By the time this book hits the shelves, everything will have changed. Instead, I'll list some of the standards, acronyms, and buzzwords that you should keep an eye on, and, for a chuckle, I'll spout off some of my predictions for each. Table 6-17 lists some more general Web-related reference libraries for your perusal.

CSS

Cascading Style Sheets (CSS) are the Web equivalent to the style sheets you probably have encountered, if not used, in your word processor. Style sheets let a Web author assign formatting commands—a style—to a particular HTML tag. CSS separates, to some degree, the look of a page from the structural HTML. For example, CSS lets you define first-level headers (indicated by the <H1> tag) to appear in the font Helvetica, with a size of 24 points, in blue. CSS also allows precise positioning of page elements including text and images. Version 4 browsers from Netscape or Microsoft support some of the CSS specification, but not all. Of course, both support different elements.

My prediction: Now that there's a standard from the W3 Consortium, look for more standardized support for CSS in the version 5 browsers. CSS will catch on, at least until everyone switches to XSL.

DHTML

Dynamic HTML (DHTML) is, somewhat simplistically, the combination of HTML, CSS, and JavaScript. Think of DHTML as HTML with a really expensive makeover. The three components of DHTML give Web developers quite a lot of power in designing interactive and graphically appealing Web pages. If you have a version 4 browser, you have support for most DHTML features, although CSS and JavaScript support is inconsistent.

My prediction: You've already visited lots of Web sites that use DHTML. You will probably continue to see such pages, although many cutting-edge sites are gearing up for the switch to XML.

XML and XSL

The eXtensible Markup Language (XML) and associated eXtensible Stylesheet Language (XSL) can be pictured as HTML (and CSS) on steroids. If you want to *do* something—such as perform general computations, perhaps off-line—with information shared on the Web, HTML and DHTML don't provide enough information about the information.

An explanation of the HTML family tree might clarify matters. HTML is derived from the Standard Generalized Markup Language (SGML), an international standard for defining and describing a document's structure. In other words, SGML is a language for defining markup languages—like HTML. Because SGML is so complex, the originators of the Web used SGML to define the much simpler, static HTML; therefore, HTML was originally designed to describe a document's *structure,* not its appearance. This is why HTML has six header levels (for levels of sections and subsections) and such "orphan" tags as <BLOCKQUOTE>, <AU> (author), <CITE> (citation), and <FN> (footnote). As the Web has evolved, HTML was expanded and used ingeniously to describe a document's appearance. DHTML primarily addresses HTML's failings for describing appearance.

XML returns to the Web's roots as a means for distributing structured data. XML is also a subset of SGML, but one that allows you to define custom markup languages, called Document Type Definitions (DTDs) that specify all the tags appearing in a document. As XML becomes more widely adopted, HTML will become one of many common DTDs.

By specifying a document's structure, you also know something about what the data in the document *mean*. In particular, you can write programs that use structural information to analyze and process an XML document. XML will make it possible, for example, for Web clients to present different views of the same data based on the viewer type. WebTV, palm personal organizers, and other nontraditional Web browsers can be programmed to make more intelligent decisions about displaying XML documents. XML will also allow intelligent "hyper-Web" sites that tailor information discovery to an individual's needs by bringing together information from many different Web sites and databases.

My prediction: XML is coming fast. The version 5 browsers will support at least some XML capabilities, and organizations that manage a lot of data resources will turn to XML to integrate those resources. In the not-so-distant future, the next generation of Web portals and search engines will use XML-based applications to allow more complex queries.

VRML and X3D

The Virtual Reality Modeling Language (VRML) is a Web standard for displaying 3-D worlds in a VRML browser or a Web browser with the appropriate plug-in. Like HTML files, VRML "worlds" are text files, but these text files describe the 3-D scene. The VRML browser or plug-in translates the description of the scene into a 3-D world you can navigate.

I mention VRML here because frankly I'm a little bitter that the Macintosh was never well supported by the VRML developer community. The only surviving VRML browser plug-in for Macintosh is a perpetually beta version of Cosmo Player 2.1 by Cosmo Software (*www.platinum.com/cosmo/mac.htm*). On Macs that predate the blue-and-white G3 towers, Cosmo Player works well, but I've had no luck getting it to run on a blue-and-white G3. However, Cosmo Player's existence may be in question since Cosmo Software was acquired by Platinum Technology, which was subsequently bought by Computer Associates. Platinum made Cosmo Player open-source and handed it off to the Web 3D Consortium.

The only consolation is that VRML seems to be fading in popularity across the board. The keepers of the VRML 2.0 specification, the Web 3D Consortium, are working on a successor specification called X3D (eXtensible 3D) to complement XML. With the addition of the OpenGL graphics libraries to the Mac OS, I have hopes that future 3-D Web standards will be better supported on the Mac.

JavaScript

Originally called LiveScript, JavaScript was developed by Netscape to let Web pages take advantage of Navigator's capabilities that were beyond the scope of HTML. (It was renamed JavaScript about the time Java appeared on the scene by virtue of Netscape's licensing of the "Java" name from Sun.) JavaScript is a programming language that lets Web developers include "scripts" or sets of commands inside Web pages. The Web browser carries out the scripts once the page is downloaded.

The main problem with JavaScript has been the browser battle between Microsoft and Netscape. In the fray, Internet Explorer and Navigator handle JavaScript differently. Microsoft also promoted its own scripting languages, VBScript and JScript. Web developers, for their part, had to worry about whether their scripts would work in both browsers. Much of this has settled down as standards organizations have begun narrowing in on a "standard" JavaScript known by the catchy name of ECMA Script.

My prediction: ECMA Script may become the standard, but everyone will call it JavaScript. And JavaScript is not going away anytime soon—it lets Web pages perform some very useful functions (form input verification) and flashy but not-so-useful clutter (such as the scrolling messages at the bottom of browser windows).

Java

Don't let the names fool you. The Java programming language is nothing like JavaScript. The Java language is a complete programming language developed by Sun Microsystems, and you need programming skills to use it effectively. The unique feature of Java technology is that a Java program can run on any platform or within any Web browser for which there exists a Java compiler (or interpreter). The Mac OS includes a Macintosh Runtime for Java (MRJ) that can run Java programs rather quickly.

Generally, you'll encounter Java programs, called applets, within Web pages. The main distinction to note on a Macintosh is that Internet Explorer uses Apple's MRJ to run applets while Navigator uses its own much slower Java runtime system. Reports have it that Apple is working with Netscape to let Navigator use Apple's MRJ.

While the Java language can be used to write any type of application, the emergence of XML as a common language for describing data coincides well with the Java language as a common language for cross-platform programs. It's not hard to imagine a hyper-Web site that uses XML to collect and compile information sets and then provides Java applets for analyzing that information on the fly. For example, a user might query a Census Bureau database for population statistics and the American Cholesterol Council Web site for food purchase trends. Then a Java applet would be available for a statistical analysis that estimates propensities for heart disease.

My prediction: The Java technology family—the Java programming language, JavaBeans, Java Grande—will soon exhaust the supply of coffee-related nomenclature. The Mac's Java technologies will benefit when Netscape begins using Apple's MRJ. And programmers more creative than I will write all sorts of unique Web applications once they get all the scrolling text marquees and related window dressing out of their systems.

Perl

Like the Java language, Perl is a full-fledged programming language. Unlike the Java language, which originated from a sole source (Sun Microsystems), Perl grew more haphazardly out of an open-source community effort. Perl is very handy for processing text and strings of characters, such as the text and characters that Web surfers enter into Web-based forms. As a result, Perl is one of the most common languages for extending the capabilities of Web server software.

However, although Perl software is available for many platforms, including the Mac OS, it is not completely cross-platform. A Perl program written for a UNIX machine probably will not run on a Macintosh as a MacPerl program. The amount of changes required might range from minimal to extensive. On the other hand, it is often easier to port a UNIX Perl program to MacPerl than to write it from scratch.

If you aren't interested in programming, you probably won't need to worry too much about Perl. It's included here because you almost certainly will run across a reference to it in your Web travels. And I wanted to make sure Mac programmers were aware that MacPerl is available.

IN SHORT, YOU SHOULD...

For a smoother cross-platform experience, I recommend these steps for working with Web and non-Web documents and applications:

- Learn a few Windows file extensions and use them when you're creating files that will be shared. These extensions may be just as helpful for reminding *you* of a file's format.

Table 6-17. Web Authoring and Standards Resources

Description	Location
General References, with Information on All or Most Standards	
The World Wide Web Consortium, the official keepers of all things Web	*www.w3.org*
HotWired's WebMonkey	*www.webmonkey.com*
Web Developer's Virtual Library authoring references	*www.stars.com/Authoring*
Web Reference	*www.webreference.com*
CNET's Builder.com	*www.builder.com*
CSS, DHTML, XML, VRML	
Dynamic HTML Lab	*webreference.com/dhtml*
Web Design Group guide to Cascading Style Sheets	*www.htmlhelp.com/reference/css*
MacWeb3D, Web3D group focused on the Mac platform	*www.macweb3d.org*
Web 3D Consortium, keepers of the VRML and X3D specifications	*www.web3d.org*
W3 Consortium's XML pages	*www.w3.org/XML*
XML.org non-profit site	*www.xml.org*
JavaScript, Java, and Perl	
JavaGoodies has JavaScript information. (Go figure.)	*www.javagoodies.com*
JavaScripts.com also has JavaScript info.	*www.javascripts.com*
Sun's Java pages	*java.sun.com*
Apple's Mac OS Java pages	*www.apple.com/java*
JARS.com for Java examples and reviews	*www.jars.com*
The Perl Institute	*www.perl.org*
The MacPerl pages	*www.ptf.com/macperl*

- Limit the number and type of fonts you use to a set that most people have. The Microsoft Web fonts are a good choice.
- Be aware of the idiosyncrasies of the extended ASCII character sets. If you often use such characters, experiment with and learn the cross-platform settings for the e-mail and other applications you use.

If you are aware of these potential stumbling blocks, most cross-platform applications can open, read, and edit files and documents that were created on either Mac or Windows.

Similarly, there are a number of platform-independent file formats that work pretty well (if not perfectly) for exchanging files. Choose the format based on your reasons for sharing the file. If you want to edit the shared file, use plain text, RTF, or possibly HTML; for viewing the file, use PDF; for printing, PostScript. Graphics formats are also better for some uses than others. For viewing a file, try GIF or JPEG. For editing, use PNG or TIFF. For printing, use TIFF or EPS.

Finally, the Web is sprouting platform-independent standards like nobody's business. As a Web surfer, your best tactic is to use a relatively recent version of your Web browser. You don't need to follow every little upgrade—from 4.5.1 to 4.5.2, for example—but if your Mac can run it, you should get a version 4 browser. (Both the Netscape and Microsoft version 4 browsers are significantly better and, to a degree, less demanding on your hardware, than the version 3 browsers.)

In short, with a few simple adjustments, it's quite possible to exchange and work with files across platforms as long as you expect it to work pretty well and not perfectly.

CHAPTER 7

Camouflaging Your Mac

*W*hen all else fails, it's time to bring out the big guns. Your Mac is talking to a Windows NT file server, it's reading PC-formatted disks like nobody's business, and you've worked out the optimal file formats for sharing your documents. Then someone throws you a curve: You have to run a non-Mac application to fulfill your job requirements or complete a specific task.

Don't count your Mac out yet. In this digital world, you've got a few more options, ranging from connecting your Mac to a Windows application server, logging in remotely to a UNIX or mainframe, or even running the Windows operating system on your Mac.

Simple Windows Tricks

Sometimes the problem that Windows users have with the Mac has less to do with a visceral dislike for the Mac than the learning curve associated with moving from a familiar interface to one they don't know. As a result, you hear gripes about how "The Mac can't do this" or "Windows does it this way." With some basic instruction and a few pieces of shareware, it's possible to make Windows users more comfortable in front of a Mac.

GUI Orientation

I won't get into the argument of which graphical user interface (GUI) is best. We all know whose was first (Xerox PARC). What does matter is helping a Windows user mentally adjust from one to the other. Figures 7-1 and 7-2 show Mac and Windows screen shots with labels indicating roughly comparable elements of the interfaces.

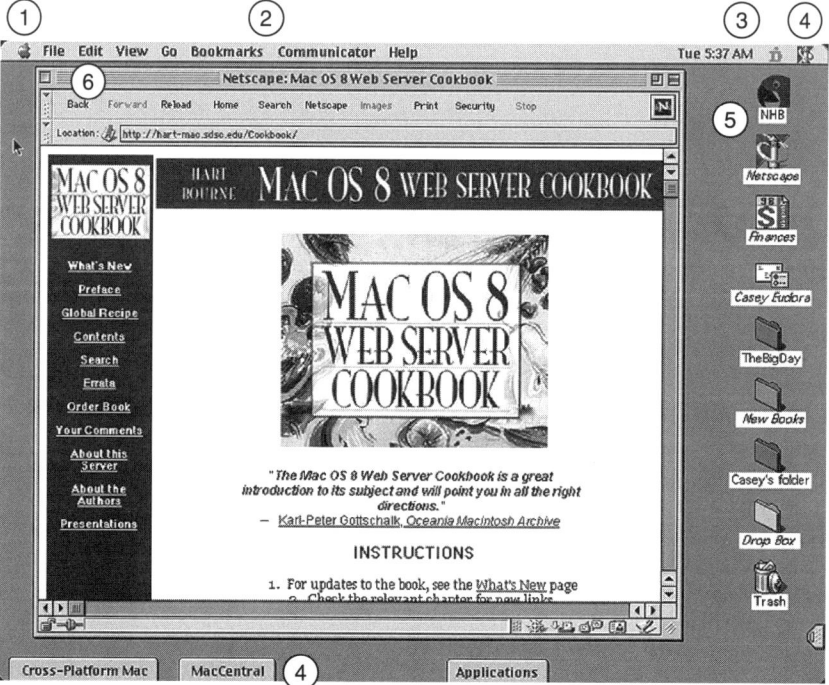

Figure 7-1. Mac OS interface

Simple Windows Tricks

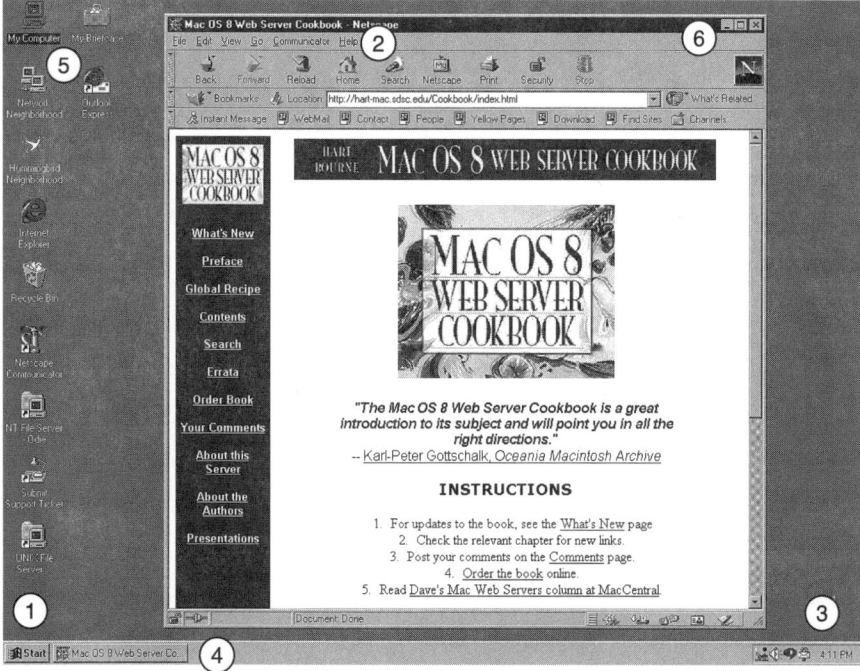

Figure 7-2. Windows NT interface

1. The Mac OS "Apple" menu (upper left corner) is roughly equivalent to the Windows "Start" menu (lower left corner by default). You can make the Apple menu more familiar with a few basic additions, described below.

2. The Mac OS menu bar (across the top of the screen) is context sensitive and provides the menu commands for the active application, including the Finder. Windows application menus are contained within the main application window.

3. The Mac clock and other system indicators appear in the upper right, while the Windows equivalents appear at the lower right.

4. The Mac application menu (upper right corner) shows the current application and lets you switch among open applications. The closest Windows equivalent is the task bar (bottom of the screen), which shows all of the open application windows. The Mac's pop-

up folders (bottom) also provide some functionality similar to the Windows task bar.

5. The Mac desktop icons line up along the right side of the screen, from top to bottom. Overflow columns are added from right to left. Windows desktop icons line up along the left side of the screen, from top to bottom. Overflow columns are added from left to right.

6. A basic Mac OS window has the title centered and three buttons in the title bar: close (left), resize (second from right), and window shade (right). A basic Windows window has the title at the left and three buttons at the right end of the title bar: minimize (leftmost), maximize (center), and close (right). Mac "window shade" and Windows "minimize" are roughly comparable, as are Mac "resize" and Windows "maximize."

GUI Adjustments

While there are similarities between the Mac OS and the Windows interfaces, it's possible to make the Mac OS look even more like Windows. You may be asking yourself, "Why would anyone want to tamper with the perfection that is the Mac OS 8 'platinum' appearance and make it look like Windows?"

I can give you one scenario that happened to me. My wife left her job at a Windows software developer, where—obviously—Windows computers were the standard. From there she moved to a Mac-based public relations firm. She was cut off from PCs and found herself forced into Macs, both at work and at home, where I had a Mac. No matter how pleasant the Mac interface, being forced into it is awkward at best. A few adjustments helped make her transition easier.

Apple Menu. With the basic Mac OS installation, the Apple Menu has a mish-mash of items—including the occasionally handy Key Caps and Calculator and the almost-never-used Jigsaw Puzzle and NotePad. Other key items are missing. You can fix this easily enough.

1. Open your System Folder and locate a folder called Apple Menu Items. Whatever is inside this folder appears in the Apple Menu.
2. Open the Apple Menu Items folder and, from the View menu at the top of the screen, choose "as List." This is just to make the folder contents look more like the actual Apple Menu.
3. Make a New Folder (command-N), and change its name to Accessories. Put all those random little applications inside, except for perhaps Chooser, Network Browser, and Sherlock (or Find File). Your Apple Menu looks better already.
4. Create another New Folder, and name it Applications. Inside this folder, place aliases for all your commonly used applications.
5. Finally, add an alias of your main hard drive. (Click once on the hard drive icon and type Command-M, or Option-Command-click on the icon and drag it into the folder.) Another tip: Change the alias name by inserting a space at the beginning. This will make the hard drive alias be alphabetized first.
6. Done. Close the Apple Menu Items folder, and check out your new Apple Menu. It now very closely approximates the Windows Start menu, with access to your hard drive, major programs, control panels, and recently used items.

Makeshift Task Bar. Windows users get addicted to the Windows task bar, and there are a few ways to approximate this feature on the Mac. Option 1 is to use the Launcher control panel. You can add applications to the Launcher and move it to the bottom of the screen. However, I don't like the way that the Launcher clutters up the screen, so I made my own in Mac OS 8.

1. Open the Apple Menu Items folder (inside the System Folder).
2. Open the Applications folder that you created above (with all your most common application aliases), and from the View menu, choose "as Icons" if it's not that way already. Select "View Options…" to choose the larger icon size.

3. Resize this window to be very wide and flat, and arrange all of the icons, single-file, in one (or possibly two) horizontal rows. To get them close together, you might want to shorten the names.
4. Click on the window's resize button (upper right) to fit the window around your icons.
5. From the View menu (at the top of your screen), choose "as Buttons." Select "View Options…" to choose the smaller icon size. (You can use large buttons if you like.)
6. Click on the title bar of the Applications folder window and drag it to the bottom of your screen until it becomes a pop-up tab.

Now you have a basic application launcher. Mine is shown in Figure 7-3. You click the tab to pop it up for launching or switching between applications, but it stays out of the way when you're not using it. You can also drag files and folders onto the tab to pop it up. Note that you don't *have* to use the Applications folder from the Apple Menu Items folder; you could create another. I just use the same one so I only have to update one folder if I want to add a new application.

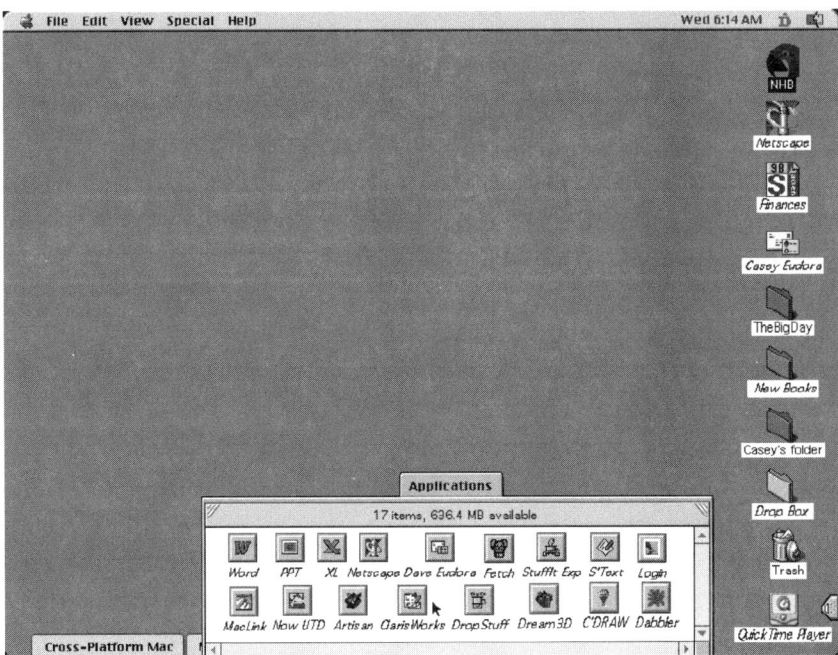

Figure 7-3. Makeshift Windows "task bar"

I should also mention that there are various shareware utilities that do all this and more, including the popular DragThing shareware by James Thomson, listed in Table 7-1.

Actual Task Bar. If jury-rigging the Apple Menu and task bar isn't enough, you can add an actual Start button and task bar to the Mac OS with the GoMac utility from ACTION Utilities. GoMac replicates quite closely the Windows Start menu, task bar, and even keyboard application switching—pressing command-tab (like Windows alt-tab) brings up a dialog that lets you switch between applications with the arrow keys.

The keyboard application switching by itself is also available in the LiteSwitch freeware from Proteron (the original developer of GoMac).

Ultimate Windows Camouflage. For the most complete Windows camouflage without actually running a Windows emulator, get the Kaleidoscope shareware that lets you redesign the look of the Mac OS interface, as shown in Figure 7-4. A predefined scheme will eerily reproduce the Windows look. Combine this with the GoMac utility and only the Mac OS menu at the top of the screen will remind you that you're using a Mac.

Table 7-1 provides you with pointers to the tools described here for modifying the Mac OS interface.

Table 7-1. Mac Interface Tricks

Description	Location
DragThing, docking and launching shareware by James Thomson	*www.dragthing.com*
GoMac from ACTION Utilities, a Windows-like task bar and Start menu	*www.actionutilities.com*
Kaleidoscope, Mac OS interface redesign shareware	*www.kaleidoscope.net*
LiteSwitch, keyboard task switching freeware from Proteron	*www.proteron.com*

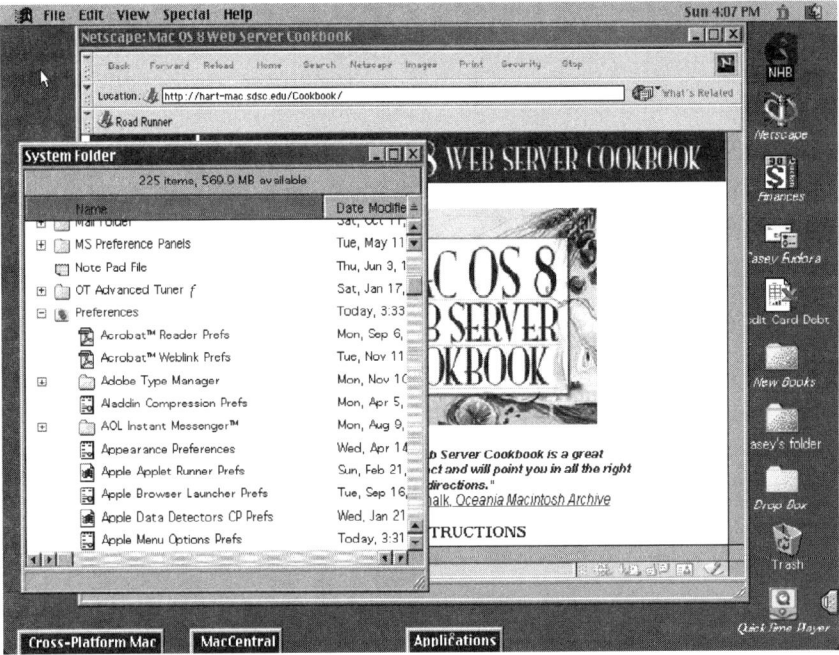
Figure 7-4. Windows 98 scheme for Mac by Kaleidoscope

TERMINAL EMULATORS

A terminal, at least in the world of computers, refers to a device that looks like a computer, but actually is just a display (for output) and keyboard (for input) for a remote computer, such as a mainframe. The terminal needs no hard drive or processor, applications or operating system, other than that needed for controlling the screen and connecting to the "real" computer. In the past, "dumb" terminals—stripped-down monitors and keyboards for timeshared IBM or DEC mainframes—were much more common. These days, software lets your Mac impersonate many types of terminals. Table 7-2 shows some of these software options.

Most UNIX computers, for example, support the VT-100 or VT-102 terminal standards, which display the command-line interface on a screen that is 80 characters wide and 25 lines high. Another common terminal type is tn3270, which is more common with IBM mainframes. But that's not all. We could talk

Terminal Emulators

about tn5250, the VT-52 and other VT terminals, or the family of terminals for Hewlett-Packard systems.

Table 7-2. Telnet and Terminal Software

Description	Location
5PM Term from White Pine can emulate terminals for IBM mainframe, AS/400, UNIX, VMS, and HP hosts.	*www.wpine.com/products/5PM-Term*
BetterTelnet, freeware from Rolf Braun, with Kerberos support available. SSH module not distributed.	*www.cstone.net/~rbraun/mac/telnet*
Black Knight, shareware from Raine Storm Networks	*www.kagi.com/raine*
CelView the new Mac RUMBA, from Cel Corporation, supports SNA and TCP/IP access to IBM mainframes.	*www.celcorp.com*
ComLink, 1996 shareware from Will Price	*ftp://ftp.primenet.com/users/w/wprice/*
DataComet, shareware from databeast, supports Kerberos.	*www.databeast.com*
F-Secure SSH from Data Fellows offers SSH connection clients for the Mac.	*www.datafellows.com/f-secure*
NiftyTelnet SSH, a freeware enhancement of NiftyTelnet by Jonas Walldén of Sweden. Because of U.S. regulations, it cannot be used in the U.S.	*www.lysator.liu.se/~jonasw/freeware/niftyssh*
NiftyTelnet, freeware from Chris Newman, supports Kerberos.	*andrew2.andrew.cmu.edu/dist/niftytelnet.html*
ProTERM Mac from Intrec includes an integrated text editor and many terminal types.	*www.intrec.com*
RunTime Plus and MultiTerm Pro from Vicomsoft	*www.vicomsoft.com/hostcon/host.macos.html*
tn3270, 1995 freeware from Peter DiCamillo, available from Info-Mac mirrors	*ftp://mirrors.aol.com/pub/info-mac/-comm/tcp/tn3270-25b2.hqx*

Connection Protocols. Your Mac's terminal emulation software must also support the appropriate protocol for communicating between the host system and your Mac. By far, the most common protocol is called Telnet. Telnet is a widely used TCP/IP application protocol that lets you log into and use a remote system. However, Telnet is not the only protocol in town. You might encounter, for example, a mainframe that must be accessed via an SNA-based connection. Once connected by Telnet or another protocol, the display and keyboard interface is determined by the terminal type.

Secure Connections. Many computing centers these days, including the San Diego Supercomputer Center, are concerned about the security of their networks and systems. Telnet, it turns out, is not the most secure protocol. It sends the keyboard commands and display information across the network as plain text, and hackers have developed tools that can "sniff" Telnet traffic for passwords and other information. To close this security hole, the Kerberos and SSH (secure shell) protocols are the most widely used secure protocols.

If you need a secure connection, your options are more limited, mainly because of U.S. restrictions regarding the distribution of strong cryptography software. SSH is much easier to use, but only the commercial Data Fellows F-Secure package is available to U.S. users. Kerberos, while more complicated to configure, is supported by more freeware and shareware.

APPLICATION SERVERS AND CLIENTS

Most terminal software described in the previous section is designed for text-based interaction with the UNIX command line or mainframe operating systems. On the other hand, most Windows and many UNIX applications have a graphical user interface. If your workplace demands that you run such a UNIX or Windows application, it is possible to do so by running the application on a UNIX or NT server and have the GUI appear on your Mac.

In a completely general case, the client computer need not have *any* operating system, Mac OS or otherwise. Called a network computer or thin client, such terminals don't have any of their own applications and only run applications from the central server. Booting a roomful of iMacs from a central Mac OS X Server is a comparable situation. A number of companies make terminals for Windows or UNIX servers.

X Window System

The UNIX world's version of such an environment, the X Window System, has been around since the early 1980s. The open, cross-platform X Window System manages a windowed graphical user interface between a client and a server in a distributed network.

Typically, the client user logs into a UNIX machine—using a Telnet connection and appropriate terminal software—and starts an application that can communicate with a machine running X Windows. The application then sends screen display information to the client's machine, which the client has identified to the UNIX machine. The client machine runs an application that listens for and displays the graphical interface instructions. (Technically, the client-server relationship is reversed. On your Mac, you will run an X display *server,* and the application on the UNIX machine acts as a client that makes screen display requests of your X server. I mention this only to explain why the software packages I'm about to mention are referred to as X servers.)

There are three readily available X Windows applications. MacX from Apple and eXodus from White Pine are two commercial packages. MI/X is a freeware version from Micro Images. Figure 7-5 shows the MI/X X server displaying a Netscape window from a UNIX machine.

Windows Terminal Server

Because the X Window System is an open, cross-platform solution that has been around for fifteen years, it only makes sense that Microsoft chose not to use X Windows for Windows NT Server, Terminal Server Edition. The idea behind the Windows Terminal Server is the same as with the X Windows System: The application runs on the Windows Terminal Server, and a client system interacts with the application remotely. The client may be another computer—Windows Terminal Server supports Windows NT Workstation, Windows 95/98, Windows 3.11—or a Windows-based terminal device.

Even if an organization has Windows client computers, it can benefit from running Windows applications remotely by making system administration easier. The administrator has to configure only the central server, not every client system.

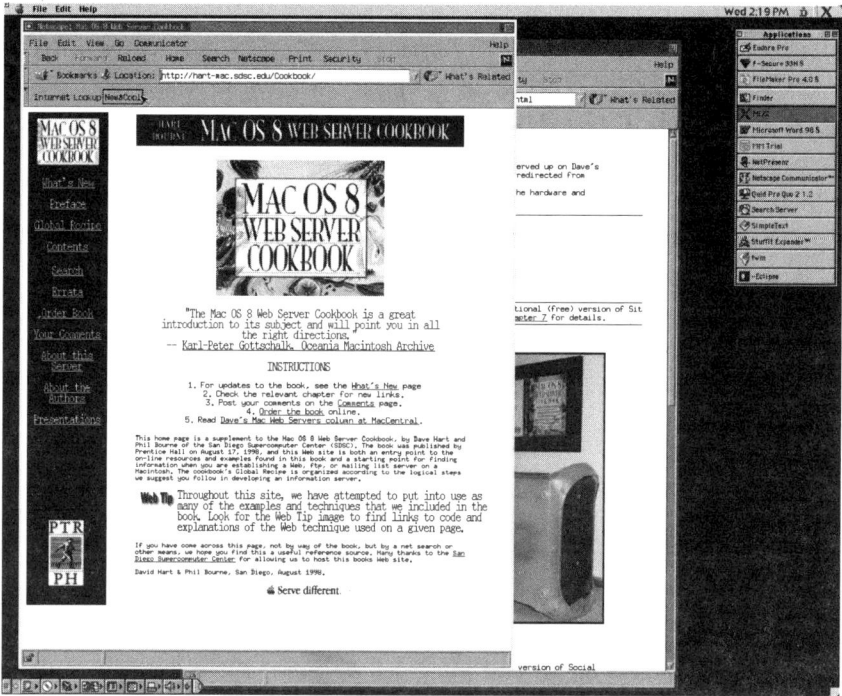

Figure 7-5. MI/X X server for the Mac, courtesy MicroImages, Inc.

For a mixed-platform environment, such as the San Diego Supercomputer Center, the MetaFrame or WinFrame software from Citrix extends the Windows Terminal Server and allows Mac OS, UNIX, OS/2 Warp, and other systems to run applications from the server, as shown in Figure 7-6. With MetaFrame or WinFrame on the Windows Terminal Server and the free Citrix ICA (for Independent Computing Architecture) client on client systems, the Mac can become a Windows terminal. The ICA protocol sends only keystrokes, mouse clicks, screen updates, and audio across the network.

Citrix reports that the ICA software allows clients to run remote applications over even a dial-up connection. From my experience, the apparent Windows application performance depends on the speed of the Windows Terminal Server, which is to be expected. A heavily loaded server will likely feel sluggish even over a fast network connection.

Application Servers and Clients

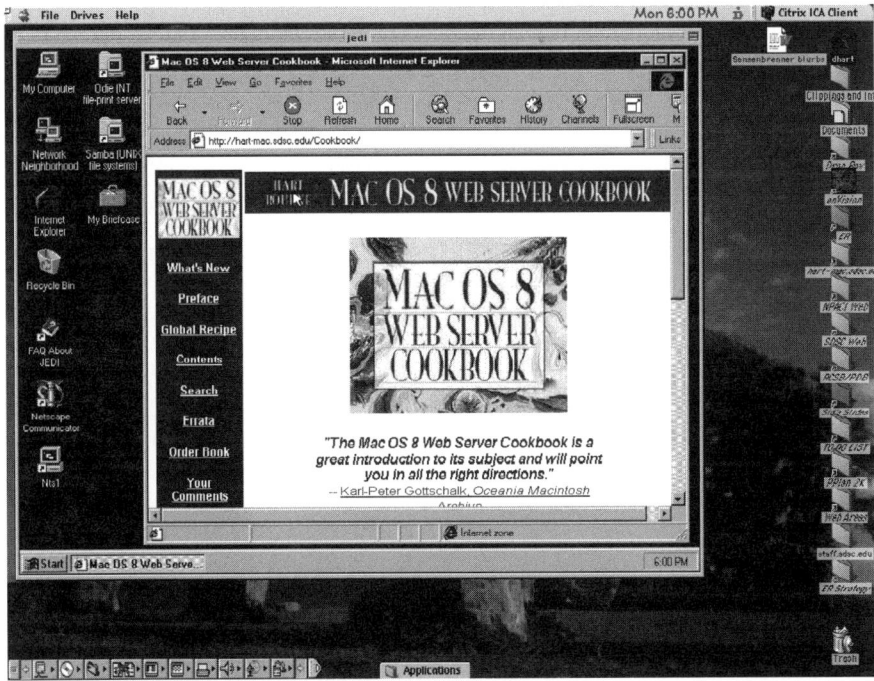

Figure 7-6. Citrix ICA client for Macintosh

To use a standard X Window System connection to a Windows Terminal Server or Citrix MetaFrame server, Network Computing Devices offers NCD WinCenter, which installs on top of Windows NT or on top of MetaFrame. NCD WinCenter allows any system that supports X Windows to run Windows applications—no special client software needed.

Remote Control

The advantage of running applications from a UNIX machine using X Windows and Windows using Windows Terminal Server or Citrix products is that more than one user can be running those applications. However, if you are a solitary user in this situation—maybe you have a Mac at home and a Windows machine at work—you have a few other options.

Timbuktu Pro from Netopia gives you remote control of one computer from another. Install Timbuktu Pro on your Windows machine at work and your Mac at home, and you can run Windows applications from the comfort of your home office.

A comparable, free, and multi-platform option is the Virtual Network Computing software from AT&T's Cambridge Laboratories. VNC also requires that software be installed on both the application server—possibly a UNIX, Windows 95/98/NT, or even Mac system—and the UNIX, Windows, Mac, or Java application client. On UNIX, VNC acts as an enhancement to the X Window System. You must log in to the UNIX machine, start the VNC server, and then start your UNIX applications. Because UNIX is, by default, multi-user, more than one UNIX user can start a VNC server on the same machine. On a standard Windows or Mac OS machine, which allows only one logged-in user, VNC works more as a single-user remote control environment.

Table 7-3 lists Mac software for X Windows, Windows NT Terminal Server, and remote control of systems.

Table 7-3. Windows and X Windows Clients

Description	Location
X Window System definition	*whatis.com/xwindow.htm*
X.org, keepers of the X Window System standard	*www.x.org*
eXodus from White Pine	*www.wpine.com/exodus*
MacX from Apple	*www.apple.com/networking*
MI/X freeware from Micro Images	*www.microimages.com/freestuf/mix*
Windows NT Server, Terminal Server Edition	*www.microsoft.com/ntserver/terminalserver*
MetaFrame and Mac ICA client from Citrix	*macos.citrix.com*
NCD WinCenter from Network Computing Devices	*www.ncd.com/pwin*
Timbuktu Pro from Netopia for remote control	*www.timbuktupro.com*
Virtual Network Computing, freeware from AT&T Cambridge Laboratories	*www.uk.research.att.com/vnc*

Non-Mac Operating Systems

If you're not part of an organization that has a central application server, the ability to run Windows or UNIX software from a server doesn't do you much good. And a slow server may not be your favorite option if you need to use a Windows or UNIX application regularly. The next option is to have your Mac emulate a Windows environment. Emulation is the Nirvana of the digital world: You can simulate physical hardware—such as an Intel Pentium chip—entirely in software. You can also run UNIX and Linux operating systems directly on your Mac hardware.

Windows Emulators

In the Windows emulator arena, there are two major contenders and two upstarts. The upstarts, at the time of writing, aren't ready for the big leagues just yet. Both the Blue Label PowerEmulator and MacBochs are getting better, but you should give them a shot only if you don't mind fiddling with the idiosyncrasies of early releases.

The two major contenders here are Insignia, makers of SoftWindows and RealPC, and Connectix, makers of VirtualPC. The two companies have taken different approaches to the task of emulating a Windows or DOS machine.

Insignia's products run the PC operating system—Windows 95/98 for SoftWindows, DOS for RealPC—by replacing the drivers that DOS or Windows use with versions that interact with the Mac OS. In other words, SoftWindows hands off Windows and DOS hardware commands to the Mac OS.

VirtualPC by Connectix takes emulation one level deeper. VirtualPC emulates a PC at the hardware level, so Windows or DOS can use their native driver software and "see" the right PC hardware. You can purchase VirtualPC with either DOS or Windows.

Note that both companies offer versions that include only DOS—RealPC and VirtualPC—as well as versions that include Windows 95/98—SoftWindows and VirtualPC (with Windows). The DOS versions target gamers; many PC games bypass the performance overhead of Windows and run right from DOS. The Windows versions are more useful for so-called "productivity" applications—the software you have to use at work that needs Windows.

Now for the Great Debate: Which is better, SoftWindows or VirtualPC? The answer depends on whom you ask. Both are comparable in terms of performance, but SoftWindows seems to be faster on older Macs, while VirtualPC can be faster on fast new G3 machines. Both also offer good (and getting better) compatibility, but the vagaries of the PC world mean that eventually you'll run into some piece of software that conflicts with something.

As a rule, most reviews of both products rank them as acceptable for what they are: workarounds for not having a PC when you want or need to run a Windows or DOS application. Each works well for casual use. However, if you demand top-of-the-line PC performance for your games or other applications, you need a top-of-the-line PC, not an emulator. Table 7-4 provides links to Windows emulators.

UNIX and Linux for Mac

Unlike Windows 95/98/NT, which must be emulated, your Mac hardware can run UNIX and Linux as a non-emulated operating system. In most cases, you can choose between the Mac OS or Linux/UNIX during start-up and sometimes switch between the two without rebooting. In this category, there is one UNIX virtual machine, two flavors of the BSD UNIX system, and two variants of Linux for the Mac. Table 7-5 points you to the relevant Web sites.

Table 7-4. Windows Emulation for the Mac

Description	Location
Blue Label PowerEmulator, from Lismore Software Systems, emulates DOS, Windows, and UNIX—you provide the OS.	*www.lismoresoft.com*
MacBochs, David Batterham's Mac port of Kevin Lawton's Bochs PC emulator	*members.xoom.com/macbochs*
RealPC, from Insignia, emulates DOS (included). You can add Windows.	*www.realpc.com*
SoftWindows 98, from Insignia, emulates Windows 98 (included).	*www.softwindows.com*
VirtualPC, from Connectix	*www.connectix.com*

A word of caution: UNIX is not designed as a user-friendly operating system, and while there are some nice Mac touches in some of the UNIX and Linux versions for Mac, you should be aware of the learning curve. If you are a novice, you may not want to experiment with UNIX on your primary Mac system.

MachTen. Let's start with Tenon Intersystem's MachTen, a UNIX virtual machine for PowerPC and older 68K-based Macs. MachTen is a small family of fifteen shared libraries consuming about 1.2MB of memory. With MachTen, you can operate as if you're on a UNIX machine running the Mach kernel and BSD 4.4. A major advantage of MachTen is that you can switch easily between the Mac OS and the MachTen UNIX environment, because MachTen runs as another Mac OS application. For the same reason, MachTen is probably the safest version of UNIX for non-experts.

NetBSD and OpenBSD. NetBSD and OpenBSD are two open-source projects to develop and distribute UNIX-like operating systems based on the BSD 4.4 system. Both initiatives have versions for 68K-based Macs and the PowerPC architecture. NetBSD, however, cannot share the hard drive with the Mac OS. OpenBSD should be able to, but expect to spend some time repartitioning your hard drive prior to installing OpenBSD. Again, you should attempt this on your own only if you are familiar with UNIX and comfortable with the intricacies of your hardware. And, please, back up your hard drive before you try this.

MkLinux and LinuxPPC. Originally started by Apple and the Open Software Foundation, MkLinux runs a Linux environment on top of the Mach microkernel, while LinuxPPC is a monolithic Linux OS. Both versions of Linux should run the same applications without changes, and both will co-exist with the Mac OS, letting you choose between the Mac OS and Linux when you boot your system.

You might choose between them for several reasons. If you have an older NuBus-based Mac, MkLinux is the only Linux that will work. If you have a Mac clone, LinuxPPC is the better option. If you own a PCI-based Mac, you can choose between LinuxPPC and MkLinux. And because MkLinux incurs the overhead of using the Mach kernel, MkLinux might be a tad slower than LinuxPPC.

Table 7-5. UNIX and Linux for Mac Hardware

Description	Location
MachTen BSD 4.4 UNIX virtual machine from Tenon Intersystems	www.tenon.com/products/machten
NetBSD, an open-source version of BSD 4.4 UNIX	www.netbsd.org
OpenBSD, an open-source project for BSD 4.4 UNIX	www.openbsd.org
MkLinux from Apple and the Open Software Foundation	www.mklinux.org
LinuxPPC from LinuxPPC, Inc.	www.linuxppc.com

Other Emulators

Since it's possible to emulate the latest and supposedly greatest operating system from Microsoft, you'd think that it would be possible to emulate older computers—perhaps that Apple II that you used in high school. And as a matter of fact, it is.

For emulating just about anything besides a Windows or DOS PC—from a Commodore VIC-20 (I had one of these!) to a ColecoVision game system or a Texas Instruments calculator—visit the *emulation.net* site of John Stiles, a truly amazing spot for developing the ultimate in cross-platform environments. Check Table 7-6 for more resources.

Table 7-6. General Emulation Information

Description	Location
Emulation Excitement, where you can get games for game system emulators	www.emux.com
Emulation.net by John Stiles	emulation.net
MacPC Online by Kevin Liu	www.macpconline.com
MacWindows emulator page	www.macwindows.com/emulator.html
The Pure-Mac emulation page	www.pure-mac.com/emu.html

PC Cards and Cheap PCs

If you've gotten this far and you still haven't gotten that Windows application running on your Mac, or if the options thus far aren't fast enough for you, I hate to say it, but you are running out of options. At this point, you need to start looking at some Intel-based hardware. Table 7-7 lists some of your options.

If space is at a premium, Orange Micro is the long-time maker of OrangePC compatibility cards, basically a PC motherboard on an expansion card. You have processor options ranging from a 100-MHz Intel Pentium to a 400-MHz AMD K6-3. There are three main advantages to using an OrangePC card: speed, space, switching. Running Windows on PC hardware is faster than running Windows on emulated hardware, hands down. OrangePC cards fit inside your existing Mac case and make it easy to switch back and forth between the Mac and the PC. The OrangePC cards, of course, let you use your Mac monitor and keyboard. However, you should expect to pay anywhere from $775 to $1,200 for this option.

On the other hand, if price is your overriding concern, and you really, really need to run some Windows-only software, you have one last course of action, which I will only touch on. You can buy a low-end PC for around $500 these days. It seems like they give them away with a full tank of gas at some places. (You get what you pay for, though.) And if you have a Mac, you can share your existing monitor with little or no trouble. (It's possible to share a single keyboard, too, but the cost and hassle may not be worth it.) You can visit the MacWindows Web site for tips on sharing a monitor between two computers.

Table 7-7. Mac-PC Compatibility Hardware

Description	Location
OrangePC compatibility cards from Orange Micro	*www.orangemicro.com*
MacWindows tips for sharing monitors and keyboards	*www.macwindows.com/keytips.html*

CAMOUFLAGE RECAP

There are a number of steps you can take to make your Mac behave more like a Windows machine. For Windows users who are uncomfortable with the Mac, you can customize parts of the interface by hand or with utilities for the Windows task bar, for example.

If you need your Mac to run an occasional application on another platform, you have some other options, roughly in order of increasing complexity:

- A terminal emulator will let you connect to servers and mainframes that have text-based interfaces.
- An X Windows or Windows Terminal Server will let you run UNIX or Windows applications on a remote server and see the graphical user interface on your Mac.
- Connectix and Insignia have products to let you run Windows (or DOS) on your Mac by emulating the underlying interface to the PC hardware. (You can run UNIX without emulation on your Mac.)
- If all else fails, you can install an OrangePC card, which has the hardware for an entire PC on a single board, or punt completely and buy an inexpensive PC and share your monitor and possibly your keyboard between your Mac and PC.

CHAPTER 8

The Expanding Digital World

From the days when a single computer filled a room the size of a cafeteria and was coddled by dozens of human attendants, we've come full circle. Today, a single hypothetically well-connected person can walk down the street with half a dozen computers in tow—a pager, cell phone, and Palm Pilot clipped to a belt, a PowerBook tucked into a shoulder bag, a CD player in a pocket, and a digital camera for some souvenir snapshots.

Computers are popping up everywhere and in all sorts of gadgets, some useful—digital cameras, for example—and some you want to hit with a sledgehammer—Furbys and virtual pets to name two. For the sake of this chapter, we'll consider devices that you don't wish would be run over by a truck, but that you wish would be able to cooperate with your Mac.

Starting with peripherals that are designed to plug into a computer, we'll move into accessibility devices, other computing devices, and the telephone realm. Finally, we'll finish up the book with ways to connect other electronic devices to your Mac.

Peripheral Matters

Mac computers have a number of plug-in connections, called *ports*, available for expanding the capabilities of your system. In general, any device you plug into one of these ports is called a *peripheral*, which sits on the periphery of the box holding the main processor and boards, hence the name. Technically speaking then, your monitor, mouse, and keyboard are also peripherals, although somewhat more necessary than, for example, the devices more commonly called peripherals, such as printers and scanners.

When you're looking to add a device to your Mac, you should be prepared to navigate an alphabet soup of port and interface names. The port determines the type of connector on the device and, therefore, whether you can plug it into your Mac. Here we'll run through the major Mac options.

ADB

Until the recent arrival of the iMac and blue-and-white G3 towers, Macs used Apple Desktop Bus (ADB) ports for plugging in slow input-output devices, such as the mouse and keyboard, or alternatives such as trackballs or graphics tablets. Because the ADB ports can only transmit data at a rate of about 10 thousand bytes per second (kbps), ADB ports are insufficient for devices, such as disk drives, that require a speedier interface.

For faster connections, at around 230 kpbs, older Macs have modem and printer ports, which only look like ADB ports, that support LocalTalk connections. If you have an older Mac, until recently, you had to be sure that any printer or modem is Mac-compatible—meaning that it will plug into the Mac's non-PC connectors. These days, however, many products let you add USB ports to your PCI-based Mac.

USB

The Universal Serial Bus (USB) is the standard peripheral port on the new generation of Mac hardware. In fact, it's the only option on the iMac. (The G3 towers do have an ADB port for backward compatibility.) Keyspan makes an adapter that adds Mac ADB and printer ports to your USB port.

Because USB can send data at 12 million bits per second (Mbps), it is fast enough not only for the mouse and keyboard, but also printers, scanners, and even disk drives. Hence the "universal" in the USB name. USB has the added advantage that it is a cross-platform standard. Since it was originally developed by PC computer manufacturers—even though the iMac made it more widely known—USB has expanded tremendously the number of options available to Mac users.

Table 8-1 lists some makers of PCI cards that will add USB ports to your beige Mac. These cards work only for PCI-based Macs, which include all but the earliest Macs with PowerPC processors. I did not find an option for providing USB ports to older Macs.

SCSI

The Small Computer System Interface (SCSI) is a cross-platform standard that was the standard on all Macs prior to the introduction of USB. SCSI was used for high-speed external devices; the variants of SCSI can transfer data at rates between 5 megabytes per second (MBps) and 40 MBps. While SCSI is fast, it was more commonly recognized as being a more expensive connectivity option.

Many SCSI-based peripheral options, particularly for disk drives, remain, since the slowest SCSI speed (5 MBps) is more than three times faster than USB. (Watch out for megabytes versus megabits! SCSI's 5 megabytes per second equals 40 megabits per second; 1 megabyte per second equals 8 megabits per second.) It is, however, possible to find adapters that will let you plug SCSI devices into a USB port. They won't be nearly as fast, but you won't have to throw them out.

FireWire

FireWire is the popular name for the IEEE 1394 standard, which moves data at up to 400 Mbps (or 50 MBps). At 35 times faster than USB, FireWire is the heir apparent to SCSI. FireWire is standard on the new blue-and-white G3 towers, and is becoming commonplace as the connector for digital cameras and camcorders. If you have a PCI-based PowerMac, you can add FireWire ports. If you have an iMac, you cannot, according to Apple's support Web pages.

Table 8-1 lists makers of cable adapters and expansion cards that let you use ADB and SCSI devices with USB ports and add USB and FireWire ports to PCI-based Macs. I probably missed a few, but this should be plenty to get you started. More information is given at the end of this chapter.

Table 8-1. USB and FireWire Adapters

Description	Location
Entrega Mac products, USB to Mac serial ports and 4-port USB PCI card	*www.entrega.com*
Griffin Technology iMate USB to ADB adapter	*www.griffintechnology.com*
Inside Out Networks USB to Mac serial ports	*www.ionetworks.com*
KeySpan USB to serial adapter, USB PCI card	*www.keyspan.com*
Macally USB input devices, USB PCI card	*www.macally.com*
Belkin USB PCI card	*usb.belkin.com*
XLR8 USB PCI card	*www.xlr8.com*
ADS Technologies USB PCI card	*www.adstech.com*
Ariston USB PCI card, USB to SCSI adapter	*www.ariston.com*
Second Wave USB to SCSI adapter	*www.2ndwave.com*
Newer Technology uSCSI USB to SCSI adapter	*www.newertech.com*
Adaptec USB to SCSI adapter, and PCI to SCSI/FireWire	*www.adaptec.com*
Apple's FireWire Kit, PCI to FireWire	*www.apple.com*
Orange Micro's HotLink, PCI to FireWire card	*www.orangemicro.com*

ACCESSIBILITY AND ASSISTIVE TECHNOLOGY

Standard computer hardware is not designed to meet the needs of users who have physical disabilities, from poor eyesight to paralysis. You could argue that standard computer hardware isn't always ergonomically designed for users *without* special accessibility requirements. On the other hand, in the same way that the digital world makes your choice of computer platform somewhat irrelevant, computers and related hardware can provide entry into the digital world, and expand the connection to the physical world, for users with all sorts of accessibility needs.

The general category of accessibility lumps together a wide variety of computing needs, ranging from enlarged screen graphics for users with poor eyesight to alternate input devices for users who cannot manipulate a keyboard or mouse. There are software and hardware products that cover the spectrum, and I can't cover them all in part of a chapter.

However, I have collected in Table 8-2 a selection of Web sites dedicated to accessibility software and hardware for Macs, starting with Apple's own Disability Resources page, which includes a database of accessibility products.

I'll mention only a handful of products here. First, Apple produces two control panels for the Mac OS—CloseView and Universal Access (formerly Easy Access). CloseView magnifies screen contents by up to 16 times for visually impaired users. Easy Access allows users to alter the Mac mouse and keyboard interface to assist users who have difficulty using the mouse or keyboard.

Table 8-2. Mac Accessibility Resources

Description	Location
Apple's Disability Resources page	*www.apple.com/disability*
Center for Applied Special Technology. Web site has links to many accessibility resources.	*www.cast.org*
Macintosh Disability Shareware and Freeware page by Scott Norris	*www.ecnet.net/users/gnorris/place.shtml*
Pure-Mac disability software page	*www.pure-mac.com/disabilities.html*
TRACE Center at the University of Wisconsin	*trace.wisc.edu*
Virtual Assistive Technology Center's Mac page	*www.at-center.com/MAC.html*

COMPUTING DEVICES

Besides the Windows NT or UNIX workstation on your co-worker's desk, or the spare Windows 95 system at home, you may encounter a need to connect your Mac to a less massive, but just as handy portable or handheld computing device. You might have a Palm VII, a Windows CE device, or maybe even one of Apple's former Newtons or eMates. There's no reason these devices can't complement the services of your Mac.

Palm Computing Organizers

The Palm Computing series of personal digital assistants (PDAs), originated by USRobotics and since merged with 3Com, have become the most popular handheld computing devices, with around 70 percent of the handheld computing market as of mid-1999, despite Microsoft's continued push for Windows CE (see the next section). The Palm organizers' appeal stems from a number of factors—their size, the simplicity of the Palm OS, and the battery life of one or two months.

For Mac users, Palm organizers are Mac-friendly. In fact, as I was writing this book, there were rumors circulating about a Palm OS device to be sold under the Apple name. However, if you're a Mac owner who tried connecting a Palm device with version 1 of the Palm Desktop and HotSync software for the Mac, your initial experience may not have been so pleasant.

MacPac version 1, the name for the combined software, left much to be desired. Owners of both a Mac and a Palm PDA should be sure to use Palm MacPac version 2. The new version of the HotSync software fixes many bugs, the Palm Desktop software is based on an enhanced version of Claris Organizer (which 3Com bought when Claris reorganized into FileMaker, Inc.), and many more third-party Mac products can synchronize with the Palm OS. The MacPac version 2 software is available free—whether you own a Palm PDA or not—from the Palm Computing Web site, listed in Table 8-3 along with other Palm and Mac resources.

Synchronization is the key activity with Palm devices, because they were designed not so much as portable computers but as portable extensions to your desktop computer. With a Palm PDA, you can carry your important information for the day—appointments, notepad, and phonebook, for example—while your

Mac keeps a master copy from the Palm Desktop or your favorite organizer software, along with all your major computer applications. Synchronization, via the HotSync manager, makes sure that the information on both your Palm device and your Mac is the same. Mac utilities let you convert Palm documents to formats readable by your Mac applications. Third-party personal information managers, such as Consultant from Chronos, can also be synchronized with your Palm device.

Even though the Palm MacPac software is a free download, you still need to spend $15 for the MacPac to get the adapter cable that will let you connect your Palm organizer to your Mac. The cable from 3Com connects the Palm device to a Mac serial port. Those of you with iMacs or G3 towers might be wondering how that helps you with your computer's USB ports. It doesn't. However, KeySpan and Entrega make PDA to USB cable adapters for around $40, and at

Table 8-3. Mac to Palm Resources

Description	Location
3Com Palm Computing Macintosh page	*www.palm.com/macintosh*
Consultant, commercial personal information manager software from Chronos	*chronos.iserver.net/consultant*
Entrega USB to serial DB9 adapter	*www.entrega.com*
KeySpan USB to PDA adapter cable	*www.keyspan.com*
Mac/Pilot info from strout.net	*strout.net/info/macpilot*
"Mac's Best Friend," August 1998 *MacWorld* article by David Pogue	*macworld.zdnet.com/pages/august.98/Feature.4408.html*
Palmac	*www.execpc.com/~krugd/palmac.html*
PalmCentral	*www.palmcentral.com*
PalmGear HQ	*www.palmgear.com*
PalmPilot: The Ultimate Guide, by David Pogue	*www.davidpogue.com/dpbooks.html*
PilotMac site	*home.earthlink.net/~xbpr/PilotMac*
Visor handheld devices, from Handspring, Inc.	*www.handspring.com*

the time of writing, 3Com had announced plans for a PDA to USB cable adapter for both Windows and Mac connectivity.

Once your Palm organizer is connected to your Mac, adding software is a two-step process. First, download the compressed files from a software site such as PalmCentral and uncompress them. Next, tell the HotSync Manager software, which resides on your Mac and is shown in Figure 8-1, to install the Palm application the next time you synchronize your Palm with your Mac. The Palm OS takes care of everything else.

Since my goal here is to show that you *can* connect your Palm PDA to your Mac, and how to do that, I'll wrap this up. If I were to go further, I'd just be explaining how to use your Palm device, a task better left to other sources. You might want to check out *PalmPilot: The Ultimate Guide* by well-known Mac author David Pogue. (Trivial note: The book title notwithstanding, PalmPilots aren't called PalmPilots anymore, due to the trademark enforcement of the Pilot Pen company. Now they're just Palm Computing devices.)

As this book was going to press, a new player entered the Palm OS market. Founded by the ex-Palm Computing team of Donna Dubinsky and Jeff Hawkins, Handspring, Inc. released the Visor family of products—cheaper, faster, and more expandable Palm OS-based handheld devices. The Visor promises to be even more Mac-friendly, with Mac software being included on the included CD-ROM and sporting a USB-connected cradle.

Windows CE Devices

While Palm Computing devices and their kin (such as the IBM WorkPad) can be used easily with a Mac, the same cannot be said for Windows CE handheld and palmtop devices. A fairly thorough search of the Windows CE world on the Web turned up only a handful of possibilities, none of them particularly elegant.

If you are a Mac user, there aren't many advantages to using a Windows CE device. If you must have a color screen, that's one feature in favor of Windows CE. You could also argue the larger number of manufacturers of Windows CE devices is an advantage. Most other features are stacked against Windows CE, as far as Macs are concerned: a battery life measured in hours, a Windows-like interface, and inelegant Mac connectivity. While the full-grown Windows versions (95, 98, and NT) have some ability to play nice with other operating systems,

Windows CE does not like to work with anything but its grown-up Windows siblings.

However, it's not impossible to connect a Windows CE device (I am working very hard to resist the urge to abbreviate Windows CE as "WinCE") to your Mac. The most popular solution is to run Windows 95, 98, or NT under an emulator such as Connectix VirtualPC or Insignia SoftWindows (see Chapter 7) and install Windows CE Services—the synchronization and transfer software from Microsoft. Windows CE Services is available through the manufacturer of your handheld device.

To make the actual connection, you need a cable. PDA Concepts makes the only cable specifically designed for this purpose that I found, but it connects to the Mac serial port. However, Windows CE devices connect to a PC-standard serial communication port, a DB-9 RS-232 port. Any cable that will convert from DB-9 RS-232 to a Mac serial port should do the trick. For iMacs and those Macs with USB ports, any cable that connects DB-9 serial ports to USB will work. Keyspan and Entrega, as well as other companies listed in Table 8-1, make cables designed to connect a PDA to a USB slot.

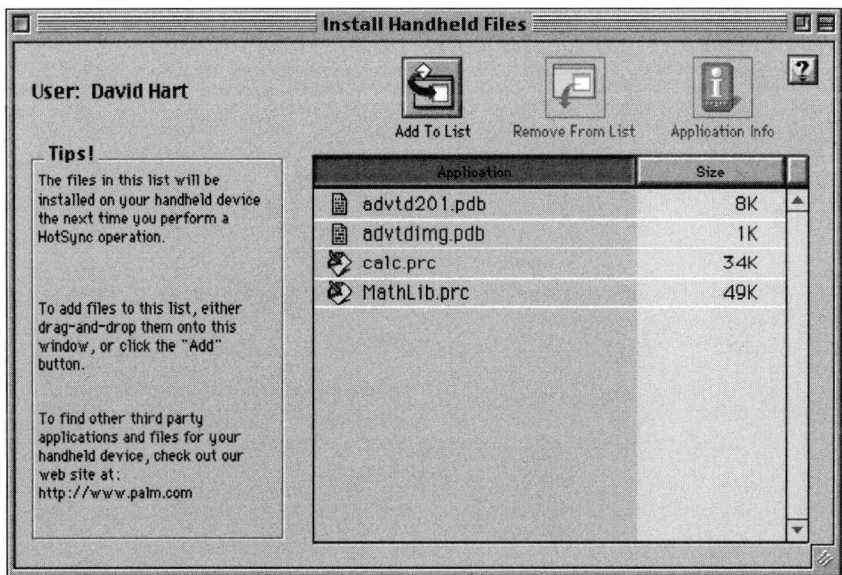

Figure 8-1. Palm HotSync Manager for Mac

The only option for connecting a Windows CE device to a Mac that does *not* involve running Windows on your Mac comes from a Japanese company, Reudo. Reudo's XIN/XOUT III provides both a Mac serial to DB-9 serial converter cable and the XIN/XOUT III software. Small applications run on both the Windows CE device and on the Mac, and they allow you to transfer files between the two and perform basic file translation. It does not support date book or address book synchronization. And as far as I can tell, you will have to mail order this product from Japan.

Table 8-4 lists some of the very few Mac and Windows CE options, as well as a place to start exploring Windows CE Web sites.

Table 8-4. Windows CE Options for the Mac

Description	Location
USB to PDA cable from Entrega	*www.entrega.com/con_serial9.html*
USB to PDA cable from Keyspan	*www.keyspan.com/products/usb/PDAadapter*
WinCE to Mac cable from PDA Concepts	*www.pda-concepts.com/otherproducts.html*
Windows CE Web ring	*www.windowscewebring.com*
XIN/XOUT III cable and software from Reudo	*www.reudo.co.jp*

Newton

The Newton family of portable computing devices became a casualty on Apple's road back to profitability. However, many Newton owners truly adore their Message Pads, and it's still possible to find software and even some accessories for Newton products online.

Newtons have standard serial ports, so any Mac serial cable that will connect an eight-pin port to an eight-pin port should work here. (The Newton Message Pad 2000 series and eMates come with an adapter for connecting the serial cable.)

The Newton OS has software that can communicate with the Mac; however, the reverse is not true. You need to find Mac OS software that will let your Mac communicate with the Newton. The official software for Newton OS 2.0 is the Newton Connection Utility, available for purchase from Apple by calling 1-888-273-3594. However, Newton user and software developer Matthew Vaughn of Lightyear Media does not recommend the Apple utility. Alternative software utilities for the Newton—MacDownload has more than a hundred—provide Newton-to-Mac connectivity, as well as extend your Newton's capabilities. Table 8-5 points you to Apple's support page for Newton products and other Newton sites.

Desktops and Laptops

To cover all the bases, while we're talking about linking computing devices to your Mac, I might as well mention briefly that it is possible, without any Internet connection at all, to connect another computer to your Mac.

Connecting another Mac, whether it's a PowerMac, PowerBook, or iBook, is straightforward. You can connect one Mac to the other by a cable between the modem and printer ports. Set the AppleTalk control panel on both machines to "Connect via" whichever port you choose. Turn on File Sharing with the File Sharing control panel on both Macs, and you can use the Chooser and AppleShare to access shared folders on each Mac.

Table 8-5. Newton Resources

Description	Location
Apple's support info for Newton products	til.info.apple.com/techinfo.nsf/artnum/n26179
Arizona Mac User Group's Newton page	www.amug.org/amug_newton.html
LandWare software for Newtons, including X-Port connectivity software	www.landware.com
Lightyear Media, software for Web-based Newton Personal Data Sharing	come.to/lightyear_media
MacDownload for Newton applications	www.macdownload.com
NewtInTouch	surf.to/NewtInTouch
Newton Connection Utilities guide	til.info.apple.com/techinfo.nsf/artnum/n24299
Newton OS 1	newtonos1.webjump.com
The Newton Source	www.oldschool.net/newton
Planet Newton	www.planetnewton.com

You can also connect two Macs by connecting the Ethernet ports, if both are so equipped. Most Macs purchased in the past few years have an Ethernet port built in. The Apple Technical Information Library article listed in Table 8-6 describes how to make the connection. The most important point is to use a special type of Ethernet cable, called an Ethernet crossover cable, which lets you avoid using an Ethernet hub. You can buy crossover cables from electronics stores. If you want to connect more than two Macs via an Ethernet, you will have to use a hub with standard Ethernet cables. Once connected, set the AppleTalk control panel to Ethernet, turn File Sharing on, and you should be in business.

It is also possible to connect a Mac computer and a Windows computer directly, either through serial ports, modems, or Ethernet. The options here are more complicated, and the article on peer-to-peer networking at the MacWindows Web site details the various cabling and software options. Once connected, it's possible to use the Miramar System's PC MACLAN (on the Windows machine) or DAVE from Thursby Software Systems (on the Mac) to get both computers to speak the same file sharing language (see Chapter 4). The Star Gate utility, installed on both the Mac and Windows machines, will also let you transfer files back and forth.

Table 8-6. Mac Peer-to-Peer Networking

Description	Location
Apple TIL article on peer-to-peer Ethernet connection	*til.info.apple.com/techinfo.nsf/artnum/n30820*
Peer-to-peer networking tips from MacWindows	*www.macwindows.com/peertips.html*
Star Gate by Kevin Raner	*www.home.aone.net.au/krs/sg.html*

TELEPHONIC MAC

In the digital word, one of the new buzzwords is "convergence." Convergence means, for example, that the distinction between computer networks, the telephone system, and the television cable delivery networks is becoming blurred. Digital mobile phones and pagers, telephone and cable modems, and satellite relays are some early points of convergence. In particular, the connections between computers and the phone system have gone far beyond modems calling into computer networks.

Now, it's not all that earth-shattering to learn that a modem allows your Mac to use the phone line to dial into an Internet Service Provider (ISP) for Internet access. Many Macs have modems built in. If your Mac does not have a modem, external modems that plug into your Mac's modem port are readily available from retail outlets and on-line stores. Chapter 3 discusses some of the control panels and options for configuring your modem.

Besides talking with other computers, your modem also lets your Mac communicate with the many other devices connected to the telephone system—pagers, fax machines, digital phones, and voicemail systems. From your Mac, you can send e-mail messages to pagers and mobile phones, send faxes, record and forward voicemail, or make long distance audio and video phone calls across the Internet. PowerBook owners can dial into an ISP via 3Com's cellular modems. Table 8-7 lists some of the telephony software available for the Mac, divided into somewhat arbitrary categories.

- **Multi-function telephony packages.** Stalker's CommuniGate and Smith Micro's MacCommCenter Plus provide paging, digital phone messaging, faxing, and voicemail messaging in one application. CommuniGate can provide these capabilities, along with e-mail, Web, and other Internet services, to an entire office through its server gateway.

- **Single- and dual-function telephony packages.** These applications focus on paging, voicemail, faxing, or limited combinations of those functions. They are lumped together here because otherwise I'd have to put each in its own category. The PageNOW! family of products, for example, lets you send pages, as shown in Figure 8-2, but can also be tied into a fax, e-mail, or voicemail application. For example, PageNOW! might send a page in response to getting an e-mail message.

- **Internet phone and conferencing.** With these packages you can teleconference or videoconference over the Internet instead of over a telephone line. With a camera and microphone attached to your Mac, you can participate in on-line conversations and see the folks you're talking to. Figure 8-3 shows the ClearPhone interface.

Table 8-7. Mac telephony resources

Description	Location
Multi-function telephony packages	
CommuniGate from Stalker Software	*www.stalker.com/CommuniGate*
MacComCenter Plus from Smith Micro	*www.smithmicro.com/products/macplus.htm*
Single- or dual-function telephony packages	
CoMa Voice/Pro from Germany's Softbär	*home.t-online.de/home/Softbaer*
FaxSTF from STF Inc.	*www.stfinc.com*
MegaPhone, Bonzer, and Voice Messenger from Bing Software	*www.bingsoftware.com*
Notify! Classic, pager software from AirMedia (formerly Ex Machina)	*www.exmachina.com*
PageNOW! software family from Mark/Space Softworks	*www.markspace.com/pagenow_mac.html*
ValueFax, shareware from Pancomm	*members.aol.com/valuefax*
Internet phones and conferencing	
ClearPhone Internet phone	*www.clearphone.com*
CU-SeeMe from White Pine Software	*www.wpine.com/Products/CU-SeeMe*
Internet Phone from Vocaltec	*www.vocaltec.com/mac/web/mac.htm*
iVisit audio/video conferencing software for Mac OS and Windows	*www.ivisit.com*
PGPfone, encrypted Internet phone	*www.pgp.com/products/PGPfone.cgi*
Related resources	
3Com Megahertz 56K cellular modem PC cards for PowerBooks	*www.3com.com/client/mcd/products*
Metricom's Ricochet wireless networks support Macs (limited service areas).	*www.ricochet.net*
Pure Mac telephony software page	*www.pure-mac.com/telephony.html*

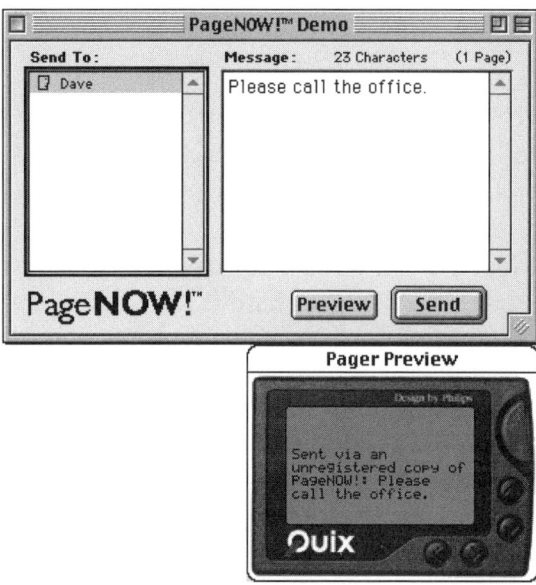

Figure 8-2. PageNOW! interface and message preview, courtesy Mark/Space Softworks

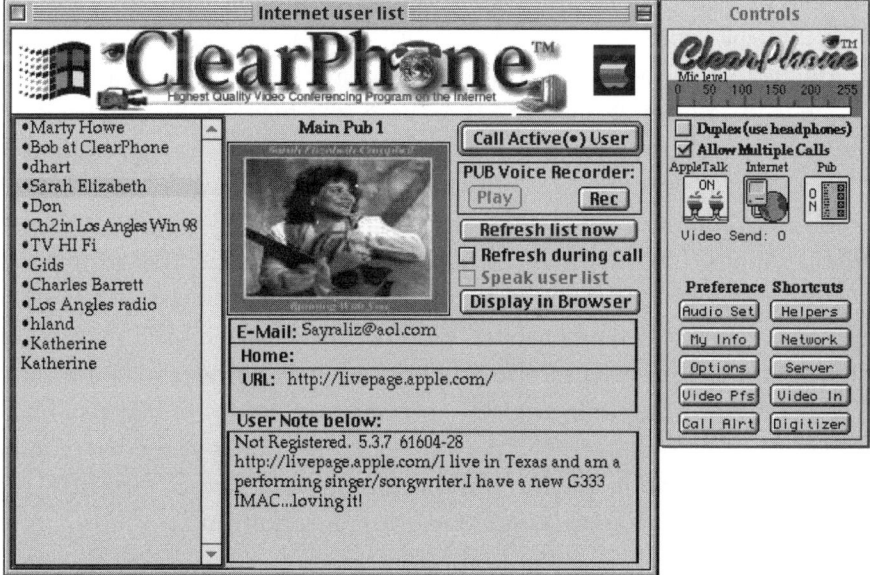

Figure 8-3. ClearPhone Internet phone, courtesy Engineering Consulting

AUDIO-VISUAL MAC

In the digital world, more music and video are coming at us as bits and bytes. Consider Compact Discs, Digital Versatile Discs, and High-Definition Television. Most Macs of the past several years have come with a CD-ROM drive and software to play audio CDs. Just this year, personal computers, including Macs, have started to come with DVD-ROM drives for playing DVDs, as well as CDs.

This section covers some newer software and hardware accessories for up and coming digital media, including MP3 music, television, and digital still and motion photography.

MP3 Players

The music format that swept the digital world in 1999 is MP3, short for MPEG-1 Audio Layer-3. MP3 is a compressed audio file format (file extension *.mp3*), in the same way that GIF and JPEG are compressed graphics file formats. I'm not sure what caused MP3 to catch on so suddenly in 1999, because the format has been around for about ten years, but catch on it did. MP3 lets you compress sound files by a factor of twelve while retaining CD-quality sound.

For listening to MP3 sound files, you have the option of playing them on your Mac with a software player or downloading them to a portable device designed to load an hour or more of MP3 audio into memory for playback. (Some of these devices also receive FM radio broadcasts.) The players, both software and hardware, give you the capability to collect and play sets of MP3 files, almost as if you're compiling your own custom CDs. For simply playing a single MP3 audio file, Apple's latest QuickTime software recognizes the MP3 format.

Creating an MP3 file is only slightly more complicated. To do so, you need a piece of software called an encoder. Some of the software MP3 players include an encoder utility, but you can also purchase separate encoder software.

Table 8-8 provides links to MP3 software and hardware players. There are a number of other portable MP3 players on the market, but the two companies listed here, I-JAM Multi Media and Diamond Multimedia, explicitly support Macs through USB connectors and Mac OS control software.

Table 8-8. MP3 Players and Software

Description	Location
Definition of MP3	whatis.com/mp3.htm
Audion shareware MP3, CD, and network audio player from Panic Software	www.panic.com/ppack/audion
I-JAM player and Jam Station software from I-JAM Multi Media	www.ijamworld.com
MacAMP and MacAMP Lite MP3 player software from @soft	www.macamp.net
N2MP3 encoder from Proteron	www.n2mp3.com
QuickTime from Apple	www.quicktime.com
Rio PMP300 and Rio 500 players from Diamond Multimedia	www.rioport.com
SoundJam MP software player and encoder from Casady & Greene	www.soundjam.com
Sites for more MP3 information	www.mp3.com mp3.lycos.com

TV Tuners and Video Capture Cards

The next step from audio is full audio plus video, either from television or from a video camera. Maybe you'd like to capture digital video on your Mac, watch CNN financial news while you work, or participate in a videoconference. A number of expansion cards and external USB devices are available—at prices within the range of the average consumer's checkbook—that will let you watch TV or capture digitized video from just about any video camera, camcorder, VCR, or any device with a standard video-out port.

While some camcorders and devices produce digital video directly, most such cameras and virtually all VCRs have standard analog video output. To view, save, and edit video from these sources, your Mac needs hardware to convert the analog video to digital format. Traditionally, this hardware has come on expansion cards installed inside your Mac, but newer products connect to the Mac's USB ports.

Depending on your needs, you might choose a device that only digitizes video input, but several of these products also incorporate cable TV tuners.

Without the TV tuner, you can still route signals from a TV or VCR into the digitizer through standard video connectors; however, you will have to change channels on the TV or VCR (or with the respective remote control). With a built-in tuner, you can control the television signal in software.

Another factor to consider is the demand that video capture places on your system. At minimum, you need a Mac new enough to have PCI expansion slots. Even better would be a Mac with a G3 or G4 processor. Typically the video capture cards, with their on-board hardware and direct PCI connection, can also capture video at higher resolutions. The USB options are limited to an image size of 320 by 240, but that resolution should suffice for video clips destined for the Web and comparable uses. Table 8-9 lists several video capture and TV tuner devices for the Mac.

Table 8-9. TV Tuners and Video Capture

Description	Location
Buz from Iomega	*www.iomega.com/buz*
Interview USB-based video capture from XLR8	*www.xlr8.com/interview*
ixTV and ixTV FM expansion cards from ixMicro	*www.ixmicro.com/products/tvtuners.html*
My Capture and My TV USB devices from Eskape Labs	*www.eskapelabs.com*
Xclaim VR 128 card and Xclaim TV from ATI Technologies	*www.atitech.com/ca_us/products/mac/xclaim_vr_128*

Digital Cameras

Digital cameras fall into two categories. The core technology in both types of cameras is essentially the same: Images are captured in digital form on a charge-coupled device (CCD) rather than in analog form on chemically coated film. The image from the CCD is saved to more permanent storage.

Cameras in the first category are designed to capture still photographs, much like traditional film-based cameras, except the digital photographs are "developed" by downloading them to a computer. Typically, these cameras are what people think of when they hear the term "digital camera." Other features of these cameras are their portability, high-resolution (at least for the high-end models), and the ability to store several dozen images internally before having to download the photos. These digital cameras are also relatively expensive.

The high-end digital cameras are approaching a quality that can replace traditional photographs for many applications. For this reason, companies long associated with film-based cameras manufacture many of the best digital cameras. Table 8-10 lists several companies who produce digital cameras that can be used with Macs.

The second category of cameras, for lack of a better term, I'll label "Web cams." While technically they are also digital cameras, they fill a completely different niche. They do not necessarily have to be used in Web applications, but that is one common use. Web cams are typically low-resolution, tethered by a cable to a computer, and lacking internal storage of their own. (They can be portable only if attached to a portable computer.) However, by sacrificing portability and resolution, Web cams can cost considerably less than other digital cameras. In addition, these cameras often can capture motion video in addition to still photos. Table 8-10 also lists several Web cam models that are compatible with Macs.

MACS AT WORK

As we enter the book's home stretch, I've crammed in a number of special-purpose electronic accessories. All of these accessories serve a dedicated purpose, but not all are just for fun. Some items, like bar code scanners and data acquisition cards, play key roles in the office or laboratory.

This section runs through a handful of accessories that make your Mac a central part of your workplace. There are bar code scanners for inventory control or retail sales, boards and interfaces for data acquisition and research, and global positioning system (GPS) interfaces for real-world navigation. These hardware accessories are obviously only part of a complete system, and I've included some resources for further information. You should also consult the Macintosh Products Guide (described later in this chapter) for more options and options tailored for specific applications.

Table 8-10. Digital Cameras and Mac Connectivity

Description	Location
Digital Cameras	
Agfa digital cameras	*www.agfa.com*
Canon PowerShot digital cameras	*www.powershot.com*
Casio digital cameras	*www.casio.com/digitalimaging*
Kodak digital cameras	*www.kodak.com*
Nikon Coolpix digital cameras	*www.nikonusa.com*
Panasonic digital cameras require a separate Mac cable.	*www.panasonic.com*
Sony Digital Mavica cameras	*www.sel.sony.com/SEL/consumer/dimaging*
Toshiba digital cameras	*www.toshiba.com*
Web Cams	
Ariston iSee USB Digital Camera	*www.ariston.com*
Logitech QuickCam Pro and QuickCam VC	*www.logitech.com/us/cameras*
iRez Kritter camera	*www.irez.com/kritter.html*
Reardon Technology SiteCam software and SiteZAP Web cam	*www.rearden.com*
Pixera Personal digital camera	*www.pixera.com*

Bar Code Readers and Point-of-Sale Software

A Mac (or iMac) can serve a small business for inventory control and tracking by attaching a bar code scanner to read universal product code (UPC) symbols. Some scanners can work independently and collect data that will later be downloaded to the Mac, while others remain connected to the computer. To turn your Mac or iMac into a full-fledged cash register, add a cash drawer, credit card reader, receipt printer, and some point-of-sale software.

Table 8-11 lists makers of Mac-compatible bar code readers and point-of-sale software from MacPOS, ExecUtron Development, and EES Companies. POS Direct is a reseller of point-of-sale software and hardware, including bar

Table 8-11. Mac Bar Code Scanners and Point-of-Sale Software

Description	Location
Mac-Barcode Company	www.mac-barcode.com
MacPOS	www.macpos.com
Order Manager POS software from Colin Chong's Visual Imaging	homepages.ihug.co.nz/~cchong
P.I.M.S. from ExecUtron Development Corp.	www.execution.com
POS/OE software and connectors from EES Companies, Inc.	www.posoe.com
P.O.S. Direct barcode reader retailer	www.posdirect.com
River's Edge Corporation barcode readers	www.riversedge.com
Sixth Sense POS and Sixth Sense Café restaurant software	www.SixthSensePOS.com
Silicon Valley Bus Co. barcode readers	www.svbus.com

code scanners, credit card readers, cash drawers, and receipt printers. Figure 8-4 shows the sales order screen from the MacPOS software.

Data Acquisition Interfaces

Since my day job involves writing about scientific research, I wanted to make sure I worked that subject into this book. Consider it done. Long a mainstay on university campuses, Macs continue to play important roles in the research laboratory. Data acquisition is a key part of the scientific process, and several companies produce hardware and software for data acquisition with Macs. Data acquisition hardware can also be used by non-scientists and hobbyists. Sensors can provide information about the energy consumption for maintaining the temperature inside buildings, or control information for robotic navigation.

National Instrument, for example, has 34 boards for data acquisition, image acquisition, motion control, and instrument control from which researchers can construct their measurement systems. To make use of the boards, LabVIEW is a general-purpose graphical programming tool for measurement and automation, while HiQ provides numerical analysis.

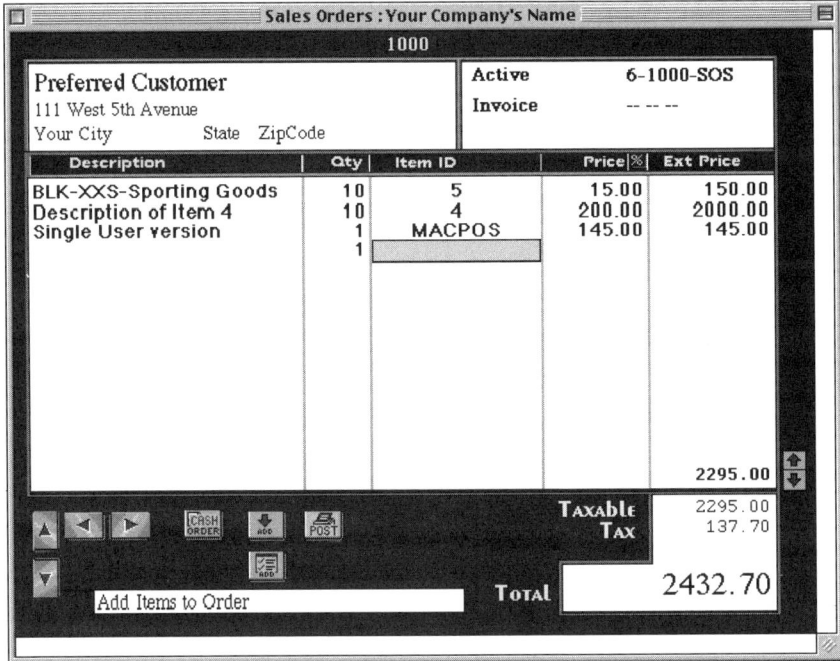

Figure 8-4. MacPOS point-of-sale software, courtesy MacPOS.com

Remote Measurement Systems produces the ADC-1 sensor interface and control software. Their Web site includes a useful section on how to set up systems to measure everything from temperature to soil moisture to room occupancy.

Table 8-12 has links to Mac data acquisition products, such as the free data acquisition and analysis software from WartHog Systems, which will work with hardware from National Instrument, Remote Measurement Systems, and other makers. The MacSciTech Users Association Web site is a good resource for more Mac-related scientific and technical software and hardware.

Global Positioning System

To help launch and track nuclear warheads, the U.S. Department of Defense launched a system of 24 NAVSTAR satellites that orbit the Earth more that 10,000 miles overhead. These satellites, combined with five fixed ground stations, send out signals from which a receiver can calculate its precise location anywhere on the Earth. This Global Positioning System (GPS), like computers themselves, has evolved from purely military applications to many commercial and individual uses. Since only a few small computer chips are required to interpret GPS signals, GPS receivers are turning up everywhere—in cars, phones, and handheld receivers, for example.

The GPSy and Mac GPS Pro are two software packages that let you use your Mac for advanced mapping, logging, and data transfer with portable GPS receivers. Both companies also make cables for connecting the GPS device to the Mac serial ports. (For USB ports, you'll need a USB to Mac serial adapter.) GPS devices can also provide information to navigation and charting software that supports GPS input. Table 8-13 lists these and other Mac GPS resources.

Table 8-12. Mac Data Acquisition and Measurement

Description	Location
MacSciTech, general resource for scientific uses of Macs	*www.macscitech.org*
National Instrument data acquisition and measurement	*www.natinst.com/mac*
Remote Measurement Systems ADC-1 data collection device and Mac control software	*www.measure.com*
WartHog Systems data acquisition and analysis software	*cnas.ucr.edu/~bio/faculty/Warthog.html*

Table 8-13. Global Positioning System Resources

Description	Location
All About GPS tutorial by Trimble Navigation Limited	*www.trimble.com/gps*
GPSy and GPSy Pro, software and cables for Mac GPS Communications	*www.gpsy.com*
Mac GPS Pro software and cables for Garmin GPS receivers from James Associates	*www.csn.net/~lwjames*
NavimaQ, electronic marine charting software from Quintessence Designs	*www.quintessencedesigns.com*

MACS AT HOME

Your Mac can also be pressed into service around the house. You might use it to control your lights, your remote control television, or a ham radio. You can also use your Mac as a makeshift home security system. Others devices, however, would more traditionally be called gadgets—functional, but not truly necessary. We'll start with some of the more serious items and finish up with the fun ones.

Home Automation

If you spend a lot of time at your Mac, you've probably been annoyed by having to run through the house to start a pot of coffee or turn off the lights. Wouldn't it be nice to turn off the lights downstairs without a trip down the steps, turn on the coffee maker in the kitchen, or even turn down the stereo when the remote control is sitting across the room. You have a couple of options. The Keyspan IR card allows you to connect an infrared receiver and up to seven infrared transmitters for controlling televisions, VCRs, CD changers, and other devices. You'll have to buy the infrared receivers and transmitters from an electronics retailer, but Keyspan provides programming interfaces for AppleScript and C as well as infrared code files.

The X10 standard provides another way to control devices in your home. X10 is a powerline carrier protocol that allows devices to communicate with each other via the existing electrical wiring in the house. With X10 interface boxes plugged into your home's power outlets and the XTension software from Sand Hill Engineering, shown in Figure 8-5, and MouseHouse from MouseHouse Electronics, you can send commands from your Mac to appliances throughout your home. Many of the X10 modules are available from electronics retailers such as Radio Shack and Fry's. MouseHouse Electronics also sells a complete starter kit including X10 modules and the MouseHouse control software. You can also buy parts and software from SmartHome.com.

For a truly dedicated gadgetophile, you can connect a wireless microphone, your Mac, and X10 components into a system that will let you control appliances in your home by voice commands. You'll have to buy the May 1999 issue of *MacAddict* magazine and read the article by David Reynolds for the full details. Without revealing all of the article's tips, I can tell you that, in addition to X10 modules and the XTension software, you'll need a lamp or appliance to be controlled, the AppleScript and Speech Recognition software with the Mac OS, a wireless audio link, a lavalier microphone, and audio cables.

Table 8-14 has links to tools and tips for Mac-based home automation.

Table 8-14. Mac Home Automation

Description	Location
"Command Your Mac" by David Reynolds	*MacAddict magazine, May 1999, www.macaddict.com*
Keyspan IR card lets a Mac be used as a universal remote.	*www.keyspan.com/products/ir*
Mac software and X10 modules from SmartHome.com	*www.smarthome.com/mac.html*
MouseHouse from MouseHouse Electronics	*www.mousehouse.net*
X10 Technology and Resources Forum	*www.x10.org*
XTension, from Sand Hill Engineering	*www.shed.com*

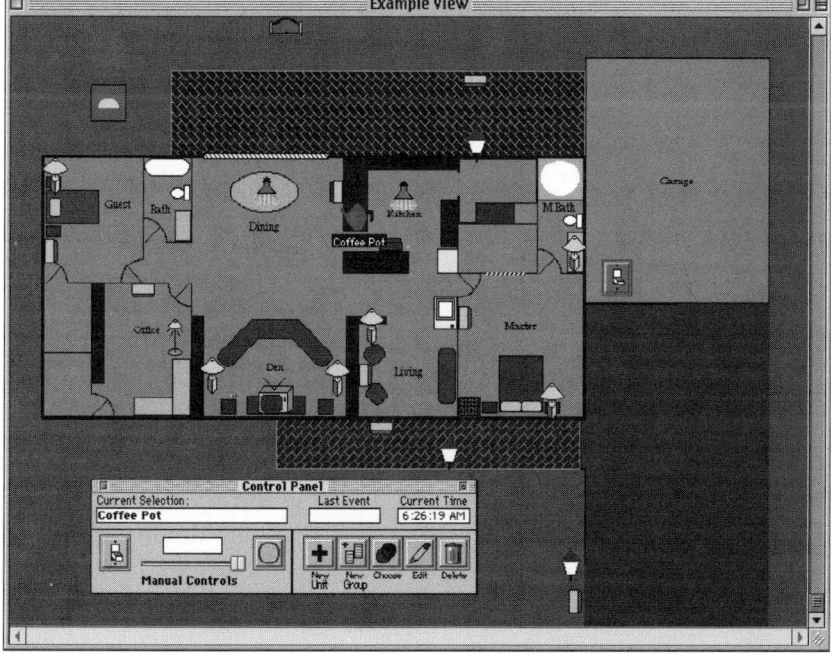

Figure 8-5. XTension X10 home automation software, courtesy Sand Hill Engineering, Inc.

A Note on Jini. With all the discussion on the X10 protocol for home automation, I felt I should briefly mention Jini connection technology, the latest idea percolating out of the world of Java technology. Jini connection technology (see *www.jini.org* or *java.sun.com/jini*) lets devices interact in an impromptu, plug-and-play community without any human intervention. Jini devices, in other words, have a bit of "self-control." When a Jini device is plugged in, it first checks to see what other devices are already in the community and then joins the community by posting information about the services it can provide.

On the other hand, X10 is a communication language that can be sent over electrical wiring. X10 gives you *remote control* of connected devices, but without external intervention—such as from a timer, a human, or computer software—an X10-enabled device won't do anything at all. However, you could imagine Jini and X10 being used together. Rather than rewiring a house to provide Ethernet links for the Jini-aware lamps, coffee maker, and clock radios, Jini devices might use the X10 protocol to communicate over existing electrical wiring.

I won't go any further into Jini technology here because, like all Java technology, it is designed to be platform independent. In fact, it is designed for non-computer devices such as lamps and dishwashers. There are also not many Jini-enabled devices available yet. Perhaps in this book's second edition, I'll have a section on how to get your Mac to work with the Jini-supported Blender OS.

Home Security

If you don't own a dog or you don't have the resources to spring for a full-fledged home security system, your Mac can also be pressed into service as a digital watchdog. Table 8-15 has pointers to Mac home security resources.

Microcosm's StopIt! software turns your Mac into a stand-alone security device. By listening to noise levels through a microphone and movements of the mouse and keyboard, StopIt! sounds an alarm when your computer hears unexpected sound or unauthorized movement.

The ADC-1 sensor interface provides a way to construct your own home security system from a variety of sensors. The Remote Measurement Systems Web site has a basic introduction to the possibilities. Vibration detectors, pressure pads, magnetic switches, and infrared and ultrasonic detectors can be combined and customized for your home.

Table 8-15. Mac Home Security Resources

Description	Location
MouseHouse from MouseHouse Electronics	www.mousehouse.net
Remote Measurement Systems introduction to home alarm sensors and detectors	www.measure.com/sensors/sensor-security.html
StopIt! from Microcosm Software	www.thesanctuary.com/microcosm/stopit.html
X10 modules and home security sensors from SmartHome.com	www.smarthome.com/mac.html
XTension, from Sand Hill Engineering	www.shed.com

The X10 standard offers a third option for building a home security system through your Mac. X10 modules and sensors sold by SmartHome.com can be combined with the XTension or MouseHouse software to alert you to unwanted movement or entry into your house. You can even buy the ReX-10 barking dog alarm to add a virtual watchdog to your security system.

Amateur Radio

Way before there was the Internet, there was amateur radio. Better known as "ham radio," ham radio operators have been communicating over great distances since the early 1900s. Today, amateur radio operators send signals via satellite, as well as over the air, and can also transmit computer networking signals through wireless "packet radio" communication.

For the hundreds of thousands of ham radio operators who also own Macs, I'll just tell you about Dog Park Software and Black Cat Systems, developers of amateur radio software for Macs. They have software available (listed in Table 8-16) for controlling radios, tracking satellites, sending packet radio messages, and learning Morse code, to name a few.

Table 8-16. Amateur Radio Resources

Description	Location
Ham radio software from Black Cat Systems	www.blackcatsystems.com
Ham radio software from Dog Park Software, Limited	www.interlog.com/~dogpark

FOR MORE INFORMATION

I'm sure there are Mac users out there who feel I overlooked their own special-interest community of professionals, hobbyists, or advocates. For example, I didn't mention Mac accessories for private pilots or the medical profession. I also didn't go into such major Mac strongholds as printing, movie editing, or music. I assume full responsibility for that oversight. In my defense, there would have been no way to cover them all.

However, to make up for the missing piece of information that you were interested in, Table 8-17 provides a few resources that helped me in researching this book. If all you've got to work with is a cryptic acronym, *whatis.com* is a great place to start. Of course, there are also the major Web search engines—including Yahoo!, AltaVista, and Lycos, but for Mac-specific information, Apple maintains a useful database of software and hardware in the Macintosh Product Guide. For more software, you might try the Pure Mac directory or the ZDNet Macintosh Software Library (a.k.a. MacDownload.com). For questions related to Mac networking and connecting Macs to Windows systems, you should check out the MacWindows site.

Table 8-17. More Mac resources

Description	Location
Pure Mac software directory	*www.pure-mac.com*
ZDNet Macintosh Software Library	*www.macdownload.com*
The Macintosh Products Guide	*guide.apple.com*
Whatis.com	*whatis.com*
MacWindows	*www.macwindows.com*

APPENDIX

Mac OS Networking Primer

*T*his appendix is here because there was no easy way to talk about cross-platform networks without getting into lots of network and Internet terms. And rather than explaining them one at a time, this appendix collects them all and puts them in relationship to all the other terms. You don't need to memorize the terminology to connect to the network, so if you start feeling drowsy, you might skim through it now and refer back when the terms pop up in the book.

A word of caution: because this is not a detailed treatise on network technologies, some of the definitions here may not be as precise as a networking professional might like. But they are generally correct and should give you a good feel for the high-level networking picture.

GENERAL NETWORK TERMS

A **network** is a system of computers and other devices, connected so they can exchange data. The computers and devices on the network are also called **hosts**. When networked computers are not connected to the same physical cable, **routers** help deliver messages to addresses on other networks. A **local-area network (LAN)** connects devices over a geographically small area, typically in one building or a part of a building. A **wide-area network (WAN)** links LANs together. The **Internet** is the term that describes the largest worldwide system of connected networks.

All hosts have **addresses** so messages can be delivered from the sender to the intended recipient. On many networks, messages are broken into small, easy-to-handle chunks, called **packets**, for sending across the network. A **protocol** is a standard set of rules for exchanging data or packets. A **protocol stack** is a group of protocols and the relationships between them.

MAC NETWORKING AND INTERNET TERMS

Now we must get into specifics, and here's where it gets a little tricky. We'll start with a diagram. Figure A-1 shows many of the protocols (and acronyms) that you might encounter in the Mac networking world.

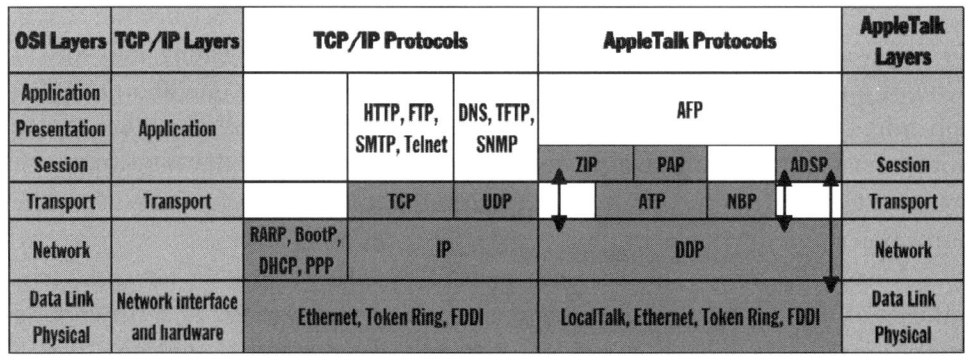

Figure A-1. Network layers, protocols, and relationships

The Networking Layer Cake 181

The first column in Figure A-1 shows the standard picture that network programmers use to talk about protocols and protocol stacks. The Open Systems Interconnection (OSI) model describes networking software in terms of seven layers. The second and fifth columns show the layers of two important protocol "families," TCP/IP and AppleTalk. **TCP/IP** is the protocol family of the Internet, with protocols for the World Wide Web, file transfer, and e-mail built on top of it. **AppleTalk** is the set of protocols built into all Macs that lets you share files, use printers, and find network services on Macintosh networks. Novell-based networks use the **NetWare** family of protocols (not shown).

The third and fourth columns show the relationships between TCP/IP and AppleTalk protocols. The term *protocol stack* reflects the layered relationships between the protocols. A given protocol generally communicates via the protocol directly below it in the protocol stack (unless shown otherwise via arrows).

Open Transport. In addition to the protocol rules, a computer needs software to turn the rules into instructions that the computer and network hardware can understand. On Macintosh computers, that software is called Open Transport. The shaded regions in the third and fourth columns of Figure A-1 show the protocols that Open Transport implements. Mac OS 8.1 comes with Open Transport version 1.3; Mac OS 8.5 comes with Open Transport 2.0. In general, with more recent versions of Open Transport, you will experience better networking performance. (If you have Mac OS versions before Mac OS 8, see the note on "classic" Mac networking and MacTCP at the end of the Appendix.)

Sustainable Softworks produces a number of shareware tools for tuning or monitoring your Mac's Open Transport performance. However, unless you have a lot more networking experienced than what you learned in this appendix, you should not attempt to tune your network software yourself.

THE NETWORKING LAYER CAKE

For a completely non-technical analogy, you might think of a protocol family as the recipe for baking a layered networking cake. TCP/IP protocols bake one type of cake, say, chocolate, while AppleTalk is a recipe for carrot cake. In both cases, you get dessert, but each is a unique flavor. Now, the part you've been waiting for—definitions of the wonderful layers, protocols, and acronyms in Figure A-1. (In the interest of sanity, we gloss over some of the acronyms and leave them for Table A-1.) We'll start from the bottom up.

Data-Link and Physical Layers. The data-link and physical layers describe the actual wires, connectors, and circuitry for a network connection, as well as the software for converting a digital message for transmission across the connection onto the network. Ethernet and Fast Ethernet hardware is built into all new Macintosh computers, including the iMac. Ethernet can transfer data at 10 million bits per second, while Fast Ethernet handles 100 million bits per second. For information on other high-speed Mac network interfaces, see the "High-Performance Mac Networking" section in Chapter 3.

Network Layer. The network layer specifies how an individual data packet is delivered from the sender to the receiver. The network layer protocol for TCP/IP is the **Internet Protocol (IP).** Computers on an IP network are identified by an IP address that looks like 132.249.202.135. (This is my office Mac's IP address, in fact.) AppleTalk defines a comparable protocol, **DDP**, and NetWare has **IPX**.

TCP/IP also defines a number of protocols that networks use to assign IP addresses automatically: **BootP, DHCP,** and **RARP**. You'll see these acronyms when you configure some of the Mac networking Control Panels. (At home, I connect to cable modem service via DHCP.)

Transport Layer. The transport layer, most importantly, provides ways to *guarantee* that messages get from the sender to the receiver. The most important protocol at this level is the **Transmission Control Protocol (TCP)** of the TCP/IP family. TCP will divide a large message into a series of packets and ensure that packets are all received without data errors and in the correct order. Or, as a more specific example, TCP makes sure the e-mail with vital Internet jokes or file attachments of dancing baby movies arrives intact. (TCP doesn't care if it's sending an e-mail message, a database file, or a Web page and graphics; TCP just makes sure it gets there in the same condition in which it left.) AppleTalk and NetWare have comparable protocols—ATP and SPX, respectively.

Application, Presentation, and Session Layers. The top-most network layers are the icing on the network layer cake. Applications such as Netscape Communicator or Microsoft Internet Explorer implement the **HyperText Transfer Protocol (HTTP)** of the Web. E-mail programs such as Qualcomm's Eudora Pro or Bare Bones Software's MailSmith implement the **Simple Mail Transfer Protocol**

(SMTP), the **Post Office Protocol version 3 (POP3)**, and the **Internet Mail Access Protocol (IMAP)**.

Unlike TCP/IP, AppleTalk defines some Session layer protocols (PAP, ZIP, and ADSP) which support the user-friendly capabilities of AppleTalk networks, such as file sharing—via the application-level **AppleTalk Filing Protocol (AFP)**—or network resource browsing. NetWare also has high-level protocols, including NCP and SAP.

We've covered most of the terms and acronyms that you'll be likely to encounter as an average computer user on the Internet, and then some. However, there are plenty more. In the text, I tossed around a number of acronyms without writing them out. Table A-1 lists them and others that appear in Figure A-1. If you need more information, you should refer to the resources in Table A-2.

Table A-1. Acronyms You Needn't Worry Much About

TCP/IP	
BootP	Boot Protocol
DHCP	Dynamic Host Configuration Protocol
RARP	Reverse Address Resolution Protocol
SLIP	Serial Line Internet Protocol
UDP	User Datagram Protocol
AppleTalk	
ADSP	AppleTalk Data Stream Protocol
ATP	AppleTalk Transaction Protocol
DDP	Datagram Delivery Protocol
NBP	Name-Binding Protocol
PAP	Printer Access Protocol
ZIP	Zone Information Protocol
NetWare	
IPX	Internetwork Packet Exchange
NCP	NetWare Core Protocol
SAP	Service Advertising Protocol
SPX	Sequenced Packet Exchange

Table A-2 provides links to more information about TCP/IP and other Internet protocols, the AppleTalk family of protocols, and Open Transport on the Mac OS. This appendix was intended only to provide some context for the networking terms that get bandied about in the Internet community. With practice, you'll be able to bluff your way out of many Internet conversations. At the very least, I hope this information makes you a little more comfortable and confident in using your networked Mac.

A Note on "Classic" Macintosh Networking

From the beginning, every Macintosh had the hardware and software necessary to communicate with other Macs via AppleTalk. And prior to Open Transport, the Mac OS implemented the TCP/IP protocol stack through MacTCP. These older networking implementations are sometimes referred to as "classic" Mac networking.

Table A-2. Networking References

Description	Location
Network glossary	*whatis.com*
Apple's reference book on Networking with Open Transport	*developer.apple.com/techpubs/mac/NetworkingOT/-NetworkingWOT-2.html*
Open Transport updates are available from Apple's software updates site.	*swupdates.info.apple.com*
Apple's AppleTalk reference	*developer.apple.com/techpubs/mac/Networking/-Networking-15.html*
Novell NetWare primer	*www.novell.com/catalog/primer/primer.html*
TCP/IP References	*www.metrowerks.com/tcpip/spec/spec-index.html*
IPNetMonitor, OT Advanced Tuner, IPNetRouter, shareware tools for Mac networking, from Sustainable Softworks	*www.sustworks.com*
Internet Engineering Task Force—source of protocol definitions (called RFCs)	*www.ietf.org*

A Note on "Classic" Macintosh Networking

If you have a Mac that still runs MacTCP, you may be fine for casual Internet use, although many current applications require Open Transport. However, if you want to use your Mac in a cross-platform office environment, Open Transport is a must. Performance boosts from the latest versions of Open Transport, the Mac OS, and PowerPC hardware all make the Mac a better cross-platform neighbor.

Index

A

Accessibility and assistive technology, 155
Adaptec USB to SCSI adapter/PCI to SCSI/FireWire, 154
ADB adapter (Griffin Technology), 154
ADB ports, 152
ADC-1 sensor interface and control software, 172
Addresses, 180
Adobe Acrobat, 94, 113
Adobe Corporation:
  customer forums, 98
  customer support, 98
  products page, 98
Adobe GoLive, 77
Adobe Illustrator 8 EPS, 94
Adobe Photoshop, 14, 98, 107, 120
  documents, 94
  mailing lists, 98
  newsgroups, 98
  plug-ins, 98
  resources, 98
Adobe Portable Document Format (PDF), 18
ADS Technologies USB PCI card, 154
ADSP (AppleTalk Data Stream Protocol), 183
AGFA digital cameras, 170
All About GPS (Trimble Navigation Limited), 173

Amateur radio, 177
Amazon.com, xix
Anarchie Pro (Stairways Software), 78
Anti-virus software, 13-14
APOP passwords, 84
Apple Computer, 9
  AppleTalk reference, 184
  Networking with Open Transport, reference book on, 184
  support info for Newton products, 161
  URL, 36
Apple Desktop Bus (ADB) ports, 152
Apple menu, 133
  approximating Windows Start menu, 134-35
Apple Network Administrator Toolkit, 25, 26, 57
Apple Network Assistant, 57
Apple Remote Access (ARA), 26, 31-33, 43
"Apple's Net Future" (*NetProfessional Magazine*), 26
AppleShare IP (Apple Computer), 37, 40-41, 44, 45, 47, 75, 80, 87, 90
  file sharing performance, 26
  Manager, 41
AppleTalk, 37, 59, 181
  addresses, 27
  advantages, 24-25
  control panel, 26-27
    connection port, 26-27

AppleTalk, control panel (*cont.*)
　　Get Info... menu option, 27
　　zone selection, 26-27
　DDP protocol, 182
　defined, 24
　disadvantages, 25-26
AppleTalk Filing Protocol (AFP), 24,
　　40-41, 183
AppleTalk-to-IP migration plan (Open
　　Door Networks), 42
Apple Technical Information Library, on
　　Open Transport SNMP, 56
AppleWorks, 94, 99
Application layer, 182-84
Application menu, 133-34
Application servers/clients, 140-44
　remote control, 143-44
　Windows Terminal Server, 141-43
　X Window System, 141
Applications, 93-107
　Adobe Photoshop, 98
　AppleWorks, 94, 99
　E-mail file exchange, 93
　FileMaker Pro, 99-101
　fonts, 95-97
　　font substitution, 95
　　handling the issue of, 96-97
　　resources, 97
　　special characters, 96
　　TrueType vs. Type 1, 95
　Microsoft Office, 101-5
　QuarkXPress, 105-7
　Quicken (Intuit), 106-7
　specific, 97-107
　Windows/Web filenames, 93-94
APS Technologies, 9
.arc, 20
Archive, 20
Archiving, 20
Ariston:
　iSee USB Digital Camera, 170
　USB PCI Card/USB to SCSI adapter,
　　154

Arizona Mac User Group's Newton page,
　　161
Asante Technologies, URL, 36
ASCII, 108-10
　extended variations, 109
ASCII Converter (Marco Bambini),
　　109-10
Asynchronous Transfer Mode (ATM), 36
At Ease for Workgroups, 57
ATP (AppleTalk Transaction Protocol),
　　183
Audion shareware MP3 (Panic Software),
　　167
Audiovisual Mac, 166-69
　digital cameras, 168-69
　MP3 players, 166-67
　TV tuners and video capture cards,
　　167-68
AutoShare (Mikael Hansen), 89
AutoStart Worm, 13-14
AVI->QT, 19

B

Bar code readers, 170-71
BarnesandNoble, xix
Belkin USB PCI card, 154
Better Finder Creators and Types, A, 15, 16
BetterTelnet (Rolf Braun), 139
.bin, 20
BinHex, 20, 82
Black Knight (Raine Storm Networks),
　　139
Black Cat Systems, ham radio software,
　　177
Blue Label PowerEmulator (Lismore
　　Software Systems), 145-46
.bmp, 118
Bonzer (Bing Software), 164
BootP (Boot Protocol), 35, 182-83
Bourne, Phil, xix, 66
Business Mac, The, 22
Buz (Iomega), 168

Index

C

California Research and Education Network (CalREN), 4
Camouflage, 131-50
  application servers/clients, 140-44
  non-Mac operating systems, 145-48
    general emulation information, 148
    UNIX and Linux for Mac, 146-48
    Windows emulators, 145-46
  PC cards, 149
  terminal emulators, 138-40
    connection protocols, 140
    secure connections, 140
  Windows tricks, 132-38
    GUI adjustments, 134-38
    GUI orientation, 132-34
Canon PowerShot digital cameras, 170
Cascading Style Sheets (CSS), 122, 123
  Web Design Group guide to, 128
Casio digital cameras, 170
CD-R/CD-RW, 9
CelView (Cel Corporation), 139
Center for Applied Special Technology, 155
CGI, 122
Character code sets, 109
Charge-coupled device (CCD), 168
Cheap PCs, 149
Claris Emailer, 83
ClarisWorks, 17
  moderated discussion list, 99
  user group, 99
  See also AppleWorks
"Classic" Macintosh networking, 184-85
ClearPhone Internet phone, 163-65
Client user, defined, 68
Client/server computing, 65-66
Clock, 133
CloseView control panel, 155
CNET's Builder.com, 128
CODECs, 20
Columbia AppleTalk Package (CAP), 54, 60

.com, 20
CoMa Voice/Pro (Softbar), 164
ComLink (Will Price), 139
"Command Your Mac" (David Reynolds), 174-75
CommuniGate (Stalker Software), 84, 87, 163-64
Compact Pro, 20
Complete Conflict Compendium, 27
Compression, See File compression
Computing devices, 156-62
  Newton, 160-61
  Palm Computing organizers, 156-58
  Windows CE devices, 158-60
Configuration Manager, Microsoft Internet Explorer, 28, 73
Conflict Catcher, 27
Connection port, AppleTalk control panel, 26-27
Consultant (Chronos), 157
Conventions, xvi
Convergence, 162-63
Conversion, *See* File conversion
Conversions Plus 4.5 (DataViz), 12
COPSTalk (COPS), 46
Core FTP Server, 80
Cosmo Player 2.1 (Cosmo Software), 125
.cpt, 20
Creator label, 15
Cross Platform utility (Sig Software), 16-17
CU-SeeMe (White Pine), 164
.cwk, 94

D

Data acquisition interfaces, 171-72
Databases, 116-17
DataComet (Kerberos), 139
Data-link layer, 182
DAVE (Thursby Software), 50-51, 162
DDP (Datagram Delivery Protocol), 182, 183

DeBabelizer (Equilibrium), 17-18
Desktop icons, 134
DHCP (Dynamic Host Configuration
    Protocol), 35, 182
DialAssist, 29
Digital cameras, 168-69
Digital information, at basic level, 2
Digital tape, 9
Disability Resources page (Apple), 155
Disinfectant, 14
.doc, 94
Dog Park Software, Limited, ham radio
    software, 177
DOS Mounter 98, 15
.dot, 94
Download Deputy (ilesa Software), 78
Dr. Solomon's Virex, 13-14
DragThing (James Thomson), 137
Dubinsky, Donna, 158
DVD-RAM, 9
DVD-ROM, 9
Dynamic DNS Network Services, 66
Dynamic HTML (DHTML), 122, 123-24
Dynamic HTML Lab, 128
DynDNS.com, 66
DynIP Internet Name Service, 66

E

EasyServe (Jason Linhart), 75
ECMA Script, 126
E-mail, 81-89
    clients, 83-86
        attachments, 85-86
        off-line features, 84
        password security, 84
        POP3 or IMAP, 81, 83-84, 86, 183
        CommuniGator (Stalker Software), 84
        eMail inChorus (SoftLink), 84
        Eudora Light (QualComm), 84
        Eudora Pro (QualComm), 82-83, 84
        Macintosh E-mail Resource Page, 84
        mailing list servers, 85-89

MailSmith (Bare Bones Software), 84
MailStrom (Tree Star), 84
Messenger (Netscape Corp.), 84
Microsoft Outlook Express, 84
most common problem with, 82-83
Mulberry (Cyrusoft International), 84
Musashi (Sono Software), 84-85
Outlook Express 4.5, 82
PowerMail (CTM Development), 84-85
servers, 85
E-mail file exchange, 93
eMail inChorus (SoftLink), 84
Emulation Excitement, 148
emulation.net (John Stiles), 148
Encapsulated PostScript (EPS) files, 18
Encoders, 166-67
Entrega:
    USB to Mac serial ports/ 4-port USB
        PCI card, 154
    USB to PDA adapter cable, 159-60
    USB to serial DB9 adapter, 157
.eps, 94
EPS, 94, 104, 118, 119-20, 129
EPStoPICT, 18
Ethernet, 182
Ethernet prots, 162
EtherShare (Helios Software GmbH), 54
Eudora Internet Mail Server (EIMS)
    (Qualcomm), 86, 87
Eudora Light (QualComm), 84
Eudora Pro (QualComm), 70, 82-85, 110,
    182-83
.exe, 20
eXodus (White Pine), 141, 144
EZQuest, 9

F

Fantom Drives, 9
Farallon Communications, URL, 36
Fast Ethernet, 182
FaxSTF (STF Inc.), 164
Fetch (Dartmouth College), 77-79

Index

Fiber Distributed-Data Interface (FDDI), 36
File compression, 19-21, 22
    formats, 20
File conversion, 14-18, 22
    compression, 19-21
    filenames/types, 14-16
    general files, 16-17
    graphics, 17-18
    movies, 19
    sound, 18
File exchange, 8-13
    Mac disks on a PC, 11-12
    PC disks on a Mac, 8-11
    UNIX disks on a Mac, 12-13
File Exchange, 8-10, 11, 15, 22
File extensions, 14-15
File formats, 107-20
    databases, 116-17
    graphics, 117-20
    PDF (Portable Document Format), 112-13
    "plain" text, 108-10
    PostScript, 114-16
    Rich Text Format (RTF), 111-12
    spreadsheets, 116-17
        ODBC, 117
File names:
    and types, 14-16
    Windows, 93-94
File sharing, 59-60
File Transfer Protocol (FTP), xvi, 24, 76-81
    clients, 77-79
    servers, 79-81
FileMaker Pro, 94, 99-101
    fonts/display, 100-101
    mailing lists, 100
    newsgroup, 100
    ODBC preview, 117
    product page, 100
    support page, 100
    technical information, 100
    Windows file names, 100

FileTyper (Daniel Azuma), 15, 16
FileWave and Asset Trustee (Wave Research), 57-58
FireWire, 153-54
FireWire Kit (Apple), 154
First Class Intranet Server (SoftArc), 75, 87
First Guide to PostScript, A, 115
5PM Term (White Pine), 139
Font substitution, 95
Fonts, 95-97
    font substitution, 95
    handling the issue of, 96-97
    resources, 97
    special characters, 96
    TrueType vs. Type 1, 95
Fore Systems (ForeRunner LE and 200E adapters), 36
Formac, 9
.fp3, 94
FreePPP (freeware), 27
F-Secure SSH (Data Fellows), 139-40

G

General files, 16-17
GhostScript (freeware), 18, 115
.gif, 94
GIF, 19, 93-94, 118, 119-20, 129
Gigabit Ethernet, 36
Global positioning system, 172-73
GoMac utility (ACTION Utilities), 137
GPS Pro (James Associates), 173
GPSy/GPSy Pro, 173
Graphical user interface (GUI), *See* GUI adjustments; GUI orientation
GraphicConverter (Lemke Software), 17-18, 22, 118
Graphics, 117-20
    conversion of, 17-18
    EPS, 94, 118, 119-20, 129
    FAQs from graphics-related newsgroups, 120
    format resources, 120

Graphics (*cont.*)
    GIF, 93-94, 118, 119-20, 129
    Graphics File Format Page, 120
    JPEG, 94, 118, 119-20, 129
    PNG, 118, 119-20, 129
    TIFF, 94, 118, 120, 129
Graphics File Format Page, 120
Gray, Gary, 115
Griffin Technology iMate USB to ADB adapter, 154
GUI adjustments, 134-38
    Apple menu, 134-35
    redesigning the interface, 137-38
    task bar:
        adding Start button to, 137
        makeshift, 135-37
GUI orientation, 132-34
    Mac OS interface, 132-34
        Apple menu, 133
        application menu, 133-34
        basic window, 134
        clock/system indicators, 133
        desktop icons, 134
        menu bar, 133
    Windows OS interface, 133
.gz, 20
Gzip, 20

H

Handspring, Inc., 157
Hart, David, 66
Hart, Deborah Casey, xx
Here & Now 2.0 (Software Architects), 11-12
High ASCII glyphs to HTML entities (Wolfgang Husmann), 109, 122
High-performance Mac networking, 35-37
Home automation, 174-76
Home security, 176-77
Hosts, 180
HotSync Manager, 158
.hqx, 20

HTML (HyperText Markup Language), 121-22
    HTML Goodies page, 122
    HTML Help (Web Design Group), 122
    numeric codes for special characters, 122
    resources, 122
    Webmonkey HTML collection, 122
httpd4Mac (Bill Melotti), 75
HyperText Markup Language (HTML), 68
HyperText Transfer Protocol (HTTP), 182

I

iCab, 69
I-JAM player/Jam Station software (I-JAM Multi Media), 167
IMAP, 81, 83-84, 86, 183
iMate USB (Griffin Technology), 154
Imation, 9
Inexpensive PCs, 149
InformINIT (Dan Frakes), 27
InformUser (Advanced Ideas), 57-58
Infrared control panel, 29
Inside Out Networks USB to Mac serial ports, 154
Installer VISE software (MindVision Software), 21
Intego Rival, 14
Internet, 63-90, 180
    clients/servers, 65-66
    e-mail, 81-89
    File Transfer Protocol (FTP), 76-81
        clients, 77-79
        servers, 79-81
    Internet Config, using, 67
    IP address, 64
    Personal Web Sharing (PWS) software, 74-76
    services, 66
    TCP/IP networking software, 64

Index

World Wide Web (WWW), 68-76
    Microsoft Internet Explorer, 72-73
    Netscape Communicator, 69, 70-71
    Web browsers, 69-70
    Web servers, 73-74
Internet Config (Stairways Software), 27, 29-30, 67, 85
Internet control panel, 29-30
Internet Engineering Task Force (IETF), 65, 184
Internet Mail Access Protocol (IMAP), 81, 83-84, 86, 183
Internet Phone (VocalTec), 164
Internet Protocol (IP), 64, 182
Internet Relay Chat (IRQ), 65, 66
Internet Society, 65
Interphase 5575 ATM adapter, 36
Interview (XLR8), 168
Intragy (Ascend), 54-55
Iomega, 9
    Zip and Jaz drives, 10
IP address, 34, 64
IPNetMonitor (Sustainable Softworks), 184
IPNetRouter (Sustainable Softworks), 184
iPort network adapter (Griffin Technology), 24
IPX (Internetwork Packet Exchange) protocol (NetWare), 182-83
IrDA, 29
iRez Kritter camera, 170
IRTalk, 29
ISO Latin-1 or 8859-1 standard, 109
iVisit audio/video conferencing software, 164
ixTV/ixTV FM expansion cards (ixMicro), 168

J

JARS.com, 128
Java, 125-27, 176
JavaGoodies, 128
JavaScript, 125-26
JavaScripts.com, 128
Jaz disks, 9-10
Jini, 176
Johnson, Greg, xx, 13
JPEG, 19, 94, 112, 118, 119-20, 129
.jpg, 94

K

Kaleidoscope (shareware), 137
K-AShare (Xinet, Inc.), 54-55
Kerberos passwords, 84
Kerberos protocol, 139-40
Keyboard application switching, 137
KeyServer (Sassafras Software), 57-58
KeySpan:
    IR card, 175
    USB to PDA adapter cable, 157, 159-60
    USB to serial adapter/USB PCI card, 154
K-FS (Xinet), 44, 47
Kingston Technology, URL, 36
Kodak digital cameras, 170

L

La Cie, 9
LabVIEW, 171
LandWare software for Newtons, 161
LANsurveyor (Neon Software), 57-58
LaTeX/TeX resources, 115
Launcher, 135-37
Lesch, Susan, 14
LetterRip (Fog City Software), 89
.lha, 20
LHA archive, 20
Lightyear Media, 161
LinuxPPC (LinuxPPC, Inc.), 147-48
List server software, 86-87
ListSTAR, 89
LiteSwitch (Proteron), 137
Local area networks (LANs), 39-61, 180
    Mac OS X Server, 49

194 Index

Local area networks (LANs) *(cont.)*
  Mac servers, 40-48
  NetWare servers, 51-53
  sharing over TCP/IP networks, 42-43
  sharing with Windows and UNIX, 44-47
    PC MACLAN, 16, 46, 162
    printing, 47-48
    TSSTalk, 46
    UNIX, 47
  UNIX servers, 53-55
  Windows NT servers, 48-53
Location Manager control panel, 30-31
Logitech QuickCam Pro/QuickCam VC, 170
Lotus 1-2-3 format, 116
.lzh, 20
.lzs, 20

M

Mac disks, reading on Windows PC, 12
Mac disks on a PC, 11-12
Mac ICA protocol, 142, 144
Mac networking, *See* Networking
Mac OS 8 Web Server Cookbook, xvi, xix, 65, 66, 69, 74, 89
Mac OS/AppleTalk:
  advantages, 24-25
  disadvantages, 25-26
Mac OS interface, 132
  tricks, 137
Mac OS Java pages, 128
Mac OS X Server, 49
Mac Type/Creator Database (Ilan Szekely), 15, 16
Mac Virus Web site, 13-14
MacAddict magazine, 174
MacAdministrator (Hi Resolution), 57-58
Macally USB input devices/USB PCI card, 154
MacAMP/MacAMP Lite MP3 player software (@soft), 167
Mac-Barcode Company, 171
MacBinary, 20

MacBochs (David Batterham), 145-46
MacCentral Help Forums, 102
MacCommCenter Plus (Smith Micro), 163-64
MacCommon LISP Server (John C. Mallery), 75
MacDownload, 161
MacDrive 98 (Media4), 12
MachTen (Tenon Intersystem), 147-48
MacHTTP (StarNine), 75
MacIn Tax, 107
Mac-in-Dos 3.0 (Pacific Micro), 12
Macintosh Disability Shareware and Freeware page (Scott Norris), 155
Macintosh E-mail Resource Page, 84
Macintosh Products Guide, 178
Macintosh removable media, 9
Macintosh Runtime for Java (MRJ), 126-27
Macjordomo (Michele Fuortes), 88, 89-90
MacLinkPlus (DataViz), 16-17, 22, 111
MacLynx, 69
MacNFS (Thursby Software), 54-55
MacOpener (DataViz), 12, 15, 16
MacPC Online (Kevin Liu), 148
MacPerl page, 128
MacPOS, 170-71
MacPPP (freeware from MacBel group), 27
Macro viruses, 13
"Mac's Best Friend" (*MacWorld*), 157
MacSciTech Users Association Web site, 172-73
MacServer IP (Team ASA), 50-51
MacSLIP (Hyde Park Software), 27
MacTar (freeware from Jim Strout), 21
MacTCP control panel, 31
MacWeb3D, 128
MacWindows, 178
  emulator page, 148
  tips:
    peer-to-peer networking, 162
    for sharing monitors/keyboards, 149
MacWorld, 22, 157
MacX (Apple), 141, 144

Index

MacZilla, 19
Mailing list servers, 85-89
MailSmith (Bare Bones Software), 84, 182-83
MailStrom (Tree Star), 84
Makeshift task bar, creating, 135-37
Mariner Write, 107
McAfee VirusScan for Macintosh, 14
MegaPhone (Bing Software), 164
Melotti, Bill, 75
Menu bar, 133
Messenger (Netscape Corp.), 84
MetaFrame (Citrix), 142-43, 144
MIB (Management Information Base), 56
Microboards, 9
Microsoft Excel, 15, 101-3, 105, 116
   differences, 105
   file format, 94
Microsoft Internet Explorer, 69, 72-73, 96
   Configuration Manager, 28, 73
Microsoft Office 98, 15, 101-5, 107
   compatibility page, 102
   documents, saving as HTML, 104-5
   embedded TrueType fonts, 104
   FileMaker Pro importer, 102
   font substitution, 103
   images, 104
   macro virus protection, 102
   and Microsoft Access database software, 101
   movies, 104
   newsgroup, 102
   product page, 102
   user area, 102
   Windows file name extensions, 102
   Woody's Office Watch, 102
Microsoft Outlook Express, 82, 84
Microsoft PowerPoint, 15, 102-5
   presentation (template), 94
Microsoft Universal Data Access page, 117
Microsoft Web Font Pack, 96
Microsoft Word, 14, 15, 92, 101-4
"Migrating Macintosh Networks to Internet Protocols" (*NetProfessional*), 42
MIME (Multipurpose Internet Mail Extension), 70, 82, 110
MindExpander (MindVision Software), 21
MI/X (Micro Images), 141, 144
MkLinux (Apple/Open Software Foundation), 147-48
Modem control panel, 31
MouseHouse (MouseHouse Electronics), 174, 177
Movies, conversion of, 19
MP3 players, 166-67
   definition of MP3, 167
   resources, 167
MRJ, 126-27
Mulberry (Cyrusoft International), 84
MultiTerm Pro (Vicomsoft), 139
Musashi (Sono Software), 84-85
My Capture/My TV USB devices (EsKape Labs), 168

N

N2MP3 encoder (Proteron), 167
Name servers, 34
NameCleaner (Sig Software), 15, 16
National Instruments, 171-73
NavimaQ (Quintessence Designs), 173
NBP (Name-Binding Protocol), 183
NCD WinCenter (Network Computing Devices), 143, 144
netatalk, 44
   AppleTalk suite (University of Michigan Research Systems UNIX Group), 54-55
NetBSD, 147-48
NetFinder (Peter Li/Vincent Tan), 78
NetOctopus (Netopia), 57-58
NetPresenz (Stairways Software), 75, 79-81
   configuring, 80-81
   setup, 81

Netscape Communicator, 69, 70-71, 129
NetWare, 40, 181
  IPX protocol, 182
  over IP for Macs, 53
  primer (Novell), 184
NetWare 5 for Macintosh (ProSoft
    Engineering), 26, 51
NetWare 5 services for AppleShare, 53
Netware Client 5.12 for Macintosh
    (ProSoft Engineering), 51
NetWare documentation, 52
NetWare for Macintosh client, 51-52
NetWare Loadable Module (NLM), 51
NetWare servers, 51-53
Network, defined, 24
Network administration, 55-59
  Simple Network Management Protocol
      (SNMP), 56
  tools for, 56-59
    Apple Network Administrator
        Toolkit, 57
    Apple Network Assistant, 57
    FileWave and Asset Trustee (Wave
        Research), 57-58
    InformUser (Advanced Ideas), 57-58
    KeyServer (Sassafras Software),
        57-58
    LANsurveyor (Neon Software),
        57-58
    MacAdministrator (Hi Resolution),
        57-58
    NetOctopus (Netopia), 57-58
    SNMP Watcher (Dartmouth
        College), 57-59
    Timbuktu Pro (Netopia), 57, 59
Network computer, defined, 140
Network control panel, 32
Network glossary, 184
Network layer, 182
Networking, 23-37
  addresses, 180
  AppleTalk, 181
  application layer, 182-84

configuring, 26-35
  AppleTalk control panel, 26-27
  DialAssist, 29
  infrared, 29
  Internet Config (Stairways
      Software), 29-30
  Internet control panel, 29-30
  Location Manager control panel,
      30-31
  MacTCP control panel, 31
  Microsoft Internet Explorer
      Configuration Manager, 28
  Modem control panel, 31
  Network control panel, 32
  Open Transport PPP control panel,
      32
  Remote Access control panel, 33
  Remote Access Setup control panel, 33
  TCP/IP control panel, 34-35
data-link layer, 182
general network terms, 180
high-performance, 35-37
hosts, 180
Internet, 180
local-area networks (LANs), 180
Mac OS/AppleTalk:
  advantages, 24-25
  disadvantages, 25-26
NetWare, 181
network layer, 182
Open Transport, 181
physical layer, 182
presentation layer, 182-84
protocols, 180
SDSC's cross-platform installation,
    59-61
  AppleTalk, 59
  file sharing, 59-60
  printing, 60-61
session layer, 182-84
TCP/IP, 181
Transmission Control Protocol (TCP),
    182

Index

transport layer, 182
wide area networks (WANS), 180
See also Network administration
Networkz (James Andrews), 78
Newer Technology SCSI USB to SCSI adapter, 154
NewtIn Touch, 161
Newton, 160-61
   MacDownload, 161
   Newton Connection Utility, 160
   resources, 161
Newton Connection Utilities guide, 161
Newton Source, The, 161
NeXTStep, 13
NiftyTelnet (Chris Newman), 139
NiftyTelnet SSH (Jonas Wallden), 139
Nikon Coolpix digital cameras, 170
Nisus Writer, 107
Nomai, 9
Non-Mac operating systems:
   camouflaging, 145-48
   general emulation information, 148
   UNIX and Linux for Mac, 146-48
   Windows emulators, 145-46
Norris, Scott, 155
Norton Anti-Virus, 14
Notify! Classic (AirMedia), 164
Novell NetWare documentation, 52

O

Open Database Connectivity (ODBC), 101, 117
Open Transport, 25, 181
   PPP control panel, 32
   SNMP, instructions for installing, 56
   updates, 184
OpenBSD, 147-48
Optical and magneto-optical disk, 9
Orange Micro:
   Hotlink, 154
   OrangePC compatibility cards, 149
Order Manager POS software (Colin Chong's Visual Imaging), 171
OT Advanced Tuner (Sustainable Softworks), 184

P

PageNOW! (Mark/Space Softworks), 164-65
Palm Computing organizers, 156-58
Palmac, 157
PalmCentral, 157-58
PalmGear HQ, 157
PalmPilot: The Ultimate Guide (David Pogue), 157-58
PalmPilots, 158
Panasonic, 9
   digital cameras, 170
PAP (Printer Access Protocol), 183
PC cards, 149
PC disks on a Mac, 8-11
PC-Enterprise (Platinum Technology), 54-55
PC Exchange, 8-10, 15
PC MACLAN (Miramar System), 16, 44, 46, 48, 162
PC Migrator, 16
PDA Concepts, WinCE to Mac cable, 159
.pdf, 94
PDF (Portable Document Format), 94, 111, 112-13
   Adobe Acrobat, 113
   definition, 113
   newsgroup, 113
   PDF Zone Web site, 113
Pearce, Nick, xix
Peripherals, 152
Perl, 127
Perl Institute, 128
Personal Web Sharing (PWS) software, 74-76, 90
PGPfone, 164
Physical layer, 182
PilotMac site, 157
P.I.M.S. (ExecUtron Development), 171

Pixera Personal digital camera, 170
"Plain" text, 108-10
   extended ASCII variations, 109
   solutions, 110
Planet Newton, 161
PNG, 112, 118, 119-20, 129
Point-of-sale software, 170-71
POP3, 41, 81, 83-84, 86, 88, 183
Portable Document Format (PDF), 18
Ports, 152
POS/OE software/connectors (EES Companies), 170-71
Post Office Protocol version 3,
   See also POP3
PostScript, 111
   Adobe PostScript overview, 115
   definition, 115
   files, 18, 94, 114-16
   fonts, 95
   newsgroup, 115
   resources, 115
.pot, 94
PowerMail (CTM Development), 84-85
PPP Menu, 27
.ppt, 94
Presentation layer, 182-84
Printing to a shared printer, 47-48
ProSoft Engineering, 25, 51-52, 53
ProTERM Mac (Intrec), 139
Protocols, 180
   defined, 24
.ps, 94
.psd, 94
Publishing Solutions/Packet Engines, 36
Pure Mac, 21, 22
   disability software page, 155
   emulation page, 148
   software directory, 178
   telephony software page, 164

Q

.qdb, 94
.qdf, 94
.qdt, 94
QuarkXPress, 105-7
   file format, 94
   product page, 106
   resources, 106
   technical notes, 106
   technical support, 106
   user forums, 106
Que!, 9
Quicken (Intuit), 106-7
   file format, 94
   "Invalid transaction in account:xxxx" error, 107
   newsgroup, 107
   product page, 107
   support network, 107
QuickTime (Apple), 18-20, 22, 104, 166-67
   web site, 19
QuickTime Player, 19
Quid Pro Quo (Social Engineering), 75
.qxd, 94, 106
.qxt, 106

R

RARP (Reverse Address Resolution Protocol), 35, 182, 183
RealPC (Insignia), 145-46
RealPlayer G2 (Real Networks), 123
Reardon Technology SiteCam software, 170
Remote Access control panel, 33
Remote Access Setup control panel, 33
Remote control, 143-44
Remote Measurement Systems:
   ADC-1 data acquisition device/Mac control software, 172-73
   introduction to home alarm sensors and detectors, 177
Removable media, 8
Resource fork, 15
.rgb, 118
Rich Text Format (RTF), 94, 111-12
   definition, 112

Index

resources, 112
RTF 1.14 specification, 112
RTFtoHTML utility, 112
RichReader (Michael Arena), 112
Ricochet wireless networks (Metricom), 164
RingTwice4Mail (Building4Media), 87, 89
Rio PMP300/Rio 500 players (Diamond Multimedia), 167
River's Edge Corporation barcode readers, 171
Router address, 34
.rs, 118
.rtf, 94
RTFtoHTML utility, 112
Rumpus (Maxum Development), 80
RunTime Plus (Vicomsoft), 139

S

samba.org, 55, 60
San Diego Supercomputer Center (SDSC), xix, 4, 140, 142
SAP (Service Advertising Protocol), 183
SCSI (Small Computer System Interface), 153
SDSC's cross-platform installation, 59-61
   AppleTalk, 59
   file sharing, 59-60
   printing, 60-61
.sea, 20
Second Wave, 154
Self-extracting archive, 20
Service Location Protocol (SLP), 24
Services for Macintosh (SFM), 48-49
   information, 51
Session layer, 182-84
ShareWay IP Gateway (Open Door Networks), 44
ShareWay IP Professional (Open Door Networks), 42-43
Silicon Valley Bus Co. barcode readers, 171

Simple Mail Transfer Protocol (SMTP), 182-83
Simple Network Management Protocol (SNMP), 25, 56
.sit, 20
SiteZAP Web cam, 170
Sixth Sense POS/Sixth Sense Cafe restaurant software, 171
SLIP (Serial Line Internet Protocol), 183
Small Computer System Interface (SCSI), 153
SmartHome.com, 174-75, 177
Sneaker net, 7-22
   file conversion, 14-21
     compression, 19-21
   file exchange, 8-13
     Mac disks on a PC, 11-12
     PC disks on a Mac, 8-11
     UNIX disks on a Mac, 12-13
   file names/types, 14-16
     general files, 16-17
     graphics, 17-18
     movies, 19
     sound, 18
   history of, 7
   removable media, 8
   virus software, 13-14
SNMP Watcher (Dartmouth College), 57-59
Software Architects, 10
SoftWindows98 (Insignia), 145-46, 159
Sonic Systems, URL, 36
Sony Digital Mavica cameras, 170
Sound, conversion of, 18
SoundApp (freeware), 18, 22
SoundJam (Casady & Greene), 167
Sparkle, 19
SparQ, 9
Special characters, 96
   in Mac file names, 15
Spreadsheets, 116-17
   ODBC, 117
SPX (Sequenced Packet Exchange), 183

Stalker Internet Mail Server
    (Stalker Software), 86, 87
Star Gate (Kevin Raner), 162
StopIt! (Microcosm), 176-77
strout.net, 157
StuffIt Expander/StuffIt Deluxe, 20-22
Subnet mask, 34
Sun's Java pages, 128
Suntar (Sauro and Gabriele Speranza),
    13, 21
SuperDisk, 9
SyJet, 9
SyQuest, 9

T

.tab, 117
tape archive, 20
.tar, 20
Task bar:
    adding Start button to, 137
    makeshift, 135-37
TCP/IP, 64, 181
    control panel, 34-35
    defined, 24
Team ASA, 50
    Stallion adapter series, 36
    Stallion-GE adapters, 36
    URL, 36
Tecmar Technologies, 9
TeleFinder Server (Spider Island Software),
    75, 87
Telephonic Mac, 162-65
    Internet phone and conferencing, 163-64
    multi-function telephony packages,
        163-64
    related resources, 164
    single-/dual-function telephony
        packages, 163-64
Telnet, 140
Terminal emulators, 138-40
    connection protocols, 140
    secure connections, 140

Text file, 94
Thin client, defined, 140
3Com Megahertz 56K cellular modem PC
    cards, 164
3Com Palm Computing Macintosh page,
    157-58
3CX, URL, 36
.tif, 94, 120
.tiff, 120
TIFF, 94, 118, 120, 129
Timbuktu Pro (Netopia), 57, 59, 143-44
Tkchooser2, 44, 47
tn3270 (Peter DiCamillo), 139
Toshiba digital cameras, 170
TotalNET Advanced Server (Syntax, Inc.),
    54
TRACE Center (Univ. of Wisconsin), 155
Transmission Control Protocol (TCP), 182
Transmit Pro (Panic Software), 78
Transport layer, 182
Transverter Pro (TechPool Software), 18
TrueType vs. Type 1, 95
TSSTalk (Thursby Software), 46, 48
TV tuners and video capture cards, 167-68
.txt, 94, 117
Type label, 15
TypeRighter Suite (Lightning Foundry),
    15-16
TZO Internet Naming Service, 66

U

UDP (User Datagram Protocol), 183
Unicode, 109-10
Universal Access control panel, 155
Universal Serial Bus (USB), 153
University of Melbourne AppleTalk
    software, 54
UNIX, 47, 97-98
UNIX and Linux for Mac, 146-48
    MachTen (Tenon Intersystem), 147-48
    MkLinux and LinuxPPC, 147-48
    NetBSD and OpenBSD, 147-48

Index

UNIX compress, 20
UNIX disks on a Mac, 12-13
UNIX servers, 40, 53-55
   Columbia AppleTalk Package (CAP), 54, 60
   EtherShare, 54
   Intragy (Ascend), 54-55
   K-AShare (Xinet, Inc.), 54-55
   MacNFS (Thursby Software), 54-55
   netatalk AppleTalk suite (University of Michigan Research Systems UNIX Group), 54-55
   PC-Enterprise (Platinum Technology), 54-55
   TotalNET Advanced Server (Syntax, Inc.), 54
   University of Melbourne AppleTalk software, 54
   Xinet Web site, 54-55
URLs (Uniform Resource Locators), xvi, 68
USB (Universal Serial Bus), 153
USENET groups, 65, 66
Uuencode, 82

V

ValueFax (Pancomm), 164
Vicomsoft FTP client, 78
Vicomsoft Internet Gateway, 42
Virex (Dr. Solomon), 13-14
Virtual Assistive Technology Center's Mac page, 155
Virtual Network Computing (AT&T Cambridge Laboratories), 144
VirtualPC (Connectix), 145-46, 159
Virus software, 13-14
VirusScan (McAfee), 14
Visor handheld devices (Handspring, Inc.), 157-58
Voice Messenger (Bing Software), 164
VRML (Virtual Reality Modeling Language), 122, 125
VST Technologies, 9

W

W3 Consortium, 69, 122, 128
   HTML page, 122
   XML pages, 128
WannaBe Web Browser (David Pierson), 69
WartHog Systems, data acquisition and analysis software, 172-73
Web 3D Consortium, 128
Web Administration 2.0, 51
Web browsers, 69-70
Web cams, 169
Web Developer's Virtual Library authoring references, 128
Web filenames, 93-94
Web Reference, 128
Web Server 4D (MDG Computer Services), 75
Web servers, 73-74
   AppleShare IP (Apple Computer), 75
   EasyServe (Jason Linhart), 75
   First Class Intranet Server (SoftArc), 75
   httpd4Mac (Bill Melotti), 75
   MacCommon LISP Server (John C. Mallery), 75
   MacHTTP (StarNine), 75
   NetPresenz/Web/FTP/gopher server shareware (Stairways Software), 75
   Personal Web Sharing (PWS) software, 74-76
   Quid Pro Quo (Social Engineering), 75
   TeleFinder (Spider Island Software), 75
   Web Server 4D (MDG Computer Services), 75
   Webink/Webink Pro, 75
   WebSTAR (StarNine), 75
   WebTen (Tenon Intersystems), 75
Web standards, 120-27
   Cascading Style Sheets (CSS), 122, 123
   Dynamic HTML (DHTML), 122, 123-24

Web standards (cont.)
  HTML (HyperText Markup Language), 121-22
  Java, 125-27
  JavaScript, 125-26
  Perl, 127
  VRML (Virtual Reality Modeling Language), 122, 125
  X3D (eXtensible 3D), 125
  XML (eXtensible Markup Language), 122, 124-25
  XSL (eXtensible Stylesheet Language), 122, 124-25
Webink/Webink Pro, 75
WebMonkey (HotWired), 128
  HTML collection, 122
WebSTAR (StarNine), 75, 79
WebTen (Tenon Intersystems), 75, 79
whatis.com, 65, 69, 120, 178, 184
Wide area networks (WANS), 180
Windows CE devices, 158-60
Windows CE Web ring, 160
Windows emulators, 145-46
Windows filenames, 93-94
Windows NT Server Web Administration 2.0, 51
Windows NT servers, 40, 48-53
  DAVE (Thursby Software), 50-51, 162
  MacServer IP, 50-51
  Services for Macintosh (SFM) component, 48-51
    installing, 48-49
    limitations of, 49
Windows Terminal Server, 141-43
WinFrame (Citrix), 142-43
Woody's Office Watch, 102

World Wide Web Consortium (W3 Consortium), 69, 122, 128
World Wide Web (WWW), 68-76
  Microsoft Internet Explorer, 72-73
  Netscape Communicator, 70-71
  Web browsers, 69-70
  Web servers, 73-74

X

X3D (eXtensible 3D), 125
.x, 20
X Window System, 141
  definition, 144
Xclaim VR 128 card/Xclaim TV (ATI Technologies), 168
Xinet Web site, 54-55
XIN/XOUT III cable/software (Reudo), 160
XLR8 USB PCI card, 154
.xls, 94
.xlt, 94
XML (eXtensible Markup Language), 122, 124-25
XML.org, 128
X.org, 144
XSL (eXtensible Stylesheet Language), 122, 124-25
XTension software (Sand Hill Engineering), 174-75, 177

Z

.Z, 20
ZDNet Macintosh Software Library, 178
.zip, 20
ZIP (Zone Information Protocol), 183
Zip disks, 9, 20
Zone selection, AppleTalk control panel, 26-27

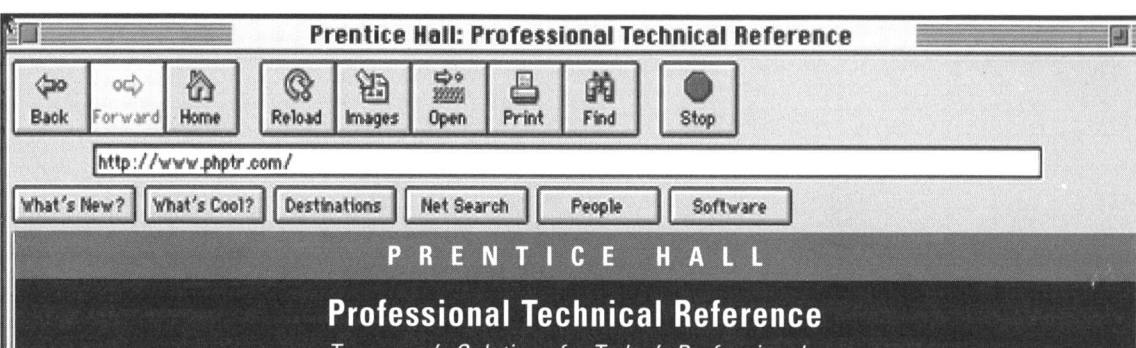

PRENTICE HALL
Professional Technical Reference
Tomorrow's Solutions for Today's Professionals.

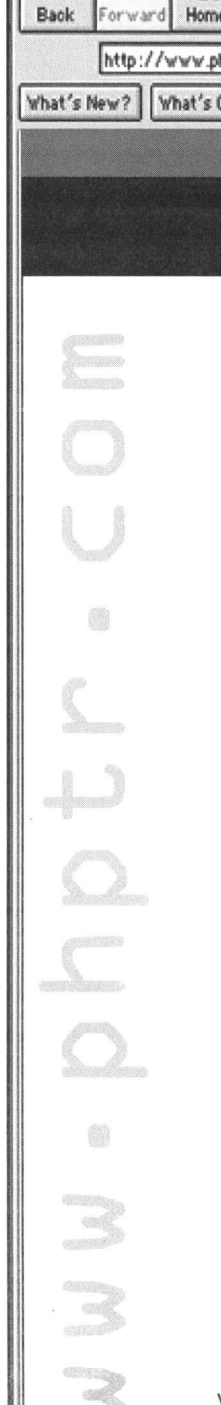

Keep Up-to-Date with
PH PTR Online!

We strive to stay on the cutting-edge of what's happening in professional computer science and engineering. Here's a bit of what you'll find when you stop by **www.phptr.com**:

- **Special interest areas** offering our latest books, book series, software, features of the month, related links and other useful information to help you get the job done.

- **Deals, deals, deals!** Come to our promotions section for the latest bargains offered to you exclusively from our retailers.

- **Need to find a bookstore?** Chances are, there's a bookseller near you that carries a broad selection of PTR titles. Locate a Magnet bookstore near you at www.phptr.com.

- **What's New at PH PTR?** We don't just publish books for the professional community, we're a part of it. Check out our convention schedule, join an author chat, get the latest reviews and press releases on topics of interest to you.

- **Subscribe Today!** **Join PH PTR's monthly email newsletter!**

    Want to be kept up-to-date on your area of interest? Choose a targeted category on our website, and we'll keep you informed of the latest PH PTR products, author events, reviews and conferences in your interest area.

Visit our mailroom to subscribe today! **http://www.phptr.com/mail_lists**